Dimensions of Sociological Theory

Dimensions of Sociological Theory

David Cheal

palgrave
macmillan

First published 2005 by
PALGRAVE MACMILLAN
Houndmills, Basingstoke, Hampshire RG21 6XS and
175 Fifth Avenue, New York, N.Y. 10010
Companies and representatives throughout the world

PALGRAVE MACMILLAN is the global academic imprint of the Palgrave Macmillan division of St. Martin's Press, LLC and of Palgrave Macmillan Ltd. Macmillan® is a registered trademark in the United States, United Kingdom and other countries. Palgrave is a registered trademark in the European Union and other countries.

ISBN-13: 978 1–4039–4305–7 hardback
ISBN-10:   1–4039–4305–2 hardback
ISBN-13: 978 1–4039–4306–4 paperback
ISBN-10:   1–4039–4306–0 paperback

This book is printed on paper suitable for recycling and made from fully managed and sustained forest sources.

A catalogue record for this book is available from the British Library.

Library of Congress Cataloging-in-Publication Data

A catalog record for this book is available from the Library of Congress.

10   9   8   7   6   5   4   3   2   1
14   13   12   11   10   09   08   07   06   05

Printed in China

This book is for Kevin, Shannon, Adrienne and Emma

Contents

Preface

This book began life as a course of lectures in sociological theory. It is therefore intended for use by students who are embarking on that grand challenge of attempting to discover what sociological theory is all about. Because it is intended to be used by students who have little previous familiarity with the theory, I have tried to write this book in a way that students will be able to read. That has meant simplifying arguments in some cases, though I hope in a manner that is not simplistic.

This book is intended to give students a taste of what sociological theory is about. It is offered as a short and affordable introduction to the field. All of the major sociological theorists are covered, and some of the minor ones, but it is not intended to provide a comprehensive or exhaustive account of sociological theory that can be found in other books.

Courses in sociological theory can be taught in a number of different ways, and this book takes a particular approach. It is the argument of this book that there have been five major debates in sociological theory. They are: (1) the debate over units of analysis; (2) the debate over modes of explanation; (3) the debate over the key factors to be used in explanations of social evolution; (4) the debate over the relationship between sociology and ideology; and (5) the debate over structure and agency. Theorists have therefore been selected in order to illustrate these debates. The material has also been organized thematically, with theorists grouped in terms of their principal contribution to a particular debate, rather than historically, according to their order of appearance in time. This means that the theorists presented here sometimes appear out of order from a historical point of view. For example, Weber comes before Marx in this book, because their work is discussed in different sections.

It is recognized that a number of instructors organize their courses historically, and it is hoped that they will still be able to use this book, with some adjustments. The discussions of each of the theorists are self-contained so that they can be read in any order that is desired. Thematic linkages between the theorists are stressed in the introduction to the book, the introduction to each chapter and in the conclusion to the book. However, the thematic discussions are not essential to reading and understanding the individual theorists. For those readers who want to take a historical approach, the following order of the theorists is recommended (by date of birth): (1) John Stuart Mill, Chapter 1; (2) Karl Marx, Chapter 4; (3) Emile Durkheim, Chapters 1 and 3; (4) Georg Simmel,

Chapter 2; (5) Max Weber, Chapter 3; (6) Karl Mannheim, Chapter 5; (7) Alfred Schutz, Chapter 2; (8) Herbert Blumer, Chapter 6; (9) Talcott Parsons, Chapters 3 and 4; (10) Robert Merton, Chapter 3; (11) George Homans, Chapter 2; (12) Robin Williams, Chapter 6; (13) Peter Blau, Chapter 2; (14) Erving Goffman, Chapter 6; (15) Michel Foucault, Chapter 5; (16) James Coleman, Chapter 2; (17) Mary O'Brien, Chapter 6; (18) Dorothy Smith, Chapter 5; (19) Zygmunt Bauman, Chapter 7; (20) Jürgen Habermas, Chapter 4; (21) Pierre Bourdieu, Chapter 7; (22) Anthony Giddens, Chapter 7.

This book can also be utilized in courses that are organized thematically by schools of thought. Thus, Functionalism is covered in Chapter 3, Functionalism: Emile Durkheim, Robert Merton and Talcott Parsons; Positivism is covered in Chapter 3, Positivism: Emile Durkheim; Marxism is covered in Chapter 4, Karl Marx; Feminism is covered in Chapter 5, Dorothy Smith, and in Chapter 6, Mary O'Brien; Action Theory is covered in Chapter 3, Max Weber, and in Chapter 2, Alfred Schutz; Critical Theory is covered in Chapter 4, Jürgen Habermas; Symbolic Interactionism is covered in Chapter 6, Herbert Blumer; Dramaturgical Sociology is covered in Chapter 6, Erving Goffman; Exchange Theory and Rational Choice Theory are covered in Chapter 2, George Homans, Peter Blau and James Coleman; Modernity is covered in Chapter 7, Anthony Giddens; Field, Habitus and Capital are covered in Chapter 7, Pierre Bourdieu; and Postmodernism is covered in Chapter 7, Zygmunt Bauman. It is hoped that whatever way instructors organize their courses, students will still enjoy reading this book and will learn from it.

DAVID CHEAL

Acknowledgments

This book was prepared with the assistance of a sabbatical from the University of Winnipeg, which is gratefully acknowledged.

Introduction

A notorious feature of sociology is that there are numerous differences of opinion between sociologists over the nature of the questions that are asked about social issues, and the answers that are given to them. It is sometimes thought that this is a result of inadequate methods, or insufficient work, or immaturity of the discipline, or avoidable bias, and it is therefore recommended that 'we need more and better science'. However, the conclusion that is more often drawn today is that different theories are the results of different experiences, assumptions, locations and social contexts. In short, there are many different 'lenses' through which to observe the social world, and they reveal different aspects of it. This does not mean that work in social studies is random, meaningless or ill-intentioned. It is possible to provide clear and sober descriptions of these different perspectives, and the reasons for them.

One way of examining the differences between theories, which will be followed in this book, is to think about them as the outcomes of a process of theory construction. Theories do not appear full-blown as complete intellectual works. Rather, they must be built up, piece by piece. It is therefore useful to consider what steps must be taken in theory construction, and how different directions taken at different points can produce quite different results. At each stage in the process of theory construction, certain assumptions must be made in answer to certain questions, if the process of theory building is to move forward. It is worth understanding what those questions are.

It is possible to show in many cases that different theories are generated from the answers that are given to a small set of questions. There are five fundamental questions that must be addressed in some fashion in the process of theory construction. Those questions are: (1) What is the unit of analysis in sociology? (2) What kind of knowledge is desired, and how exactly is the preferred form of knowledge to be produced? (3) What are the key factors that are to be used for explanatory purposes? (4) How should we understand the nature of sociology as a system of ideas in relation to other ideas in society? and (5) What are the key concepts employed in the theory? In particular, what concepts of 'structure' or alternatives to it are embedded in the theory?

The process of theory construction begins by identifying the objects that will be the subject of investigation. In one sense, this is a relatively simple task of deciding what is the topic of investigation for a particular study. The interest

1

of the sociological observer determines what is to be studied, and the only issue for debate is whether a broader or narrower conceptualization of the problem might have been more useful. However, the most ambitious theories claim to be able to say something about all, or almost all, possible topics in sociology. Theories of this broad scope face a different kind of challenge, namely that of ensuring that the choice of unit of analysis is in accord with the basic structure of the field under investigation. The unit of analysis is the *type* of object that is taken to be the proper subject matter for theorizing. Units of analysis can be defined at different levels, depending on the point at which key properties are held to emerge. If the unit of analysis is well chosen, then the theory will be productive and it will produce useful results. However, if the choice of unit of analysis does not match the structure of the field under investigation, then the results of any theorizing will be misleading.

The task of choosing the unit of analysis requires making some assumption about how social reality is organized, in advance of the process of theorizing itself. Whatever choice is made, it is therefore a truly foundational assumption that has a profound effect upon the resulting theory. In sociology, the choice of unit of analysis has often been polarized between either choosing the individual person as the basic unit or choosing instead some larger system of action that contains many individuals. Taking the individual as the unit of analysis has the advantage of focusing upon a concrete object with corporeal form that appears to be a natural starting point for enquiry. But can individuals really be conceptualized as standing in isolation? And, if not, how exactly should their interconnections be understood? Are there, in fact, supra-individual objects that account for the collective behaviour of individuals? Or, are such objects merely convenient figments of the imagination?

Occasional attempts have been made to avoid the polarization of sociology between either the individual or the collectivity as units of analysis, but they have rarely been successful. The result has almost always been ambiguity and confusion, which is the enemy of good theory development. Therefore, debate continues around this issue.

Once the unit of analysis has been decided for a particular theory, the next question to consider is the nature of the knowledge that it is desired to have about the object under investigation. Typically, the answer that is given to this question is that the kind of knowledge required is some kind of explanation of the phenomenon. We want to know what are the reasons for its existence, and why it takes the form that it does. These questions may seem straightforward, but they raise a further question. What *kind* of explanation is considered to be most appropriate?

In this book we shall consider three kinds of explanation that have been used in sociology, either alone or in combination. The first of these modes of explanation is the scientific analysis of the causes of the pattern that is of interest. Here the intent is to identify the origins of the pattern, and to do so in a manner that is rigorous and scientific. This is the approach that is sometimes identified as 'positivism'. The second mode of explanation is referred to as 'functionalism'. It seeks to explain not how things came into existence, but how they keep going, or in other words how they are maintained over time. Social patterns are believed to persist because they fulfil a function. The third mode of explanation focuses on the interpretation of the meanings of actions to the actors who carry them out. Associated with the word 'verstehen' in the German sociological tradition, this approach seeks the interpretive understanding of social life.

Following some decision about the mode, or modes, of explanation, the process of theory construction turns logically to consider which social factors have the greatest explanatory value in sociology. As any theory develops, the theorist must sooner or later turn to the question of which factors carry the greatest weight in the theory. Not all factors are equal. Some factors explain a lot, whereas other factors seem to explain very little. To put this question in positivist terms, which factors account for most of the variation in the data? Or, to put the question a little differently, which factors explain the most about how social events have been shaped and change over time? Considered here are questions about social evolution, and how, exactly, it is to be explained.

There are many answers that have been given to the question of which are the key factors in sociological explanation, and not all of them can be considered here. Attention will be focused on three approaches that have been particularly influential in sociological theory. The first approach is that of materialism. It maintains that the material conditions of life itself ultimately determine how people live their lives, and therefore the social patterns that they produce. The particular approach to materialism that is discussed here is concerned with the economy as the basic engine of society. It is thought to be the economy which drives social life forward along a definite path of evolution. Sometimes dismissed as 'economism', this approach has proven to be resilient and it continues to be influential today, albeit in altered form. The second approach is diametrically opposed to the first. It maintains that material conditions in general, and the economy in particular, have a subordinate influence on social affairs. Instead, it is claimed that cultural factors such as beliefs and values have the greatest influence on social events. The third approach is more complex, showing influences from both of the first two approaches. Its most distinctive feature is to stress the importance of communicative action as a factor in social life.

The next step in the process of theory construction is to consider how we should understand the nature of a sociological theory as a system of ideas, in relation to other ideas in society. Any theory, as it is being developed, incorporates influences from the surrounding intellectual environment. Even theorists who work alone read the works of others, and they are influenced by them. Furthermore, the theorist too has a social life and participates in the discourses in society, and he or she is influenced by these things also. An important question, then, concerns how much influence the social environment has on theory development, and what is the nature of that influence. In particular, are there any biases that are introduced in the process of social influence, and what is the direction of bias? These questions ultimately raise the difficult question about the nature of truth in sociological theory.

The above questions lead to a discussion of ideology and its influences on sociology. An ideology is a distorted view of the world, which is shaped by a particular perspective that reflects a specific social position in the world. If sociologists as social actors are influenced by their social world, then is all sociological theory also ideological? One approach to this question is to claim that all theories are ideological except for the author's own theory. Not surprisingly, this approach has met with some opposition, and incredulity, and it has been argued that it should be replaced by the view that all theories are ideological. The question then becomes, to what extent are particular sociological theories ideological, and are there any significant differences among them in this respect? Contrasting with this approach, there is another approach which dismisses all discussions about ideology as misleading because they have become confused. Instead, it proposes to describe the ways in which all ideas are shaped in discourses. Lastly, there is an approach rooted in feminism, which asks us to consider the extent to which male biases enter into sociology, and how exactly this happens. This approach seeks to clarify the theoretical grounds for women, and the ways in which women can speak the truth about their own lives.

The last step in the process of theory construction discussed here is the use of key concepts to identify and describe selected features of the social world. Concepts are terms and their related meanings that are the building blocks in theoretical arguments. There are many concepts used in sociology, but one in particular has been both widely used and widely debated. That is the concept of 'structure'. Social structures can be conceptualized as fixed arrangements of the parts of a social system that constrain the actions of actors in that system. Debates around this concept have taken several different directions. One criticism has been that concepts of structure, especially when connected to concepts of functionalism, are conservative since they stress the stability of the social order. Alternatively, some critical sociologists have used structural concepts to identify aspects of society that are resistant to change, but that it is believed should be changed through a process of struggle. Feminist accounts of the structure of patriarchy are one illustration of this point.

A second criticism of the classical concept of structure is that it focuses too much on constraint, and does not allow enough room for human agency. Critics who follow this approach usually reject the concept of structure in favour of alternative concepts that stress the ways in which individuals creatively construct their own lines of action, in interaction with others. Finally, there is the criticism that societies are less fixed than is sometimes thought, and this is sometimes related to the idea that contemporary societies have become more fluid. Options taken here have been either to redefine the concept of structure or to abandon it entirely.

The five major questions discussed in this book can all be answered in different ways, and together they reveal a great deal of diversity in sociological theory. Such diversity is not a problem because it grows out of reasonable arguments advanced by serious scholars. However, it does constitute a challenge to understanding. It is hoped that the present book will increase that understanding.

Dimension One

Units of Analysis

1

The Individual vs Social Facts

The most basic questions for any theory are: What is the object of study? Where does the process of description and explanation begin? Does it begin at the macro-level of entire societies or other large systems of action, or does it begin at the micro-level of individuals and the ways in which they take account of other individuals in constructing their unique lines of action? Or, is there some middle way between these two extremes that can identify an alternative unit of analysis, or that somehow combines both of them? In this chapter we will begin to see that there have indeed been very different answers to the question of what is the unit of analysis in sociology. This chapter examines the classical contrast between the Utilitarianism of John Stuart Mill, for whom the individual was the basic unit of analysis, and the work of Emile Durkheim whose units of analysis were holistic social facts. Durkheim's work is described in detail due to his profound influence upon the development of sociology.

The unit of analysis in any theory is the building block from which the theory is constructed. It is the fundamental phenomenon about which key assumptions are made, and from which key arguments are developed. Because of its foundational importance, the choice of unit of analysis has a profound effect upon the manner in which the theory is developed and the direction that it takes.

In sociology, there has been a classic division of opinion over the unit of analysis, between those who stress methodological holism and those who stress methodological individualism. According to the holistic thinkers, there are systems of action which possess properties (sometimes called 'emergent properties') that are different from those of the individuals who make up the system. It follows from this that a system of action cannot be explained by reference to the properties of individuals. Rather, it must be understood in its own terms and explained by reference to the connections between elements of the system.

On the other hand, according to the methodological individualists, any system of action can only be explained in terms of the properties of its constituent parts. In human societies, these parts are individuals. It follows from this that the approach to explanation should be to reduce the study of the complex whole to the study of individuals (sometimes known as 'reductionism').

In practice, few theoretical approaches are entirely consistent in the choice of unit of analysis, but nevertheless the dominant thrust is usually clear enough. In sociology, the dominant tendency in sociological theory (though not necessarily in sociological research) has been some variant of methodological holism. Especially following the influential work of Emile Durkheim, many sociologists have concluded that social phenomena have a distinct reality which makes their study different from the subject matter of psychology (Poggi, 2000). However, there have always been important challenges to this point of view. It is with one of these challenges that we will begin our description of the changing positions in the debate on units of analysis.

John Stuart Mill

In England in the late eighteenth and nineteenth centuries, the English philosophers and economists Jeremy Bentham (1748–1832) and John Stuart Mill (1806–1873) developed a theoretical approach that came to be known as Utilitarianism. The most important principle of this approach was the Greatest Happiness Principle. As expressed by John Stuart Mill, this principle held that 'the ultimate end, with reference to and for the sake of which all other things are desirable (whether we are considering our own good or that of other people), is an existence exempt as far as possible from pain, and as rich as possible in enjoyments' (Mill, 1969: 214). This principle was thought to furnish both a standard of morality for ethical and political analyses and a guide to understanding the actual ends, or goals, of human action. In the latter sense, the Greatest Happiness Principle provided the key assumption in a theory of how and why people act in the ways that they do. The noteworthy characteristic of this approach is that the individual is the unit of analysis, as it is individuals who decide what things they feel are painful or enjoyable.

In the work of John Stuart Mill, methodological individualism was an important factor shaping how he looked at the relationships between different disciplines, including psychology and sociology. Mill did not take seriously the idea that sociology should be a separate discipline with its own research leading to the discovery of distinctive scientific laws. Instead, he thought of sociology as a deductive discipline, that is to say, as a discipline whose major propositions are deduced by logical argument from more basic propositions. And those basic propositions, he thought, must be psychological in nature.

According to Mill,

> The laws of the phenomena of society are, and can be, nothing but the laws of the actions and passions of human beings united together in the social state. Men, however, in a state of society, are still men; their actions and

passions are obedient to the laws of individual human nature. Men are not, when brought together, converted into another kind of substance, with different properties...Human beings in society have no properties but those which are derived from, and may be resolved into, the laws of the nature of individual man. (Mill, 1974: 879)

Among the laws of the nature of individual man are what Mill called the laws of mind, studied by psychology. Psychology was conceived of by Mill as a basic science of observation and experiment, in which induction from observation could be used to discover fundamental, scientific laws about individual human beings.

In contrast, social science, including sociology, could not be a basic research discipline. Social phenomena are constantly changing, and it would be impossible to separate experimental changes from changes caused by other factors. Mill concluded that there were simply too many complicated factors to be taken into account to permit the use of experimental methods of investigation in sociology. As a result, conclusions about society must be arrived at in a different way, by applying the laws of mind to understanding individuals in their social relationships. According to Mill, sociology is a deductive science in which the actions and feelings of human beings in their social life must be explained from psychological laws, as well as derivative laws about the formation of human character.

John Stuart Mill's position on the nature of sociology, and its relation to psychology, has been most influential, including among some sociologists. We shall see later how certain utilitarian ideas re-appeared in sociology in the second half of the twentieth century, notably in exchange theory. However, this point of view has not gone unchallenged, and for much of the history of sociology the dominant point of view was quite different. Among the classical sociologists of the nineteenth century and early twentieth century, Emile Durkheim clearly departed from the utilitarian approach in insisting that sociology had an independent existence as a science of social facts.

Emile Durkheim

Emile Durkheim (1858–1917) was a French sociologist who was a methodological holist. He strongly believed that there are properties of society that are independent of the individual, and that sociological explanations therefore cannot be reduced to psychological explanations. Durkheim went further than this in his opposition to reductionism, by reversing the direction of causation. He argued that, in fact, the characteristics of individuals are often determined by their social conditions, which he referred to as social facts.

Social Facts

Durkheim adopted a rigorous view of sociology, in which social facts were identified as the proper subject matter for sociology. As a scientist, Durkheim thought that key concepts should be defined carefully, and he set out to do this in his book on *The Rules of Sociological Method* (1964a). He defined a social fact in the following way: 'A social fact is every way of acting, fixed or not, capable of exercising on the individual an external constraint; or again, every way of acting which is general throughout a given society, while at the same time existing in its own right independent of its individual manifestations' (Durkheim, 1964a: 13). According to this definition, a social fact is different from an individual fact because: (a) a social fact is general, or in other words practiced by a number of people; (b) it exists independently of the actions of any particular individual; and (c) it constrains the individual, or in other words limits his or her freedom of choice.

The latter characteristic was especially important for Durkheim because it identified those facts which are truly collective in nature as opposed to being merely general, or common. It was in this way that Durkheim made his crucial distinction between the individual and the social fact as the unit of analysis. Social facts determine the individual, not the other way round. In an important statement, Durkheim says that a social fact 'is a group condition repeated in the individual because imposed on him. It is to be found in each part because it exists in the whole, rather than in the whole because it exists in the parts' (Durkheim, 1964a: 9). In other words, patterns of behaviour are to be found repeated in individuals because they are imposed by the whole society, and they are not found in society because they are practiced by individuals.

Because Durkheim did not take the individual seriously as the unit of analysis, he also rejected psychological explanations in sociology. Unlike John Stuart Mill, Durkheim argued that 'every time that a social phenomenon is directly explained by a psychological phenomenon, we may be sure that the explanation is false' (Durkheim, 1964a: 104). There are three main reasons why Durkheim thought that psychological explanations must be inadequate. First, he believed that psychological facts are the results of social facts, not the reverse. Second, Durkheim claimed that social facts are external to individual consciousness. And third, he held that social facts impose themselves upon the individual. We will examine each of these claims in turn.

Durkheim was very concerned about the numerous psychological explanations for patterns of social behaviour that existed in his day. Examples that he gave included theories that explained family life from the natural feelings that parents have for their children and that children have for their parents and that explained economic life from the individual's desire for wealth. The problem with these, and similar explanations, in Durkheim's view, is that they are misleading because they have got cause and effect the wrong way round. Psychological states, Durkheim claimed, are not the causes of social phenomena, but they are the consequences of social phenomena. The proof for this, Durkheim thought, lies in the fact that history shows any supposedly universal motive of individuals (such as love for parents) may sometimes be absent or only weakly developed. Therefore, we need to understand how certain motives are produced under certain conditions, but not under other conditions.

The conditions that Durkheim was interested in were, of course, social facts. Durkheim was convinced of the reality of social facts because he thought it was possible to identify properties of the whole society which are independent of the specific individuals in the society. According to Durkheim, these are 'ways of acting, thinking, and feeling that present the noteworthy property of existing outside the individual consciousness' (Durkheim, 1964a: 2). Durkheim advanced four main arguments in support of this claim.

First, social facts 'function independently of my own use of them', as Durkheim put it (1964a: 2). Examples that illustrate Durkheim's point well include language, law and money. These are all systems of symbols which are used by many, or all, of the individuals in society, but no one individual controls how they develop. All we can do as individuals is to participate in these systems, use them to our advantage, and perhaps contribute with others to their development. But we do not control them. The evident proof for this is that if one of us dies these systems do not stop. They continue to function without us.

Second, some social facts become crystallized and take a fixed form that does not vary between the different individuals who use them. Popular sayings which are repeated over and over again in the same form are one example. A more important example is when social facts, such as laws, are set down in writing. Passed from one person to another, and applied in different ways, the laws nevertheless remain the same in their written form. Furthermore, they remain the same even if they are never applied.

Third, many important social facts could not possibly have been created by the individuals who are alive today because they have been inherited from the past and passed on to us through education. Religious beliefs and rituals illustrate this point. The fact that many beliefs and rituals have ancient origins demonstrates the extent to which they are independent of the individual wishes of people today, even if people still conform to them and accept them.

Fourth, the independence of social facts from individual consciousness is demonstrated by the fact that certain social facts which are relevant to us may nevertheless be unknown to us. In that case, we would have to consult the people who Durkheim refers to as the 'authorized interpreters' (1964a: 1). People such as lawyers, counsellors and priests may need to be consulted about the rules that define the proper ways of managing death or divorce, for example. Our dependence upon these experts to interpret and apply the rules of our society shows, again, how separate the social facts and individual consciousness can be.

The separation of social facts from individual consciousness in Durkheim's theory paves the way for his claim that social facts impose themselves upon the individuals in society. Different kinds of facts impose themselves in different ways. The kinds of facts that Durkheim was often most interested in are the collective representations, which together make up the collective conscience, or collective consciousness. Collective representations are shared ways of thinking which are more or less obligatory upon members of a particular group or society. In many cases, these shared ideas are willingly accepted and agreed to by the individuals involved. It could therefore be argued that there is no constraint or coercion here, and instead we are simply looking at the combination of voluntary choices made by separate individuals. However, Durkheim argues that is not the case because the constraint exercised by society becomes evident as soon as anyone decides to think outside the box and act in a deviant way. Society then reacts against us, to prevent our actions or to repair the damage that we have caused. When we conform to what is expected of us we do not feel the pressure of society, but that does not mean that it is not there all along. The pressures of society may be subtle at some times, and brutally obvious at others, but they are always there, according to Durkheim. In Durkheim's view, if we willingly conform to society and are therefore unconscious of the power of external coercion exercised upon us, 'We are then victims of the illusion of having ourselves created that which actually forced itself from without' (Durkheim, 1964a: 5).

Durkheim saw himself as undertaking the task of dissipating such illusions and providing concrete explanations of how, exactly, collective representations constrain behaviour. He thought that there were four ways in which this happened. First, collective representations are taught to us through instruction, or in other words socialization of the individual. In Durkheim's view, parents and teachers are merely the representatives and intermediaries of society, whose job it is to produce a child who can take up a place within that society. Accordingly, the child is constrained from birth to begin eating, drinking and sleeping at regular hours which are convenient to others. Later, the child is taught other requirements, such as the need for cleanliness, the importance of doing what he is told to do, respect for others and so on. In all these ways, both small and large, the child is submitted to constant pressure from the environment. Eventually, if the process of socialization is successful, the child develops habits and patterns of self-control that make external controls unnecessary. Constraints from parents, and behind them society, are therefore felt less and the child feels to have more freedom. But the power of society is nevertheless the source of the socialization of the human being.

The second way in which collective representations constrain behaviour is internally, within the mind of the individual. As a result of the external constraints of socialization, 'society is represented inside us as well', as Durkheim put it (1995: 16). The authority of society represented inside us causes us to reject changes to fundamental ideas that we have learned. The fundamental ideas that we have learned take on a sense of reality, to the point that we may question the sanity of anyone who challenges them, and doubt our own sanity if we are tempted to follow alternative beliefs. Our mind therefore resists any tendency to deviate from the basic moral and logical consensus of our society.

Third, if individuals do deviate from the norms of society despite the effects of socialization, then the power of society is exercised through surveillance and sanctions to limit the extent of their deviance. Durkheim is at pains to point out here that he is not referring only to the punishments inflicted by formal agents of social control. He indicates that subtle pressures of public opinion and ridicule are equally effective in dealing with minor offences against custom and conventional morality.

Finally, the fourth way in which collective representations constrain behaviour is the practical necessity they impose upon us to adapt our behaviour to existing practices, if we want to have a comfortable existence. The fact that everyone around us acts in a certain manner may mean that it is very difficult, if not impossible, to do otherwise. For example, if everybody is speaking English, then to persist in trying to speak French would be to invite misunderstanding and incomprehension. We would be unable to communicate our wants, and therefore unable to obtain the things that we need to live. The social fact of language thereby constrains us, and limits our freedom of action. Similarly, Durkheim points out that it would be difficult to survive by setting up a business using out-of-date technology. In practical terms, it becomes impossible to resist the dominant way of doing things because to change it would require widespread co-operation, and why would people want to change something that is successful?

We can see that Durkheim was convinced social facts have effects upon individuals that are both broad and deep. Durkheim therefore always looked to social facts first in order to explain patterns of behaviour. We can see this most clearly in his work on the division of labour.

Division of Labour

The increasing specialization of work was a prominent topic for nineteenth century theorists because they could see that the world of work had been profoundly and irreversibly altered. Instead of subsistence agricultural economies in which most people grew or made most of the things they needed, the leading European societies had become industrial economies in which more and more people toiled away in factories and other establishments doing more and more specialized kinds of work, based on a detailed division of labour. Theorists therefore asked questions about this new type of economy. What factors caused the division of labour, and why was it progressing at such a rapid rate?

Economists of Durkheim's day explained the division of labour as resulting from the inherent characteristics of individuals. In the first place, individuals naturally possess different skills and abilities, as well as different interests and ambitions. Secondly, all individuals are presumed to be motivated by the desire for wealth, and they will realize that they can make themselves better off by specializing in making the things that interest them and for which they have higher productivity, and exchanging the products of their labours with others. Co-operation in the division of labour is therefore believed to be based on separate individuals rationally pursuing their private interests.

Durkheim dissented from this point of view in *The Division of Labor in Society* (1964b, 1997), and he claimed that the division of labour had to be explained by social facts. In his view, both the differences between individuals and the co-operative relations of exchange between them must be understood as the products of society.

Durkheim pointed out that individuals who decide to specialize in the work that they do are never truly isolated and independent. They are constantly engaged in transactions with other people, and indeed the division of labour is only made possible by agreements between them about who will do what tasks. Since ongoing interaction implies some kind of social organization, Durkheim concluded that the division of labour must be a social phenomenon and not an individual phenomenon. In his words, 'The division of labour can therefore only occur within the framework of an already existing society' (Durkheim, 1997: 218).

If the division of labour is to be harmonious, which Durkheim assumed is normally the case, then the individuals who are dividing their labour must engage in interaction with one another to ensure that everything that was previously done continues to be done, but now without any overlap in tasks between them. Furthermore, conflict will have to be avoided over which particular individuals do which specific tasks, and this too will require co-operative interaction. Durkheim was acutely aware of the possibility of conflict in human affairs whenever two or more individuals approach the same situation with different interests. Therefore, Durkheim concluded that there must be some force from society, greater than the individuals themselves, which compelled them to co-operate. As Durkheim put it, 'Thus there is a social life outside of any division of labour, but one that the latter assumes' (1997: 219).

This social life outside the division of labour, but upon which the division of labour depends, includes in the first place the legal regulation of contracts. Durkheim insisted that although economic life appears to consist of private agreements freely entered into without any social agency, nevertheless in the long run contracts are only made possible by legal regulations which ensure their harmonious nature. Legal provisions exist which enable people to enforce their contracts, or to obtain compensation if the contracts are broken. Durkheim referred to this type of law as 'restitutive law'. It is one of two types of law that we will describe next, due to their importance for Durkheim's overall theory of society.

Mechanical Solidarity and Organic Solidarity

It is a characteristic of Durkheim's theory, upon which we have already remarked, that he tended to stress the conditions favouring the harmonious operation of society. He was therefore very interested in the condition which he referred to as solidarity. Social solidarity refers to how people get along together, how they co-operate with one another and ultimately how societies hold together without being torn apart by conflict. For Durkheim, this is one of the most important things that we need to understand about society, for it is the basis for all social organization and all human progress. Solidarity is the essential basis for society itself, and therefore for all the human achievements that society has made possible.

Durkheim thought that history showed there were two types of solidarity, mechanical solidarity and organic solidarity. These two types tended to occur at different periods of history, with mechanical solidarity coming first, followed by organic solidarity later.

Mechanical solidarity is based on people thinking and feeling in the same way, and therefore identifying with one another. People co-operate because they believe that they belong together as the same people. Mechanical solidarity is characteristic of traditional societies in which people share the same religious beliefs and myths. This type of society has what Durkheim called a strongly defined state of the collective conscience, or common conscience.

The collective conscience is an important social fact in Durkheim's theory of society. He used this concept to indicate that society is more than the sum of the individual minds, or consciences, of the people that make up society. There is also a collective pattern of thinking that goes on between people, for example, in their shared religious beliefs.

Durkheim thought that the collective conscience could be strong or weak. Where the collective conscience is strong, most people share the same ideas, and they take them seriously and act upon them. Where the collective conscience is weak, on the other hand, people believe many different things, and there are few ideas which are truly common. And, those ideas which are shared are not taken very seriously. A strong collective conscience is the essential basis for mechanical solidarity.

Organic solidarity, on the other hand, is based on interdependence. Here, people co-operate because they realize that they depend on each other. People depend on each other because they cannot make everything that they want for themselves, and they have to obtain most of the things that they need from other people. On this basis a positive attraction can develop between people who each lack something that the other possesses. Organic solidarity, then, occurs as a result of people specializing in making different things, or in other words as a result of the division of labour.

Durkheim thought that the long-term trend in human societies was a gradual shift away from mechanical solidarity and towards organic solidarity. This was occurring for two reasons. First, the collective conscience gradually declines over time. As societies become more diverse, and as social controls become weaker, there are fewer beliefs which are truly collective. Second, the decline of the collective conscience does not produce a crisis of falling solidarity because at the same time organic solidarity is increasing due to the progress of the division of labour, which is constantly increasing.

Durkheim used his theory of the division of labour not only to talk about solidarity but also to discuss the law. Laws were important social facts in Durkheim's theory. He argued that societies based on mechanical solidarity and societies based on organic solidarity relied on different types of laws. Here Durkheim distinguished between repressive law and restitutive law.

Repressive law, as the name implies, consists of forcibly repressing people to follow the same rules as everybody else. It is the kind of law found in societies with mechanical solidarity. In mechanical solidarity, based on likeness, anybody who is different is a threat to social order and must be forced back into line, or expelled, or killed.

On the other hand, societies based on organic solidarity do not need extensive repressive law because it is more accepted that people will be different. People make different things, and therefore work in different ways, and probably think in different ways also. However, social order would be threatened in organic solidarity if people failed to honour their agreements in exchanging with one another. Therefore, societies based on organic solidarity need a different type of law, namely restitutive law.

Restitutive law consists of laws, such as laws of contract, which enable an aggrieved party to obtain recompense if an agreement is broken. The importance of restitutive law is that it provides the means for enforcing contracts, thus providing for orderly economic exchange between people who have divided their labour.

Immediate Causes of the Division of Labour

Restitutive law plays an important part in Durkheim's theory of the causes of the division of labour. Without it, the contracts between people would only be promises that carry just as much weight as the word, and good will, of the parties involved. Durkheim clearly thought that such contracts would be unreliable. Restitutive law, on the other hand, lends the power of society to intervene and uphold contracts when necessary. Contracts therefore receive more respect than would otherwise be the case, and people can trust that the agreements into which they enter will be honoured. This encourages them to consider new and more specialized ways of working that involve new forms of exchange, and thus promotes the extended division of labour.

In addition, trust in economic life is also encouraged by the way in which society adds to contracts and regulates them. As Durkheim put it, 'the contract is not sufficient by itself, but is only possible because of the regulation of contracts, which is of social origin' (Durkheim, 1997: 162). Examples with which Durkheim would have been familiar include rules defining legal weights and measures of goods for sale. Since Durkheim's time, this body of law has been greatly expanded and includes such things as truth in advertising laws, laws regulating the purity and safety of drugs and laws regulating the reliability and safety of automobiles. All these laws are reinforced by sanctions, such as compulsory recall for repair of motor vehicles whose parts are found to be defective. The sociological significance of this growing body of law lies in the way in which it minimizes the possibility for disruption and conflict in economic exchange. The effects of contracts on people in the present and in the future are controlled, reducing the possibilities for unpleasant surprises and a sense of injustice that would otherwise fuel dissatisfaction with economic life and lead to a breakdown in trust. In these ways laws play an important role in facilitating the progress of the division of labour.

Despite the importance which Durkheim attached to the law as a social fact in the division of labour, he did not think that it was entirely responsible for the regulation of contracts. In addition, there are the customs and conventions of occupational groups, such as professional associations. Good examples, which have become more prevalent since Durkheim's day, are the codes of ethics which have been developed by many occupational groups. Occupational codes of conduct require people in positions of responsibility to put the interests of other people ahead of their own under certain conditions. Such rules, therefore, have the effect of encouraging clients to trust those whose services they seek, and thereby encourage more people to seek out the services of specialized professionals.

Laws and occupational rules which regulate contracts are not the only social conditions favouring the division of labour. In an insightful analysis, Durkheim also argued that the division of labour can only develop if people are free to act differently. If everyone is required to think and act in the same way, then innovation is inhibited and new, more specialized ways of working will not emerge. In short, for the division of labour to occur, it is not enough for individuals simply to possess different abilities and interests. They must also be able to express those differences in practical behaviour.

Expressing individual differences is difficult whenever the collective conscience is strong and well defined. The stronger the state of the collective conscience, the greater the resistance will be to any attempts to act differently. And, the more well defined the collective conscience is, the less room that is left for individual variation. Therefore, Durkheim claimed that the expansion of the division of labour was unlikely under conditions of high mechanical solidarity.

It follows from this that Durkheim believed the progress of the division of labour must depend upon the decay of the collective conscience. Durkheim thought that this was indeed what was happening in France and in the other European societies with which he was familiar. His analysis of this shift was connected to his analysis of changes in religion. The decaying of the collective conscience was connected to the declining influence of traditional religion, and the associated rise in what Durkheim referred to as the worship of the individual. We will therefore turn next to examine Durkheim's theory of religion, before returning once more to complete our discussion of his theory of the division of labour.

Religion

Emile Durkheim's emphasis on social solidarity as an essential feature of all societies is evident in his theory of religion, and especially in his definition of religion in *The Elementary Forms of Religious Life* (1965, 1995). Durkheim defined religion in the following way: 'A religion is a unified system of beliefs and practices relative to sacred things, that is to say, things set apart and forbidden – beliefs and practices which unite into one single moral community called a Church, all those who adhere to them' (Durkheim, 1995: 44). In a religion, people gather together in large groups to carry out their major rituals, and thereby express their unity as members of a moral community. This is unlike magic, where magicians either practice their craft alone or with individual clients, Durkheim concluded.

Durkheim was looking for a very basic definition of religion that would be true for all societies. He thought he had found this in the universal belief in a division between sacred objects and profane objects. Sacred things are things which are protected and isolated, for example they must be treated in special ways and perhaps only by special people. Profane things are ordinary objects which do not receive any special treatment, and for this reason they must be kept at a distance from sacred things.

Religion is an important social fact, in Durkheim's view. Like any other social fact, Durkheim rejects a psychological explanation and he insisted that one social fact must always be explained in terms of other social facts. He therefore asked what social fact could be responsible for the feeling of dependence that people have upon their sacred objects and the divine beings and forces which they represent. Durkheim thought that this feeling of dependence upon something more powerful than themselves must have its origin in people's feelings of dependence upon society, which is so much more powerful than any individual. Therefore, Durkheim argued that it is the power of society itself which is the cause of religion.

Religion may be a universal phenomenon, in Durkheim's view, but this does not mean that it is equally important in every society. Durkheim was convinced that religion had been more important in earlier societies than it was in modern societies. In his words: 'if there is one truth that history teaches us beyond doubt, it is that religion tends to embrace a smaller and smaller portion of social life' (Durkheim, 1964b: 169). Originally, religion pervaded all areas of social life. Then, political, economic and scientific functions gradually separated themselves out as specific activities which took on a more and more worldly character. This happened because the collective conscience has been steadily declining. There are fewer and fewer beliefs and values which are sufficiently widely shared and held strongly enough that they could provide the basis for religious faith. As a result, the individual really feels less acted upon, by God or society, and he therefore becomes more a source of spontaneous activity.

This does not mean that religion completely disappears, or that it is likely to disappear. Rather, the old religions tend to be replaced by a new type of religion that Durkheim referred to as the worship of the individual. Durkheim claimed that: 'As all the other beliefs and practices assume less and less religious a character, the individual becomes the object of a sort of religion. We carry on the worship of the dignity of the human person, which, like all strong acts of worship, has already acquired its superstitions' (Durkheim, 1997: 122). A contemporary example of the 'superstitions' that Durkheim had in mind is the tendency to introduce and expand human rights legislation. Such laws protect the individual against certain kinds of actions by powerful organizations, and thereby elevate the status and freedom of the individual.

The significance of this for the progress of the division of labour is that an acquired individual autonomy enables individuals to diversify in freedom, thereby developing the distinctive interests and abilities that are necessary for highly specialized ways of working. Here we see how effectively Durkheim challenges any reductionist theory of the division of labour that would begin with 'natural' differences between individuals. For Durkheim, whatever differences exist between individuals they are not truly natural or inevitable, but they are only made possible by society, under certain social conditions. Those conditions include the weakening of the collective conscience and the associated decline in the influence of religion.

Determining Causes of the Division of Labour

We have seen that Durkheim sought to analyse the division of labour as a social fact to be explained by other social facts. The immediate causes of the division of labour therefore include such things as contract law, which facilitates orderly economic exchange, and individual liberty, which facilitates the development of a variety of individual interests and aptitudes. In addition, there are other causes of the division of labour identified by Durkheim, which lie at a deeper level.

Durkheim argued that 'The determining cause of a social fact should be sought among the social facts preceding it and not among the states of the individual consciousness' (Durkheim, 1964a: 110). In particular, Durkheim concluded from his investigations that the determining causes of social facts must lie in the fundamental properties of association between individuals in groups. Living in groups is the bedrock of human existence from which every-thing else flows, Durkheim concluded. He thought that it was impossible to conceive of the isolated individual as the basic unit of analysis for sociological theory, for the simple reason that individuals are never really isolated.

All we know about human beings presumes their association with others. As far back as we can look in history, our knowledge of human beings is a knowledge of people in groups, large or small. And, most importantly, Durkheim says that in the life of each individual, 'As a consequence of my birth, I am obliged to associate with a given group' (Durkheim, 1964a: 104). In other words, as soon as we are born somebody picks us up and cleans us, and feeds us, and from that moment on we are members of a social group. Durkheim's point is that to base any sociological theory on assumptions about isolated individuals is completely unrealistic because people have never existed in isolation. From the moment they are born, they interact with others and are continuously and profoundly affected by social life. It is therefore impossible to separate individual reactions from social facts because all individuals are inevitably social by virtue of living in groups.

Durkheim pursued this line of argument in a logical manner. If the basic fact of life is living in groups, he reasoned, then ways of living should vary according to variations in the patterns of association found in different groups. Or, in other words, the social environment should determine the ways in which individuals live. Durkheim then sought to identify what features of the social environment could influence the patterns of social life. He concluded that there are two pre-eminent factors. They are: (1) the number of people in a society, or in other words the size (or volume) of the society; and (2) the degree of concentration of a group, or what he referred to as 'dynamic density' (Durkheim, 1964a: 113).

The size of a population is self-explanatory, but Durkheim's concept of dynamic density is a little more complicated and it deserves a note of explanation. By dynamic density, Durkheim means the extent of interaction among the members of a group. That is because, as he puts it, 'Social life can be affected only by the number of those who participate effectively in it' (Durkheim, 1964a: 114). If people participate only marginally in the interactions within their group, then they are not likely to be affected much by it.

Dynamic density is given by the number of people in a group who have social relations with one another, or in other words it is a result of the number of social ties that exist between the individuals in the group. For example, in a group of four people if each individual forms a partnership with just one other person then only two partnerships will form and there will be only two social ties. This is a situation of low dynamic density. On the other hand, if everyone in a group of four people interacts with everyone else, then there would be six social ties in total. That would be a situation of high dynamic density.

Dynamic density, and population size (or volume), are determining causes of the division of labour, in Durkheim's view. Durkheim expressed this point in the following general proposition: 'The division of labour varies in direct proportion to the volume and density of societies and if it progresses in a continuous manner over the course of social development it is because societies become regularly more dense and generally more voluminous' (Durkheim, 1997: 205). Durkheim believed that the size of a population and the extent of interaction within it are directly related to the extent of the division of labour. Furthermore, he thought that since population size and dynamic density were steadily increasing over time, it follows that the extent of the division of labour must also be increasing.

The reason why Durkheim believed that the size of a population and the extent of interaction within it are directly related to the extent of the division of labour is because these two factors caused a more intense struggle for existence, to which the increased division of labour is one solution. The more people there are in a society, and the more people who are in contact with one another through increased trade, transportation and communications, then the greater the number of potential competitors will be for each member of the society. Competition is a great stimulant to action, and we see here once again how Durkheim sees social facts, such as population size and dynamic density, as forcing individuals to act in ways that they might otherwise not have chosen. Faced with a large number of competitors, each individual is engaged in an intense struggle for survival. And the more the competitors, the more intense the struggle for survival becomes.

The struggle for survival is most intense for those individuals who have only very general skills which are also possessed by many other people. They will face a large number of potential competitors. By comparison, individuals who have very specialized skills that few other people possess will have far fewer competitors. Therefore, one solution to the struggle for survival under conditions of intense competition is to find a new, and more specialized way of working. Those who are least efficient in performing some function will be squeezed out of it, and they must seek some other position. If they try to take up one that is already occupied by a large number of others, they are unlikely to succeed. They can be successful only if they seek some new, more specialized task. Also, two equally efficient producers in the same field will find that things are easier on both of them if they specialize so that they do not compete head-on. Under the compulsion of the struggle for survival, many individuals will therefore choose to adopt a specialization strategy, and the division of labour will accordingly increase. Furthermore, since population size and dynamic density are constantly growing, fuelling a more and more intense struggle for existence, the division of labour will continue to increase, with no end in sight.

Durkheim recognized, however, that the increased division of labour was not the only possible response to the intensified struggle for existence. Other solutions included emigration and colonization of territories where the colonizers would face fewer competitors; apathy and resignation to a precarious existence; and even suicide. Any of these alternatives would be possible, under the right conditions. Durkheim assumed that people would tend to favour the division of labour as a solution, as long as it was easily available and there were no barriers that prevented its realization. The greatest barrier would be a strongly defined state of the collective conscience that would require everyone to think and act in the same way. Therefore, Durkheim concluded that the decline of the collective conscience and increased independence of the individual was an essential secondary factor contributing to the increased division of labour.

It is an important feature of Durkheim's theory that he thought the determining factors of greater population size and dynamic density not only caused the intensified struggle for existence, but they also caused the increased independence of the individual. There are several reasons for this.

First, greater population size normally means greater variety of the environments in which people live. As a result, the collective conscience must be more general and abstract if it is to encompass the totality of the conditions in which the people exist. As the collective conscience becomes more general, people can no longer follow simple instructions but they must think about how to apply abstract rules to their particular situations. Therefore, the abstractness of the collective conscience allows more room for individual initiative and it increases individual autonomy. Furthermore, reflection upon the collective conscience encourages critical thinking so that people no longer take the collective values and beliefs as seriously as they once did. The collective representations therefore lose much of their force to compel obedience and individual diversity increases.

Second, Durkheim claimed that greater dynamic density leads to a decline in the authority of tradition, which is followed by a greater acquired individual autonomy. He argued that the force of the collective representations depends for the most part upon their being handed down from previous generations, and thereby being taken for granted without question. However, increased dynamic density occurs, in part, as a result of greater population mobility, which breaks the ties between the generations and thus weakens the authority of tradition.

According to Durkheim, 'it is the authority of age which gives tradition its authority' (1964b: 293). In other words, it is the respect that younger people have for their parents and for elders in their communities which is the basis for the respect that people have for traditions. It follows from this that prolonged contact with parents and elders is usually necessary for respect for traditions to remain strong. Geographic mobility away from the family home and community of origin weakens the influence of the older generation, and thus leads to falling respect for the collective traditions.

Durkheim thought that population change was a major factor leading to the decline of the collective conscience and ultimately greater freedom of the individual. He could see that not only were people leaving their communities of origin in rural areas in large numbers but they were also moving to cities that provided a quite different kind of social environment. It is this last point that we take up finally in Durkheim's account of how growing population size and dynamic density were contributing to the emergence of a new, and more individualistic, culture.

Durkheim observed that the cities in nineteenth century Europe contained many migrants, and furthermore their populations tended to be relatively young, as younger people were more likely to migrate than older people. Since many people in the cities were detached from the influence of older generations, he concluded that respect for the traditions of the collective conscience must be weaker in the cities. Just as important, Durkheim thought that there is less control over social behaviour in large urban centres, and therefore that individuals have greater practical freedom in what they are able to do. The difficulty with social control in the cities, Durkheim argued, is that there are too many people for it to be effective. The attention of urban dwellers is distracted in too many directions at once, and furthermore each individual has little or no interest in most of the other individuals with whom he or she interacts. Therefore, each individual in a large urban centre is watched less than someone in a village, and most of the people who do watch have little interest in getting involved in the time-consuming and difficult task of trying to control someone else's behaviour. An acquired right to individual autonomy is therefore a prominent feature of urban life.

Conclusion

In this chapter we introduced the problem of choosing the unit of analysis in sociology. We began by outlining the key elements of methodological individualism in Utilitarianism, as exemplified in the work of John Stuart Mill. For Mill, society is composed only of individuals, and therefore he thought that the study of social life should begin with the study of the individual. His approach placed the discipline of psychology in a leading role, as in principle supplying the basic propositions for the derivative discipline of sociology.

In contrast, Emile Durkheim wished to make a case for sociology as an independent discipline. He did not think that sociological studies could be reduced to psychological studies. Rather, he believed that society consists of social facts which are external to the individuals and constrain them. For Durkheim, the study of social life should begin with the description of social facts and account for how those facts shaped the lives of individuals.

In this chapter, we illustrated Durkheim's approach especially from his work on the division of labour. We saw how Durkheim claimed that the driving force for the division of labour lay in the intensified struggle for existence under conditions of increasing population size and increasing dynamic density. However, the division of labour is only one possible outcome under these conditions. The progress of the division of labour therefore depends upon the existence of facilitating factors. Durkheim argued that for the division of labour to develop there need to be differences among individuals, and co-operative relations of exchange between them. These conditions, too, have to be explained by social facts. For example, co-operative relations of exchange between individuals are made possible by the social regulation of contracts, in law, but also in professional relationships. Differences among individuals, on the other hand, are made possible by the loosening of social controls which allows individuals greater autonomy to diversify in freedom. Therefore, Durkheim thought that the weakening of the collective conscience was one of the preconditions for the rapid development of the division of labour. Durkheim believed that population change was a major factor leading to the decline of the collective conscience, and ultimately greater individualism.

Durkheim's discussion of the rise of individualism left his work with an ambiguous legacy. On one hand, he presents a logically coherent account of sociology as the study of social facts that constrain the lives of individuals. On the other hand, he acknowledges that the relation between social facts and individuals has been changing, and individuals are now less constrained than they used to be. This ambiguous situation has continued to trouble sociology through to the present day.

Further Reading

Durkheim, Emile, 1964, *The Rules of Sociological Method*, trans. Sarah Solovay and John Mueller, ed. George E. G. Catlin, New York: Free Press.
Durkheim, Emile, 1995, *The Elementary Forms of Religious Life*, trans. Karen Fields, New York: Free Press.
Durkheim, Emile, 1997, *The Division of Labor in Society*, trans. W. D. Halls, New York: Free Press.
Jones, Robert Alun, 2000, 'Émile Durkheim', in George Ritzer, ed., *The Blackwell Companion to Major Social Theorists*, Oxford: Blackwell, pp. 205–250.
Jones, Susan Stedman, 2001, *Durkheim Reconsidered*, Cambridge: Polity Press.
Lamanna, Mary Ann, 2002, *Emile Durkheim on the Family*, Thousand Oaks, CA: Sage.
Lukes, Steven, 1973, *Émile Durkheim, His Life and Work: A Historical and Critical Study*, London: Allen Lane.
Mill, John Stuart, 1969, *Collected Works of John Stuart Mill, Volume X: Essays on Ethics, Religion and Society*, ed. J. M. Robson, Toronto: University of Toronto Press.

Mill, John Stuart, 1974, *Collected Works of John Stuart Mill, Volume VIII: A System of Logic,* ed. J. M. Robson, Toronto: University of Toronto Press.

Pickering, W. S. F., ed., 2002, *Durkheim Today*, New York: Berghahn Books.

Pickering, W. S. F. and H. Martins, eds, 1994, *Debating Durkheim*, London: Routledge.

Thompson, Kenneth, 2002, *Emile Durkheim*, Revised Edition, London: Routledge.

2

Interaction and the Return of Reductionism

Durkheim's ambiguous legacy to sociology set the scene for a series of alternative discussions and debates. How could sociology develop if it is the study of social facts, yet those same social facts are declining in influence? Two broad answers to this question were developed. One approach entailed restating a reductionist position, sometimes based on the earlier position of Utilitarianism, and sometimes developing along other lines. The second approach involved trying to restate the terms of debate. The aim here was to find some middle ground that avoids polarizing the discussion between methodological holism and methodological individualism. The classical expression of this second point of view is demonstrated in the work of Georg Simmel. The present chapter therefore continues the discussion of the problem of units of analysis by examining the work of Georg Simmel, who argued for interaction as a level of analysis between the individual and social facts.

Other theorists discussed in this chapter are Alfred Schutz, George Homans, Peter Blau and James Coleman. All of these theorists represent twentieth century attempts to renew sociological studies based on the individual as the unit of analysis. Alfred Schutz represents phenomenological sociology. George Homans and Peter Blau represent exchange theory. And James Coleman represents rational choice theory.

Georg Simmel

Georg Simmel (1858–1918) was a German sociologist who defined the unit of analysis for sociology as society. It is the formal study of society, Simmel claimed, that makes sociology a distinct discipline separate from other disciplines. According to Simmel, society refers to the interaction among individual human beings. 'Society merely is the name for a number of individuals, connected by interaction', Simmel said (Wolff, 1964: 10). In contrast to

Emile Durkheim, who insisted that social facts should be treated as things (Durkheim, 1964a: 14), Georg Simmel did not think of society as a thing. What makes society is the reciprocal activity of individuals, in which one person influences another and is influenced by the other in return. As a result, society is a quantitative phenomenon, Simmel concluded. There can be more or less society, depending on the extent of the reciprocal influences that occur between individuals.

Simmel followed a complex, and sometimes tortuous, path between the extremes of sociological reductionism and sociological holism. He rejected the idea that society is just a collection of individuals, on the grounds that it imposed a false view of society as an unknowable abstraction. In opposition to this point of view, he stated that society is a reality (an 'objective unity') in its own right (Spykman, 1965: 27).

At the same time, Simmel rejected many of the assumptions that have been associated with a holistic view of society. Society is not a thing, Simmel stated, but it is an event or a process, or rather a number of processes. In other words, society is dynamic and fluid. Simmel pointed out that society does not only contain fixed structures that take on a crystallized form, but it also includes a variety of episodic events, such as asking for directions in the street. Simmel also rejected the existence of social forces such as a group mind that allegedly determines the lives of individuals. Finally, Simmel rejected any assumption about harmony as the normal state of society. Society reflects not only love but also hatred, and competition and conflict are as much a part of social life as are co-operation and friendship.

Defining sociology was an undertaking that Simmel took very seriously, including the need to differentiate sociology from psychology. He realized that sociology could not be defined simply as the study of society because there are many other disciplines which are also involved in studying various aspects of social life. He therefore looked for some further feature that could be identified as a distinctive task of sociology. Simmel's conclusion was that it is necessary to distinguish between the content and the form of society, and to use the latter as the distinguishing criterion of sociology, although he noted the difficulties of doing this (in practice, Simmel often combined the two).

The forms of interaction are the patterns of interaction that people establish as they influence one another (Simmel, 1971). Examples of forms of interaction include exchange, conflict and domination. Conflict, for instance, is a form of interaction which has specific characteristics that distinguish it from other forms of interaction. The contents of interaction, on the other hand, are the subjective interests which motivate people to engage in particular forms of interaction. In principle, the forms and contents of interaction are independent. Thus, people can participate in the same form of interaction for many different reasons. For example, people may engage in conflict out of a desire for economic gain, or to protect some object of religious faith, or to support a friend, and so forth. Simmel claimed that the distinctive subject matter for sociology was the study of social forms, not the study of their contents. He referred to this approach as the study of society in its purely formal aspect, or in other words formal sociology.

Conflict

Simmel's approach can be illustrated from the significance that he attached to the study of conflict. The study of conflict had been overlooked, Simmel noted, because of the division between methodological individualism and holism, or as he put it between two approaches which focused on 'the individual unit and the unit of individuals' (Simmel, 1955: 14). The former approach neglected social issues, whereas the latter approach emphasized the unity of society, and conflict appeared to negate that unity by undermining the wholeness of society. What was needed, Simmel concluded, was a third approach that looked at conflict as a form of social interaction. Contrary to the view that conflict is a negative factor in social life, Simmel pointed out that conflict is a form of social interaction since conflict cannot possibly be carried out by one individual alone.

The usual view of conflict is that it is a destructive process that weakens social life. It seems that if a conflict is not resolved quickly, then people may find their interactions difficult and painful, and if so they will begin to reduce the amount of time they must spend interacting with one another. Indeed, they may gradually withdraw from the relationship, until perhaps they finally break off the relationship completely. Examples of this are plentiful enough, in marital conflicts that lead to separation and eventually divorce. However, according to Simmel, conflict is not always a destructive factor, but it can contribute to the unity of a group or society, understood as specific forms of co-operation and consensus. That is because something which is negative and damaging between individuals if considered in isolation does not necessarily have that effect when viewed from a broader perspective.

For example, Simmel pointed out that legal disputes often involve intense conflicts, yet these struggles take place within a mutual agreement upon the rules within which the conflict is to be conducted. Beneath the apparent opposition of interests between lawyers representing their clients in divorce proceedings, there is a deeper agreement upon the framework of law and the protagonists' place within it. The laws make conflict possible, and sometimes inevitable, but at the same time the participants submit themselves to a set of interactions which require their co-operation in following the law.

Simmel went further than this, however, in claiming that conflict is not necessarily a destructive factor in social life. He argued that conflict can sometimes be a positive factor in creating or maintaining certain kinds of social interactions. Here, he made several kinds of arguments.

First, Simmel maintained that conflict may be an inseparable element in a relationship such as marriage. If a difficult relationship is to be endured, both individuals must find some meaning in it. Under certain psychological conditions, conflict can be a factor that gives meaning to a relationship that would otherwise be unbearable to the point of being broken off. For example, covert conflict can have this effect, where people avoid open expressions of anger but they cease doing things that the other person would like, or they try to do things that they know the other person would not like. Here, opposition to the other can give the individual some inner satisfaction, distraction from the tedium of a boring relationship or a sense of relief from oppression. 'In such cases', Simmel noted, 'opposition is an element in the relation itself; it is intrinsically interwoven with the other reasons for the relation's existence' (Simmel, 1955: 19).

A second argument made by Simmel for the positive effects of conflict is that it often causes the conflicting parties to seek out and develop relationships with third parties. Politicians, businessmen and journalists, for example, who are competing for success, are driven by their competitive struggle to develop closer and stronger ties with their publics than they might otherwise choose to do. In order to win an election fight, or a fight for economic survival, or a circulation war between rival newspapers, they are forced to find out what the voters, or consumers, or readers actually want, and to try to anticipate their needs. The struggle against one person or group becomes a struggle for the hearts and minds of other people or groups. In this way, conflicts can actually create and deepen relationships between competitors and those whose support and resources the competitors need.

Third, Simmel made an important distinction between inter-group relationships and intra-group relationships. Disputes between the members of one group and another group may divide the two groups, but within each group the conflict can serve to strengthen the sense of group unity and hence collective identity. A group which is engaged in a conflict needs to be cohesive if it is to be strong enough to succeed in its struggle. For example, groups tend to become more centralized under conflict conditions, Simmel argued. A greater need for group loyalty is felt, and dissenters are less likely to be tolerated because they divide the group. Individuals are therefore more likely to be called on to either submit to the group or be expelled from it. One effect of such conflicts is that they often prevent the boundaries of a conflict group from becoming blurred and eventually disappearing. As a result, hostilities may be deliberately created by those who have an interest in maintaining existing social conditions.

Finally, Simmel argued that conflict may not only strengthen an existing group, but it may also bring together people who otherwise would have nothing to do with one another. An aggressive and domineering group may alienate so many different people, that those who are dissatisfied are forced to come together to seek collective relief from the oppression they all suffer.

Similarly, people with disparate interests in opposition to a more powerful opponent may make common cause in order to create a combined force with the power necessary to overcome the opponent. The political logic of having allies in a struggle of overwhelming importance can be so great that people who are normally enemies may join together against a common enemy. A relevant historical example is the way in which Britain, Canada and the United States joined with the Soviet Union as allies against Germany in the Second World War. Faced with the greater threat of Nazism, the opposition between capitalism and communism was temporarily put aside in order to create a military alliance strong enough to defeat the common enemy.

Dyad and Triad

Simmel was very interested in interactions such as an alliance between two parties against a third party because he thought that it tells us something very important about social life. Patterns of relationships vary according to the number of people or groups who are involved. In particular, Simmel was convinced that there is a fundamental sociological difference between groups consisting of two parties (dyads) and groups consisting of three parties (triads) or more (Wolff, 1964).

Intimacy is really only possible in a group consisting of two people, Simmel argued. In the dyad, knowledge can be shared and confidences exchanged that take on a special significance because they are shared with no one else. As soon as a third person enters the group, the situation is entirely changed and ties of intimacy are weakened. Simmel also argued that individuals have a more immediate sense of personal responsibility in the dyad than they do in groups with three or more members. In the dyad, there is a pure and immediate reciprocity in interactions because each person responds directly to the other. Any failure to respond is immediately obvious since there is no one else to assist or intervene. Consequently, each person in the dyad feels an obligation to respond in order to keep the relationship going. In contrast, in groups with three or more people it is always possible for one individual to refrain from responding to another by claiming that what should be done is really the responsibility of someone else. It is therefore possible to avoid responsibilities in the triad in a way that is not possible in the dyad, and as a result individuals feel a lesser sense of personal responsibility.

Simmel was very interested in the changes that occur in groups as they change from dyads to groups with three people, and he therefore set out to describe the distinctive sociological features of the triad. In general, he concluded that there are several sociological features of triads that do not exist in the dyad.

First, the tie between two people can be made stronger by the addition of an indirect bond with a third person. Simmel thought this was the case in marriage, with the arrival of a child. The new tie that each parent has with the child normally links the couple together more strongly than they were before.

Of greater interest to Simmel was the potential that exists for new types of interaction in triads. One of these types of interaction is the mediation of disputes. In a dyad, any conflict between the two people has to be resolved by them alone. In a triad, however, conflict between two members can be mediated by the third person who is able to act as an impartial element in the relationship. It is therefore possible for the third person to present objective information, and to find common ground between the disputants so that they can resolve their differences more easily. A mediator, Simmel thought, is able to avoid the inflamed emotions which often enter into bitter disputes, and thus can arrive more easily at a solution than the disputing parties would be able to do on their own.

The third person in a triad is not always impartial, however, and he or she may seek to gain personally from the complex interactions involved. For example, there is the potential for gain for a third person by encouraging, or taking advantage of, competition between the other members of the group. Simmel thought this is how a market economy works. Here, competitors undercut each other's prices in order to win the favour of supplying goods to a third party. The same phenomenon can be observed in the political arena, also. Third parties may be able to extract concessions from more powerful political parties, when the major parties need the support of a minor party in order to have a majority of votes in the legislature.

The advantage enjoyed by the third element in a triad takes on an added dimension when a strategy of 'divide and conquer' is employed. Here, the third person deliberately plays one of the other parties off against the other, in order to keep both of them weak and to prevent them from combining together. This can be done, for example, by supplying special favours to one of the group members that provokes jealousy in another, thus creating a division between the two. Or, sometimes the third person may be able to provoke fights between the others by spreading rumours and by exciting feelings of hostility. Also, there is the ancient technique of joining with one party to defeat the other, and then turning against the earlier ally now that there is no alternative source of support. All of these political strategies exist in the triad, but not in the dyad.

The Metropolis

Simmel's interest in the effects of the number of people is also reflected in his analysis of life in the metropolis. A metropolis is a large urban centre which is the capital of a country, or the chief city of a region. What interested Simmel about the metropolis was the subjective effects of living in such an environment upon the mental life of its inhabitants.

Simmel believed that there were a number of subjective effects of life in the metropolis. One of them is what he called intellectualism, or in other words an attitude of dispassionate rational calculation of human affairs. In rural areas and small towns, people react emotionally to small differences in the world around them, Simmel believed. In the metropolis, however, this type of response would be very disturbing to the individual because there are so many different things happening all the time and there are so many variations in the population. Simmel thought that people's inner life needed to be protected against the constant bombardment of stimuli from the large population in the metropolis. Therefore, he claimed that people in big cities react less emotionally to events around them and are more inclined to analyse events rationally.

The tendency to analyse events rationally is accentuated by another feature of large cities, namely a highly developed economy based on the circulation of money. In cities, there is a concentration of wealth and an extensive division of labour, both of which encourage the use of money as a means of exchange. It is because of the nature of monetary relationships, Simmel believed, that they tend to be impersonal and conducted according to matter-of-fact calculations of quantities. According to Simmel, 'Money is concerned only with what is common to all, i.e., with the exchange value which reduces all quality and individuality to a purely quantitative level' (Simmel, 1971: 326). The personal qualities of people therefore tend to be ignored, and they tend to be treated as all the same, with the only important differences between them being in what they have to offer. This attitude encourages rational exchange.

In the metropolis, the rational attitude of precise calculation of quantities is carried over from the money economy into the use of time. Clocks and watches are widely diffused in the population, and become essential to the conduct of business and personal affairs. The rational calculation of time is also encouraged by another feature of life in large cities, that is, the need for punctuality. In the commercial practices of cities, and also in personal life, individuals are engaged in activities with so many other people, each of them with their own complex lives, that the timing of activities becomes a problem. The solution to this problem is to schedule activities precisely by making appointments, maintaining appointments diaries, drawing up timetables describing exactly when certain events will happen, and so on. All of this actually works efficiently only insofar as the rational calculation of time is brought into each person's consciousness, in the form of a personal code of punctuality. Following this code requires the suppression of all natural, irrational impulses that would interfere with the scheduling of activities.

One of the impulses that is suppressed in urban life, according to Simmel, is sociability with neighbours and others who are physically close. That is because people need to preserve themselves psychologically from becoming too involved with the number of people who surround them. In small towns, people know each other and maintain positive relationships with most members of their community. In large cities, in contrast, individuals maintain an emotional reserve and avoid close contact with most of the people around them. As a result, they may not talk to, or even know by sight, people who have been their neighbours for years.

Simmel has sometimes been criticized for painting a grey, negative picture of urban life. That certainly seems to be the case with his discussion of the blasé attitude. Simmel suggested that a world-weary attitude of apathy to pleasure or enjoyment is the eventual subjective response of the individual to the abundance of experiences and stimulations in the metropolis. It is also, Simmel thinks, the ultimate subjective reflection of a complete money economy (Simmel, 1978). People lose contact with the unique qualities and properties of things because everything is acquired in the same way by purchase with money. Ultimately, the value of everything comes to be judged by one common factor, namely its price. As a result, there is a probability that the entire objective world will lose much of its subjective meaning.

Simmel paints a rather bleak picture of life in the metropolis, as leading towards a grey uniformity of subjective experience dominated by money. However, that is not the entire picture. Simmel also suggests that people react against their situation in certain ways, and transcend it.

A positive outcome of life in the metropolis is cosmopolitanism, or in other words openness to the world outside one's immediate locality. As people develop more social ties, they are linked to a greater diversity of interests and experiences which widens their mental horizons. Their awareness of the world is not confined to their immediate physical environment, but it is extended to national and international areas. In this way, people in large cities have a richer mental life than people in small towns, whose social world is mainly closed within itself.

Finally, Simmel argued strongly that living in a metropolis is associated with greater individuality and more individual freedoms. This is partly due to the more extensive division of labour in large urban centres, which leads to a greater differentiation of lifestyles and attitudes. In addition, the size of the population has a direct effect on individual liberty. In small towns there tends to be a greater emphasis on unity and uniformity, accompanied by closer surveillance of the individual's attitudes and behaviour. That is because small groups tend to have a narrower way of life, and a stronger emphasis on the contrast between themselves and other groups. In large cities, in contrast, the very diversity of lifestyles and the extensiveness of contact with others outside the city produces a loosening of expectations and social controls, so that individuals have more room for independent movement.

Simmel also claimed that in the metropolis people assert their individuality as a way of distinguishing themselves from one another, in order to ensure that they do not get lost in the crowd. In a large city, in which most people are indifferent towards others, there is a real possibility that any particular individual will simply be overlooked and ignored, and that he or she will therefore become socially insignificant and socially isolated. As a result, it is also possible that people will lose their self-esteem. In order to overcome these problems, people seek to make themselves noticeable by expressing their individual uniqueness. They draw attention to themselves by engaging in unusual behaviour, which has no meaning other than to be different from others. Life in the metropolis therefore includes eccentric patterns of behaviour, which are not random but which have a definite sociological explanation.

Individuality

Despite his bleak image of the metropolis, Simmel ultimately presents us with a picture of a social world in which individuals are able to assert their individuality in order to survive socially and psychologically. This was an important theme for Simmel, since he thought that individual freedom and individual differences were generally tending to increase under modern social conditions. Simmel thought that there was a fundamental tension between the individual and society (Wolff, 1964). On the one side, societies seek to shape each individual's life to fit the goals of society as they change over time. On the other side, individuals resist the shifting influences of society as they seek internal consistency in trying to realize their own values. The result is a constant tension, in which individuals may have more or less freedom to achieve their values depending on the social conditions.

In various writings, Simmel attributed the growth of individuality under modern conditions to a number of social factors. First, as noted above in our discussion of the metropolis, Simmel thought that individuality is positively related to the number of social ties in which the members of a group are involved. As Simmel put it, 'Individuality in being and action generally increases to the degree that the social circle encompassing the individual expands' (Simmel, 1971: 252). In particular, the division of labour and attendant differences tend to increase as the number of social ties increases. For example, extending social ties from one isolated group to another group will result in a new social differentiation between those who produce for export and those who produce for the domestic market. Individuals also have greater freedom of choice in larger groups insofar as they are freed from the narrow limitations of small groups which exercise greater control over their members.

Another key factor in the growth of individuality is the expansion of a money economy (Simmel, 1978). Because it is divisible into many different amounts and can be used to obtain many different things, money is ideally suited to facilitate economic exchange. In an exchange both parties are able to obtain something that they want, and they can therefore increase their capacity to benefit from interactions and realize their personal values. Simmel also held that monetary obligations are less restrictive than obligations to provide specific goods, because obligations in kind direct the activities of the individual in certain directions, whereas financial obligations can be fulfilled in a number of ways depending on what is the easiest and most convenient way for the individual to raise the money. Likewise, receiving money in an economic exchange contributes to individual liberty because the money received can be used in many different ways, compared with a specific good whose uses are much more limited. In a similar manner, monetary exchanges contribute to individual liberty because they free the individual from personal relationships of dependence upon specific others. Money can be earned from whoever is willing to pay, and money received can be spent on whoever is willing to provide a good at a favourable price. Thus, according to Simmel,

> we are remarkably independent of every *specific* member of this society, because his significance for us has been transferred to the one-sided objectivity of his contribution, which can be just as easily produced by any number of other people with different personalities with whom we are connected only by an interest that can be completely expressed in money terms. (Simmel, 1978: 298)

The third key factor in Simmel's account of the growth of individuality is the emergence of specific meanings of individuality. Simmel concluded that in Europe in the eighteenth century, ideas about individualism emphasized the freedom of the individual from external constraint, whereas nineteenth century ideas emphasized diversity and the extent of differences between unique personalities. In both cases, the individual is driven to take the self as the ultimate point of reference by which to judge all things. That is because life has become more complicated as many different perspectives have to be taken into account, and because the individual is less and less able to find meaning anywhere outside the self. Simmel's perceptive observations on individuality were to have a wider resonance in the latter part of the twentieth century.

Alfred Schutz

Classical European sociology, in the works of Emile Durkheim and Georg Simmel, had clearly moved away from the psychological reductionism of methodological individualism found in utilitarianism. However, that approach was not dead and its basic assumptions showed great resilience during the twentieth century. This may be attributed in part to certain characteristics of modern societies, reflected in the writings of Durkheim and especially Simmel. Both Durkheim and Simmel had found it necessary to talk about individuals, as they considered the increase in individuality to be one of the hallmarks of modern society. As we have seen, Simmel considered the growth of individuality to be a subject of some importance, and he never successfully freed himself from the influence of psychology. Durkheim left sociology with the ambiguous legacy of a holistic approach that was pinned to a collective conscience which was in decline. If the growth of individuality was a long-term social trend – confirmed by the worship of the individual – then how could sociology function in the future if it did not pay more attention to individuals?

In the middle of the twentieth century, several new approaches to the study of the individual began to emerge in sociology. One of these approaches was phenomenological sociology. Phenomenological sociology is a theoretical approach that is concerned with the nature and contents of subjective human experience and social action. The leading exponent of this approach was Alfred Schutz.

Alfred Schutz (1899–1959) was a German sociologist who spent most of his career in the United States. Like all exponents of methodological individualism, he based his approach upon an assumption of individual freedom of action. Unlike Durkheim, Schutz did not believe in social facts as things of coercive character. He believed that individuals are free to decide on the course of their action, or to refrain from acting. Schutz said that 'He who lives in the social world is a free being: his acts proceed from spontaneous activity' (1970: 146). According to Schutz, after unnecessary complications are removed, 'we are left with the simple experience of spontaneous Activity based on a previously formulated project. This experience lends itself readily to sober description' (1970: 146). Schutz set himself the task of providing that description.

Schutz endeavoured to describe the individual's 'life-world' (Schutz and Luckmann, 1974). The lifeworld is the world of lived experience. It is not simply a world of private experience, but it is also a world of shared experience. Each individual has a unique biographical situation, but at the same time each individual acts upon others and is acted upon by them. This mutual relationship implies that at least some features of the lifeworld are experienced in a substantially similar way by others and by the individual. As a result, the meanings of the individual's lifeworld can be grasped not only by the actor but also by those others with whom the lifeworld is shared. This intersubjectivity of meanings makes it possible for the individual to make himself or herself understood to others, and for others to make themselves understood to the individual. It is on this basis that interactions take place in a communicative common environment. Thus, Schutz's phenomenology, which begins with the individual, includes a sociology of social action.

Schutz envisaged the lifeworld as containing multiple provinces of meaning upon which we confer the accent of reality at different times and in different places. In addition to the province of everyday life, there is the province of dreams, of theatre, of religious experience, of scientific contemplation, etc. Each of these provinces is experienced as real when it is subject to a certain tension of consciousness. Schutz was most concerned with the everyday lifeworld because he took this to be the paramount reality. This is the province of meaning that the normal wide-awake adult simply takes for granted as the context for carrying out projects of various kinds. The everyday lifeworld is the province of striving to realize goals; it offers opposition, and it requires exertion to overcome it. The natural attitude of everyday life is therefore a pragmatic attitude of getting things done. Doubt concerning the existence of the outer world is suspended, in order that the individual can engage in meaningful action.

The most important feature of the natural attitude of everyday life is that it is focused upon the realization of projects. Projects are first imagined, and their completion is rehearsed in the mind, before they are carried out in action. These projects give the individual an 'interest at hand', or 'purpose at hand', in any particular situation. That is to say, there is always something the individual is trying to achieve that motivates his or her encounter with the world and his or her responses to it. It is an interest at hand that motivates all of the individual's thinking and acting, and which establishes the problems to be solved. The interest at hand therefore structures our awareness of the world so that we focus our attention upon, and remember, those things which are relevant to our interest at hand. We need precise, detailed knowledge about those things which are most relevant to our interest at hand, whereas we need to know less about those things that are less relevant. The everyday lifeworld is therefore a stratified lifeworld, consisting of various zones of different relevance. As a result, we experience the lifeworld as a system of relevances (Schutz, 1967). This system of relevances is complicated by the fact that we rarely have just one interest at hand in a situation, but we may have several interests at hand. And these interests may change in content and importance as the action unfolds.

Schutz considered the system of relevances to be a fundamental feature of the lifeworld, which it is important to understand. He described the life-world as consisting of four zones of relevance (Schutz, 1970). First, there is the zone of primary relevance. This is that part of the world which is immediately accessible to us and within which our projects can be realized. For example, for students who are interested in obtaining a good grade in their course this includes the classroom setting within which lecture material is learned and tests are written. Careful attention is paid to details in the zone of primary relevance, as we require a clear understanding of what exactly is taking place and how we can control it to produce outcomes that favour our interest at hand (such as passing a test).

Second, there is a lesser zone of relevance consisting of objects which are not directly relevant to our interest at hand, but which supply resources or establish conditions for realizing our goals. For students, the library might fall within this secondary zone of relevance, as it can supply reading materials with which to supplement the materials presented in class. In order to satisfy our interest at hand we do not need to know everything about the library, such as how it is run or the nature of the technology employed. All we need to know is how to access the materials that we may be called upon to use. In this zone of relevance it is enough to be merely familiar with potentially relevant objects, and the possibilities that they contain.

Third, there is a zone of minor relevance, which consists of objects that for the time being are irrelevant to the interest at hand, but which might become relevant in the future under changed conditions. For instance, most students are unaware of the funding arrangements that provide financial support to their college or university. But if there was a financial crisis on campus that led to course cancellations and other cutbacks, students would become concerned. They would then quickly become informed about something that had suddenly become relevant to their interest at hand of completing their programme of studies. Schutz called objects in this zone of relevance 'relatively irrelevant', indicating that we just take them for granted without question as long as things go well. We only become aware of them, and pay attention to them, when the chances of success or failure change.

Fourth, and finally, there is the zone of things that Schutz referred to as 'absolutely irrelevant'. This zone consists of objects that are believed to have no effect at all on the interest at hand. For students taking a course in sociology in North America, the question of how much tea is produced in China would fall into the zone of absolute irrelevance. Objects in this zone are simply ignored.

Schutz's conceptualization of zones of relevance helped him to understand the amount of attention, and the quality of attention, that we pay to various objects. In order to understand the content of attention he turned to another concept, namely 'typification' (Schutz, 1964). A typification is an assignment of an object to some category, or type. We use typifications to recognize objects on the basis of the general knowledge we have of the type to which they belong. Types are classes of objects that are homogeneous with respect to certain traits. For example, we may recognize a person we meet in the street as a letter carrier. We identify the characteristics of the person as those character-istics which are typical of an object of that type. For example, we identify a letter carrier as an employee of the postal service, someone who carries a bag con-taining letters from house to house, and so on. Such typifications are based on recognizing the other as an example of an ideal type, and therefore it does not involve recognizing the unique self of the other person.

Typifications are essential features of our experiences in the lifeworld. They enable us to fill in the details of objects that we encounter for the first time, and to make predictions about how they will behave. This is necessary so that we can control the objects in order to carry out our projects successfully. Schutz therefore claimed that we experience the social world as 'a network of typifications' (1970: 119). We constantly typify people, their actions, their motives for engaging in action and the consequences of their actions.

The typifications that an individual has accumulated in her lifetime constitute her stock of knowledge. Every individual's stock of knowledge contains a large number of types that could be used in a given situation. Which types are actually used depends on the individual's interest at hand. All typification is relative to some problem that has to be solved in a particular situation, a problem which focuses our attention more upon some characteristics of objects and less upon others (Schutz, 1964, 1966). Therefore, typification is a dynamic process which unfolds as our interests at hand change in changing circumstances.

The individual's stock of knowledge is partly the outcome of his own experiences, and it is partly the outcome of the experiences of others that have been transmitted to him. Schutz thought that most of the types we use have been formulated by others, either our predecessors or our contemporaries. Knowledge of typifications, and how to use them, is an essential element in the cultural heritage that is passed on to us by parents and teachers. This cultural heritage provides the cognitive tools that are recognized as appropriate to a given way of life. Each individual draws upon this accumulated stock of knowledge in formulating responses to new events, and also modifies the stock of knowledge in the light of new experiences. Thus, there are some unique differences between individuals in their stocks of knowledge. Knowledge is not uniform, but it is socially distributed. However, there is also a common background of typifications which is shared by those who belong to the same social group. Shared typifications are especially likely to be found where they have been standardized by a group and established by means of social control. This common background helps to provide the basis for intersubjective understanding, and hence effective social interaction.

A common frame of reference of typifications is made available to us through language. According to Schutz, language involves naming things and events, and the process of naming something is also a process of typification. He said that 'By naming an experienced object, we are relating it by its typicality to pre-experienced things of similar typical structure' (1970: 117). Schutz thought that the vocabulary of everyday language contains the system of typifications, and hence the system of relevances, that has been accepted by the members of a linguistic community (Schutz, 1966). The relevances and typifications that have been validated and approved by our linguistic community are therefore transmitted to us in childhood as we learn the uses of language.

Schutz's followers were prominent in drawing the attention of sociologists to the neglected study of language. In other ways, however, the influence of phenomenological sociology has declined. In recent years, the tide of methodological individualism has turned in a different direction, towards rational choice theory.

George Homans

The intellectual tradition of utilitarianism remained strong, notably within disciplines outside sociology, such as economics and psychology. Influenced by these disciplines, there has in fact been a resurgence of methodological individualism in sociology in the second half of the twentieth century, especially in American sociology. The first of these new forms of individualism was sociological exchange theory.

Exchange theory is the term used to describe the work of a group of theorists who emphasized studying how individuals respond to rewards from others. The most notable theorists in this group were George Homans and Peter Blau. The work of George Homans will be discussed first.

George Homans (1910–1989) was a prominent American sociologist who became convinced that an essential corrective to the excessively abstract, holistic sociology of his day was to bring individuals back into sociology. Homans was explicitly critical of the intellectual tradition descended from Emile Durkheim, and he maintained that nothing emerges in social life that cannot be explained by propositions about individuals. According to Homans, 'The characteristics of social groups and societies are the resultants, no doubt the complicated resultants but still the resultants, of the interaction between individuals over time – and they are no more than that' (Homans, 1974: 12).

In the late 1950s and early 1960s, Homans began to publish work that was intended to push sociology in the direction of psychological reductionism (Homans, 1958, 1961). This work was explicitly based on a combination of ideas from behavioural psychology and economics. Homans set out his position as follows: 'Briefly, both behavioral psychology and elementary economics envisage human behavior as a function of its pay-off: in amount and kind it depends on the amount and kind of reward and punishment it fetches' (Homans, 1961: 13). People are presumed to be motivated by rewards and punishments, to engage in activities that are rewarding and to avoid activities that are punishing. Activities that are rewarding are reinforced, and are therefore repeated until the individual is satiated. Activities that are punishing, on the other hand, are likely to be given up and cease. Activities that are both rewarding and punishing will be continued if the rewards outweigh the punishments.

Homans went on to point out that when the reward or punishment that one individual receives is received from another person, then the behaviour becomes social behaviour. According to Homans, social behaviour is 'an exchange of activity, tangible or intangible, and more or less rewarding or costly, between at least two persons' (Homans, 1961: 13). When two or more people reward or punish each other's activity, and thereby influence each other's behaviour, patterns of social behaviour can be observed.

Reward and punishment are important terms in Homans' account of exchange theory. The way in which he used these terms therefore deserves some attention because it shows how Homans proposed to blend the insights of psychology and economics in his work. A reward is anything that is positively valued, and a punishment is anything that is negatively valued. Among the different kinds of punishment is one that Homans referred to as 'cost'. The cost of an activity is any negative value that the individual cannot avoid in order to carry out an activity that is rewarded. This would include, for example, having to pay money in order to acquire an object, or having to give up free time in order to meet someone. Following the economists, Homans suggested that the real cost of something is the value of the reward that could have been obtained from an alternative activity that was forgone. For example, the real cost of an activity would be the value of something else that could have been purchased with a given amount of money, or of something else that could have been done with a given amount of free time. Homans then defined the amount of reward minus the amount of cost of an activity as the individual's profit, and he argues that no exchange will continue unless both parties are making a profit.

Viewed from this perspective, regularities in behaviour are seen as the result of a stable pattern of rewards and costs in which people obtain substantial rewards for lesser costs, and they can do no better. The less their profit, the more likely people are to change their behaviour in such a way as to increase their profit. They will change their behaviour by giving up activities that are least profitable, and engaging in activities that are more profitable, until they have reached a point where there is no change in behaviour that would result in an increase in profit. At this point, their behaviour would stabilize. Homans pointed out that if this were true for all the members of a group, then the group would have a social organization in equilibrium and it would be possible for the sociologist to describe the group as having a social structure. The key point here for Homans is that social structure is not a given, or the result of social facts, but it is the result of a psychological process of individuals deciding to change or not change their behaviour.

Homans added some complexity to his analysis of equilibrium in social groups by noting that stable interactions are more complicated than at first appears. People who are engaged in repeated exchanges can be said to bargain with one another, explicitly or implicitly, and they have to reach agreement on two things. First, if an exchange relationship is to continue, the parties must reach an agreement that will give both of them a profit (i.e., their rewards must be greater than their costs). Second, they must both agree that it is a fair exchange, otherwise one or both of them will feel a sense of injustice and become angry. An angry person may become sufficiently upset that he or she decides to break off the exchange, or they may withdraw the reward of social approval previously offered to the other person. In any event, if an exchange is to persist some attempt will have to be made to address the individuals' concerns about justice and injustice.

Homans referred to this problem as the problem of distributive justice. He thought that there are two concerns that people have in comparing how well off they are with how well off other people are. They are concerned in the first place with comparing the amount of rewards that people receive in relation to their costs. If one person incurs lower costs but receives higher rewards than the other, then the other is likely to feel a sense of injustice. Second, people are concerned with comparing their situations with others with respect to what characteristics of themselves are invested in the process of exchange. For example, people with more seniority in a company are likely to feel that they have invested more in the process of exchange because they have worked for a longer period of time. Here, Homans thought that if people who believe they have invested more also believe that they profit less from the relationship, then they will feel a sense of injustice. Homans therefore defined the rule of distributive justice in the following way:

> A man in an exchange relation with another will expect that the rewards of each man be proportional to his costs – the greater the rewards, the greater the costs – and that the net rewards, or profits, of each man be proportional to his investments – the greater the investments, the greater the profit. (Homans, 1961: 75)

As can be seen from the above quotation, Homans was typically concerned with direct exchanges between two individuals. His approach to exchange theory is distinctive because he based it on what he called elementary social behaviour, or subinstitutional behaviour, and for the most part he avoided extending his analysis beyond that. By elementary social behaviour Homans meant the kind of behaviour that emerges naturally between individuals, rather than the rule-governed behaviour which is subject to deliberate social organization by large groups. The question of how institutional behaviour is related to elementary, or subinstitutional, behaviour was never really resolved by Homans, although he expressed his faith that the two were related. For example, Homans pointed out that conformity to group norms is something for which people are rewarded; however, he did not set out to explain why particular norms take the forms that they do.

Homans also maintained that some elementary social behaviour, if pursued long enough by enough people, could break through the existing institutions and replace them. He therefore concluded that social institutions probably have their origins in elementary social behaviour. However, the precise mechanisms by which this comes about are unclear. One possible mechanism that Homans did discuss was the investment of social capital by a leader. A leader who possesses relatively great resources may be able to provide rewards to other people over long periods of time in order to encourage them to develop more complex forms of social organization. The way in which this process might work was described in more detail by our next exchange theorist, Peter Blau.

Peter Blau

Peter Blau (1918–2002) was an American sociologist whose career went through several phases. In the middle of his career, he became interested in exchange theory to which he made an important contribution (Blau, 1964). According to Blau, the concept of exchange refers to voluntary social actions that depend on rewarding reactions from others. People enter into new relationships because they expect them to be rewarding, and they continue existing relationships only if they are in fact rewarding. If they are not rewarding, then the exchange ceases.

Blau acknowledged that in principle exchange theory does not attempt to account for all human behaviour. There are some types of behaviour which lie outside the boundaries of the theory, and which would have to be explained in other terms. For instance, involuntary social relationships do not fall within the terms of exchange theory. A prominent example of involuntary relationships is the kinship ties which result from the simple fact of birth into a group. They could not be described as being initiated in order to enter into an exchange. Yet even here there may be some scope for exchange theory. Although individuals may not be able to choose their kin, they can choose how, and how often, to interact with them, and these choices are likely to be influenced by the nature of exchange relationships. Another example of an involuntary relationship cited by Blau is physical coercion. In contrast, he claimed that other forms of power relationships can be considered as voluntary services provided by the less powerful person to the more powerful person in exchange for certain benefits.

It is also possible that there could be cases of genuine altruism, in which people give to others without any expectation of return whatsoever. Such cases might occur if people have internalized norms of generous or charitable giving. However, Blau suspected that in practice there is a great deal of behaviour which appears to be altruistic, but which in reality is not motivated by morality but by the desire for some return or other. For example, people may be motivated to make a gift for which no apparent return is required in order to develop a social relationship with the recipient. Similarly, people may value the social approval that follows from being known as a generous giver who does not demand repayment. In short, there are social rewards which may be expected, even if no material return is required for a gift.

Although Blau recognized in principle that exchange theory could not account for all social behaviour, in practice he believed that much behaviour is guided by considerations of exchange, and more than we usually think. Clearly, he intended exchange theory to be a general theory, with a wide relevance.

The relevance of Blau's version of exchange theory depends on his ability to show that much behaviour that we do not normally think of as exchange is nevertheless really exchange beneath the surface appearances. Blau achieved this in the first place by suggesting that in addition to primary rewards, exchange relationships are also based on social rewards such as social approval. People want approval and other signs of social acceptance, and they are prepared to give up other things in order to obtain them. Blau therefore considered such relationships as a dating relationship to be just as much an exchange of rewards as a business relationship.

Second, Blau made a distinction between economic exchange and social exchange. Economic exchanges between business associates, or between retailers and customers, are typically precise about the nature and price of what is being exchanged, and about the timing of when the transactions will take place. Social exchanges, on the other hand, are much looser and are correspondingly less visible. The most important distinction is that social exchange entails unspecified obligations. It is based on the principle that one person does another some favour in the expectation of receiving a return, but its exact nature is not specified. As Blau put it, social exchange 'involves favors that create diffuse future obligations, not precisely specified ones, and the nature of the return cannot be bargained about but must be left to the discretion of the one who makes it' (Blau, 1964: 93). In everyday social life, much exchange is social exchange that extends over long periods of time.

Third, Blau made another important distinction between direct exchange and indirect exchange. Direct exchange involves two parties who each give something to the other, and they receive something in return from the same person. Indirect exchange, on the other hand, involves more than two parties whose exchange transactions are more complicated. Here, everyone gives something and receives something in return, but the person to whom they give is not the same as the person from whom they receive. The exchange is indirect because it goes through a third party, or more than one party in the case of very complicated exchanges. In Blau's view, much exchange in organizations is of this nature. For example, somebody may perform tasks for an organization's clients but he or she is not rewarded by them directly. Rather, the clients send their individual payments to the organization's office and the office arranges for a fixed monthly salary to be paid to the worker. Clearly, looking at organizational transactions as indirect exchanges greatly expands the potential relevance of exchange theory.

Blau's ambition for exchange theory is evident in his claim to be able to use it to explain four facets of social structure. They are: integration, differentiation, organization and opposition. According to Blau, the first two (integration and differentiation) emerge directly in the course of transactions without any explicit design. The latter two (organization and opposition) emerge indirectly as a result of deliberate efforts focused on some collective goals or ideals. We shall discuss each of these facets of social structure in turn.

Integration

The starting point for exchange relations, according to Blau, is some kind of attraction between two people. This may be an intrinsic attraction, or an extrinsic attraction to something that the other person has to offer. In either case a process of exchange is likely to ensue. This is most obvious in the case of extrinsic attraction, where each party has an interest in obtaining something from the other by exchanging something that they value less for something that they value more. In the case of intrinsic attraction, each individual will be motivated to keep the relationship going by ensuring that it is sufficiently rewarding to maintain the interest of the other. In both cases, the process of exchange serves to integrate people into ongoing relationships. In particular, in social exchanges the voluntary returns for earlier favours build up relationships of trust, as each party experiences that the things they give are reciprocated.

Differentiation

Although exchange processes serve to integrate individuals into social relationships, they can also have the effect of separating people into different, and unequal, social positions. Blau was especially interested in the ways in which hierarchies of status and power emerge as a result of exchange. People who provide others with valuable resources have a claim to superior status, especially if they make essential contributions to an entire group. If the initial rewards are reciprocated in full, then no inequality in status results as the exchange is balanced. However, if the initial rewards are not reciprocated, or if they are only partly reciprocated, then an inequality of status occurs. Giving more than one receives is therefore a fundamental means of gaining superior status.

Giving more than one receives is also a fundamental means of gaining power over others, since it creates a relationship of dependence. Someone who is dependent upon another person is vulnerable to having the expected rewards withdrawn. At the same time, the person who is providing the excess rewards is unlikely to do so indefinitely unless something is received in return as compensation. The person receiving the rewards has several options. He or she may try to get along without the reward, or force could be used to induce the other to give the needed reward, or the reward could be obtained from another source. If none of these options is available, or they are not preferred, then she or he must comply with the wishes of the other in order to ensure that the flow of rewards continues.

Organization

Power gained over others gives the power holder the ability to co-ordinate the activities of a group in more effective ways, and to initiate more complex activities that bring new rewards to group members. However, such activities are likely to become stable features of the group's social organization only if power is transformed into authority.

Authority is the right exercised by a superior to give commands to subordinates who voluntarily comply because they believe it is legitimate to do so. Authority therefore rests on a set of norms of legitimate authority that define the proper relationships between leaders and followers. Like all norms, there are always some people who are tempted to break the norms of authority, but the sanctions applied by group members usually induce them to conform and thus to obey the leader. Obedience to a leader's commands is therefore compulsory from the perspective of each individual who must conform to the group, but it is voluntary from the perspective of the group as a whole as it rests on the idea that the leader has a right to expect obedience.

Peter Blau sought to explain authority relationships by looking at them as exchange relationships. He argued that leaders create joint obligations among their followers as a result of the services of leadership which they provide to the group. These services are more than just particular benefits to particular individuals, but they are services to the group such as co-ordinating group activities, setting group goals, or negotiating for group benefits with the leaders of other groups. It is important to note that Blau therefore claimed authority relationships are relationships of indirect exchange, rather than direct exchange. In authority relationships there are two exchanges. First of all, the individual group member conforms to the group by following the norms of obedience to the leader, and in return she or he receives social approval from the group. Second, there is an exchange between the group and the leader in which the group exchanges collective compliance with directives of the leader in return for the benefits of leadership. It is through this mechanism of indirect exchange that Blau claimed organization can be analysed as a process of social exchange.

Opposition

Seen as a process of social exchange, any authority relationship is vulnerable to being identified by the group of followers as an unfair exchange. If that is the case, then the exercise of authority is likely to create opposition. Blau's concept of fair exchange is similar to Homans' concept of distributive justice. People compare the rewards they receive with the investments they have made in order to procure these benefits, and if the rewards are too low then they are perceived as unfair. The main difference between Homans and Blau is that according to Blau the standards of fairness are social norms that are defined by particular social groups.

Blau attached considerable importance to the ways in which feelings and beliefs are formed within groups, as they are critical to whether or not actual opposition emerges in potential conflict situations. Isolated victims of oppression are unable to do anything about their situation, but an oppressed group with close communication is likely to be able to mobilize some resistance. As the members of an oppressed group communicate their feelings, a social consensus emerges among them that legitimates their feelings of injustice and reinforces their desire for revenge. Blau's theory of social exchange therefore begins with the individual, but in certain important respects his analysis of individual behaviour hinges on an account of social processes that take place within groups.

James Coleman

A more explicit effort to articulate the connections between processes at the level of the individual and at the level of the group was developed by James Coleman (1926–1995). Coleman was an American sociologist who occupied a prominent position in his discipline. In particular, he was an influential figure in a broad intellectual movement known as rational choice theory. Coleman was especially interested in the problem of moving between analysis at the micro-level (individual) and the macro-level (system). He proposed a three-stage explanatory process: (1) from the macro-level to the micro-level; (2) the causal analysis of linked variables at the micro-level; and (3) from the micro-level to the macro-level.

Like Homans and Blau, James Coleman was a methodological individualist, but he went further than either of them in attempting to work out a sociological approach founded on the work of economists. He used an individual-level theory of action, in which purposive action is directed towards a goal, with the goal shaped by values or preferences. Coleman said that he adopted the conception of rational action employed in economics (Coleman, 1990). This conception is based on the notion of different actions having different amounts of utility for the actor, and is accompanied by the principle that the actor chooses the action that will maximize utility.

More specifically, Coleman indicated that his model of a rational actor refers to a self-interested actor who is unconstrained by norms. This does not mean that Coleman thought that individuals are never motivated by norms. Rather, he thought that adherence to norms was something that had to be explained. Coleman asserted that much sociology takes the existence of social norms for granted, but this avoids raising the question of why and how norms come into existence. In Coleman's view, two conditions are sufficient for the emergence of a norm. They are: (1) a demand for effective norms and (2) the fulfilment of that demand.

In accounting for the demand for norms, Coleman introduced from economics the concept of 'externality'. An externality is an effect of an action which impinges upon someone who is not the source of the action. According to Coleman, an externality can be positive (i.e., it brings benefits to the other person) or it can be negative (i.e., it imposes costs on the other person). Coleman argued that a demand for norms arises when an action has externalities for a set of people, who cannot control the action in any other way. An example is non-smokers who work with a smoker. The action of smoking is controlled by the smoker, but the effects of smoking are not confined to the smoker as the non-smokers also breathe in second-hand smoke that imposes costs on them, such as ill health. Hence, there is a negative externality and a demand for effective norms to control the actions of the smoker. Such norms become effective when the beneficiaries of a norm are able to impose sanctions whose effects are greater than the cost to the actor of imposing the sanction.

Coleman's approach to sociological questions can be illustrated from his account of authority, which he defined as the right to control another's actions. How, then, is authority to be explained? Coleman said this question is easily answered. 'Individuals may, under threat or promise or because they otherwise see it as in their best interests to do so, give up the right to control certain of their actions' (Coleman, 1990: 66).

Coleman next discussed the conditions under which this occurs. One possibility is coercion, which occurs when the authoritative other holds extensive resources and is willing to use them so that non-compliance would lead to serious negative consequences. Coleman considered this situation to be a transaction in which the person who submits to authority exercises a choice, because 'Choice always exists even for persons subject to the most despotic authority' (Coleman, 1990: 71). However, this does not mean that all authority is voluntary. There can be involuntary authority, such as the authority that parents have over children from birth, or the authority that the state exercises over its citizens with respect to all acts that are declared illegal. Yet, even here, Coleman considered that choice is possible, since children can run away from home and people can leave the country in which they are born.

In the case of voluntary authority that is not the result of coercion, Coleman considered that there are two reasons why persons vest rights of control over their actions in others. First, the individual may vest rights of control unilaterally, without extrinsic compensation, because she or he believes that they will be better off by following the other's leadership. Second, the individual may transfer rights of control without holding this belief, in return for some extrinsic compensation. Coleman referred to these two possibilities as 'conjoint' and 'disjoint' authority relations respectively. In a conjoint authority relation, the superordinate's directives implement the subordinate's interests. In a disjoint authority relation they do not, and the subordinate's interests must be satisfied by extrinsic means.

Disjoint authority relations are exemplified by work relations in a bureaucracy. Here, employees vest authority over themselves in the organization, in return for a salary. There is no assumption that authority will be exercised in the interests of all the members. Rather, authority is exercised to pursue the goals of the organization as they are defined by the people at the top of the hierarchy of authority.

Conjoint authority relations are exemplified by a labour union. Each union member gives up control over certain actions, such as the right to sign a contract with the employer, in the expectation that actions on the part of the union will bring benefits. For example, it is expected that the union will negotiate wage increases that bring higher income to the members. Here, there is an assumption that the exercise of authority will benefit the subordinates in the authority relation.

Coleman thought that conjoint authority relations were vulnerable to a variant of the 'free rider' problem. The 'free rider' problem occurs when it would be rational for an individual to not participate in or contribute to an activity, in the expectation that others will do so and will bear all the costs of action. Thus, the rational individual would receive the benefits of the collective action while bearing no personal costs. Coleman therefore considered actual participation in conjoint authority relations to be a puzzle to be solved through investigation. One possibility is that the individual may have a high level of personal disorganization and may benefit directly from having his or her actions directed by another, irrespective of the benefits of collective action.

Coleman concluded that conjoint authority relations are also vulnerable to the 'free rider' problem in another sense. Once authority has been vested in a person who is believed to provide greater benefits than one could do on one's own, it would be rational for the individual to let the leader do all the work. As a result, there will be low levels of participation in conjoint authority structures, unless some special arrangement is made, such as sanctions for non-participation. Coleman considered this action by the subordinates to be a fundamental defect of a conjoint authority relation.

Similarly, Coleman believed that a fundamental defect of disjoint authority structures is that the subordinates have no intrinsic interest in the tasks they are assigned. If they are rational, they will therefore tend to avoid doing the tasks unless detailed mechanisms of supervision are established.

Coleman concluded that in both conjoint authority and disjoint authority the subordinates' interests lead to reduced levels of performance, in the absence of special correctives. However, other aspects of behaviour differ markedly. In conjoint authority structures the subordinates' interests lead to public support of norms encouraging high performance. Private behaviour, on the other hand, may not accord with these norms, and Coleman seems to have believed that it would not. In contrast, in disjoint authority structures subordinates' interests lead to no such norms. Instead, subordinates' interests may lead to norms that discourage high performance.

Coleman's discussion of authority illustrates several characteristics of his approach. First, there is the tendency to base theoretical arguments on assumptions at the level of the individual. Second, there is the tendency to use abstract models of hypothetical rationality as a basis for formulating puzzles to be solved. And third, there is the tendency to theorize at the stage of micro-level to macro-level.

Conclusion

This chapter has continued the discussion of the problem of units of analysis that was begun in the first chapter. The chapter began by considering the work of Georg Simmel, who tried to avoid the poles of methodological individualism and methodological holism by developing a characteristically complex approach. Instead of choosing either the individual or the social fact as the unit of analysis, Simmel identified sociology with the study of interaction. Simmel agreed with the reductionists that society is composed of individuals, but then he argued that what makes society possible is that the individuals are united in interaction. However, unlike the methodological holists such as Emile Durkheim, Simmel did not assume that society was a collaborative construction based on social solidarity. Simmel was convinced that conflict, too, was normal, and he tried to provide a clear and detailed description of it.

The study of conflict was one of a number of studies that Simmel conducted. Other studies discussed here include the effects of the number of people involved in interaction, life in the metropolis and the growth of individuality. Like Emile Durkheim, Georg Simmel thought there was a long-term trend towards greater individualism. Unlike Durkheim, Simmel did not attribute the rise of individualism to the decline of the collective conscience, but rather to a variety of specific factors that encouraged people to think and act individually. These factors included the number of social ties in which the members of a group are involved, the expansion of a money economy and the emergence of specific meanings of individuality.

The trend towards greater individualism in society had a significant impact on sociological theory in the twentieth century. Many sociologists responded to this shift by reinstating methodological individualism as the preferred solution to the problem of units of analysis. Examples discussed here are phenomeno- logical sociology, exchange theory and rational choice theory. It is characteristic of all of these approaches that they have tended to downplay, or even ignore, societal influences upon the individual in favour of some model that emphasizes free individual choice.

Phenomenological sociology is represented in this chapter by the work of Alfred Schutz. Schutz took a radical position on the question of individual freedom, in claiming that individuals engage in spontaneous activity. Schutz set out to describe how spontaneous activity is organized, and the structures that it assumes. He was most concerned with the everyday lifeworld within which individuals carry out projects of various kinds. These projects give people interests at hand in specific situations, as they try to achieve specific goals. Our interests at hand define for us what is perceived as relevant in the situation, and therefore what we will pay attention to and remember. The life- world is therefore a structured system of relevances. Things that are relevant to us are typified as we identify specific characteristics of objects as belonging to some class, or type, of objects that is part of our stock of knowledge about the world.

Exchange theory is represented here by George Homans and Peter Blau. Homans tried to push sociology in the direction of psychological reductionism by basing his approach on the work of behavioural psychologists, and to a lesser extent on the work of micro-economists. Homans argued that human beings are motivated by the balance of rewards and punishments, or costs, in which they seek to maximize their profit, which consists of the excess of rewards over costs. Human behaviour becomes social behaviour when two or more individuals reward or punish each other in an exchange of activity. A stable social structure emerges in human groups when there is no possible change of behaviour for any group member that would result in an increase in profit, and when the members agree that their exchange relations are characterized by distributive justice.

Peter Blau's version of exchange theory was similar in its fundamentals to that of George Homans', but Blau was more concerned with showing how various features of social structure were constructed on the basis of exchange processes. He distinguished four such features, namely, integration, differentiation, organization and opposition. Integration occurs when two individuals maintain a social relationship over time, on the basis of mutually rewarding transactions that are characterized by trust in reciprocation for benefits given. Differentiation of social positions develops as a result of imbalances in the exchange process, in which one party is unable to return as much as he or she receives. Initially taking the form of inequality in status, differentiation turns into inequality in power if the imbalance grows and is continued over time. Organization of group life develops when power is transformed into authority, through the introduction of relations of indirect exchange. Finally, opposition occurs when exchange relations are seen as unfair.

The last theorist discussed in this chapter is James Coleman. Coleman is an exemplar of an approach with links to exchange theory, known as rational choice theory. Coleman adopted the model of a rational actor from micro-economics, and he argued on this basis that social norms are something that has to be explained rather than taken as given. Social norms emerge when an action has externalities for a set of people who cannot control the action in any other way, and they are able to impose sanctions on the targets of norms. Like Blau, Coleman was interested in the sociologically important concept of authority. According to Coleman, authority relations develop when individuals see it as being in their best interests to give up the right to control certain of their actions. This is likely to occur when the individual believes that he or she will be better off by following the other's leadership, or when the individual expects to receive some extrinsic compensation. Clearly, Coleman's general approach is based upon the assumption that individuals make rational choices about their lines of action.

Although we leave the question of units of analysis here, it would be wrong to give the impression that methodological individualism has been universally victorious in the struggle for academic recognition. Both methodological individualism and methodological holism continue to be debated in sociology. Like all of the dimensions of sociological theory discussed in this book, the problem of units of analysis continues to be an open question that challenges each new generation of scholars. Which approach do you think is best, and what arguments would you make to support your position?

Further Reading

Blau, Peter, 1964, *Exchange and Power in Social Life*, New York: John Wiley.

Coleman, James S., 1990, *Foundations of Social Theory*, Cambridge, MA: Belknap Press.

Coleman, James S. and Thomas J. Fararo, eds, 1992, *Rational Choice Theory: Advocacy and Critique*, Newbury Park: Sage.

Cook, Karen S., ed., 1987, *Social Exchange Theory*, Newbury Park: Sage.

Featherstone, Mike, ed., 1991, *A Special Issue on Georg Simmel: Theory, Culture and Society*, Volume 8, Number 3, London: Sage.

Frisby, David, 1984, *Georg Simmel*, London: Tavistock.

Frisby, David, ed., 1994, *Georg Simmel: Critical Assessments*, 3 vols, London: Routledge.

Gergen, Kenneth J., Martin S. Greenberg and Richard H. Willis, eds, 1980, *Social Exchange: Advances in Theory and Research*, New York: Plenum.

Heath, Anthony, 1976, *Rational Choice and Social Exchange: A Critique of Exchange Theory*, Cambridge: Cambridge University Press.

Homans, George C., 1958, 'Human Behavior as Exchange', *American Journal of Sociology*, 63: 6, 597–606.

Homans, George C., 1974, *Social Behavior: Its Elementary Forms*, Revised Edition, New York: Harcourt Brace Jovanovich.

Lindenberg, Siegwart, 2000, 'James Coleman', in George Ritzer, ed., *The Blackwell Companion to Major Social Theorists*, Oxford: Blackwell, pp. 513–544.

Rogers, Mary, 2000, 'Alfred Schutz', in George Ritzer, ed., *The Blackwell Companion to Major Social Theorists*, Oxford: Blackwell, pp. 367–387.

Scaff, Lawrence A., 2000, 'Georg Simmel', in George Ritzer, ed., *The Blackwell Companion to Major Social Theorists*, Oxford: Blackwell, pp. 251–278.

Schutz, Alfred, 1970, *On Phenomenology and Social Relations*, ed. Helmut R. Wagner, Chicago: University of Chicago Press.

Schutz, Alfred and Thomas Luckmann, 1974, *The Structures of the Life-World*, trans. Richard M. Zaner and H. Tristram Engelhardt, Jr., London: Heinemann.

Simmel, Georg, 1955, *Conflict and the Web of Group-Affiliations*, trans. Kurt H. Wolff and Reinhard Bendix, Glencoe: Free Press.

Simmel, Georg, 1971, *On Individuality and Social Forms*, ed. Donald N. Levine, Chicago: University of Chicago Press.

Spykman, Nicholas J., 1965, *The Social Theory of Georg Simmel*, New York: Atherton Press.

Thomason, Burke C., 1982, *Making Sense of Reification: Alfred Schutz and Constructionist Theory*, Atlantic Highlands: Humanities Press.

Wolff, Kurt H., 1964, *The Sociology of Georg Simmel*, New York: Free Press.

Dimension Two

Modes of Explanation

3

Explaining Social Life

In the previous two chapters we were concerned with the problem of choosing the unit of analysis in sociology. In this chapter we take up the next task to be undertaken in the process of theory construction. Once the unit of analysis has been determined, the next question to be asked is what kind of knowledge is desired about it, and how is that knowledge to be obtained?

Three different modes of explanation can be observed in sociology, in isolation and in combination. The chapter begins by introducing positivism as the once-dominant approach to sociology, seen as the science that provides causal explanations of society. Positivism is important, and it is the first approach to be discussed here, because it was historically identified with the attempt to delineate sociology as a distinct discipline that was not to be confused with other disciplines that theorize about social life, such as philosophy. This approach is illustrated from the work of Emile Durkheim. Also found in Durkheim's work is the next mode of explanation to be examined, namely functionalism. The work of the later structural functionalists is also introduced here, with a focus on Talcott Parsons. Finally, the work of Max Weber is discussed as an important theorist who sought to combine causal explanations with interpretations of meaning. Weber's ideal type analysis is explicated as the particular means by which he strove to achieve his goal.

Positivism: Emile Durkheim

Positivism is an intellectual approach to social life that seeks to ground ways of looking at the social world in the methods of the natural sciences. Calling sociology a 'social science', for example, usually signifies a positivist intent. It signifies that the scientific method, which has been applied to the natural world so successfully by disciplines such as physics and chemistry, is now being applied to the social world.

One of the most resolute positivists in sociology was Emile Durkheim. Poggi (2000) has referred to Durkheim's book on *The Rules of Sociological*

Method (1964a) as a 'positivist manifesto'. Durkheim did not particularly care for the label 'positivism', but he nevertheless associated himself with what Poggi calls the positivist project. *The Rules of Sociological Method* was primarily intended to draw a sharp boundary between social science and other modes of discourse concerning social affairs.

There are four general features of positivism that can be illustrated from Durkheim's work. They are: (1) the goal of discovering scientific laws; (2) a belief in philosophical realism; (3) the practice of empirical research; and (4) the use of logical methods of proof for relations of causality.

Scientific laws are general statements about relationships between factors (e.g., causes and effects), which can be proven to be universally true under specified conditions, and that are usually independent of time and space. Durkheim clearly hoped, and believed, that sociology would be capable of discovering genuine scientific laws like those in physics. We can see this illustrated in his own work, in *The Division of Labor in Society*. There, Durkheim presented a scientific law explaining the division of labour, in the following manner: 'The division of labor varies in direct ratio with the volume and density of societies, and, if it progresses in a continuous manner in the course of social development, it is because societies become regularly denser and generally more voluminous' (Durkheim, 1964b: 262).

The first thing to notice about this statement is the language that Durkheim used, words such as 'volume' and 'density'. It is the language of physics, a social physics in fact. We can see here in the clearest manner how Durkheim was trying to imitate the laws of physics in his scientific sociology. The next thing to notice is the structure of the statement, and how it satisfies the requirements for a scientific law. Durkheim tells us about certain factors (the division of labour on one hand, and the volume and density of societies on the other hand), which have a definite relationship. (They vary in direct ratio, in other words, as one term increases the other term increases.) Durkheim is telling us in this statement that as the volume and density of societies go up, the division of labour will also go up. Finally, this is a general proposition that is independent of time and space. There is no indication here that Durkheim meant the scope of his proposition to be restricted to his own society, namely nineteenth century France. On the contrary, the latter part of the statement is intended to draw our attention to the fact that the proposition can be used to explain changes over time, in an unspecified number of societies. Concerning time, Durkheim draws our attention to the fact that the division of labour is constantly increasing over time (i.e., it progresses over the course of social development), which he attributes, according to his law, to the constant increase in the size and density of societies. Furthermore, Durkheim's proposition can be used to make predictions about the future. It follows that if the volume and density of societies continue to go up in the future, then so will the division of labour.

Durkheim's interest in scientific laws was made possible by a belief in philosophical realism. Philosophical realism is the belief that it is possible to have an exact understanding of how the world really works, and therefore that theories can (and should) correspond with reality. The main barrier to this goal is the possibility that subjective influences may interfere with accurate observations about the social world. If we have a strong emotional commitment to a particular point of view, we may see only what we want to see. More subtly, our limited experiences of the world may incline us to more readily recognize and identify some things, and overlook others. In either case, the outcome would be the same. Findings and conclusions would be shaped by characteristics of the observer, and not by characteristics of the real world. Theories would therefore not correspond exactly with reality, but they would be distorted to a greater or lesser extent.

Durkheim was very much aware of this problem in sociology. In fact, he realized that it could be a greater problem for sociology than it is for the natural sciences. That is because of what he referred to as 'the frequent interference of sentiment', which makes 'emancipation from lay ideas particularly difficult in sociology' (Durkheim, 1964a: 32). In particular, Durkheim thought that political and religious ideas, and moral standards, were most likely to interfere with scientific work because we cannot tolerate opposition to our points of view in these areas. Such sentiments do not convey insights, Durkheim concluded, rather they are simply strong but confused states of mind.

Durkheim's principal solution to this problem was that 'all preconceptions must be eradicated' (1964a: 31). In other words, Durkheim thought that the sociologist should set aside all preconceived ideas originating outside science in order to arrive at objective knowledge of the world as it really is.

Durkheim was not only concerned about the pre-scientific ideas of the sociological observer, but he was also concerned that the ideas of the subjects of research might also 'infect' the process of scientific understanding. If the subjects of research are asked their opinions about their behaviour, and if they are taken seriously by the observer, then subjective ideas formed in everyday life would shape the conclusions. Durkheim therefore thought that it was important to deliberately ignore the ideas of the people who are being studied, in order to avoid becoming caught up in their subjective ideas.

Durkheim followed this procedure in his study on *Suicide* (1966). He did not seek out suicide notes, or other evidence on the state of mind of the suicidal person prior to committing suicide. In his opinion, people's own interpretations of their situations are often misleading because they may be unconscious of the real reasons for their actions. In that case, their own thoughts merely rationalize a tendency to act that was initially formed for other reasons. Therefore, Durkheim believed it was necessary to ignore their interpretations of their behaviour in favour of studying the behaviour itself.

Durkheim thought that in practice it was desirable to check the influence of subjective factors by having clear definitions of the facts that are to be included in a sociological explanation. Such definitions should focus on external, behavioural characteristics rather than involving subjective judgements.

According to Durkheim, the external characteristics that are used to define the objects of research should be as objective as possible. For example, Durkheim argued that crimes should be defined in a way different from common sense, as those acts which 'evoke from society the particular reaction called punishment' (1964a: 35). In this way Durkheim avoided having to make judgements about illegality, and the motives for action, which could have entangled him in subjective issues.

Durkheim was concerned with making practical recommendations for empirical research in sociology. Empirical research involves an emphasis on supporting all claims and arguments with data drawn from systematic observation. Durkheim thought that in this way sociology would be differentiated from philosophy, with which it had been historically connected. A key difficulty with the sociology of his day, Durkheim argued, was that it was more concerned with ideas than with things. Ideas were studied as if they were real, and he accused sociology of being more or less exclusively concerned with concepts. Ideas, Durkheim concluded, are often dangerously incorrect. The only way to correct this situation, he argued, is by studying reality itself, through beginning with scientific observations about things.

One of Durkheim's recommendations for empirical sociology was that sociologists should only study phenomena with some stability that do not change too much over time. His reasoning here was that we should approach the study of social life where it offers the easiest access for investigation. Scientists need to test their ideas against data, then go back and re-work their theories, and then re-test their ideas. If the social world had changed in the meantime, then any second or subsequent tests would likely produce different results, but the reasons would be unclear and a definite answer would have to be deferred. Therefore, Durkheim recommended that 'we must establish the foundations of science on solid ground and not on shifting sand' (1964a: 46). For example, Durkheim thought that it was useful to study legal regulations because they change more slowly than the behaviour to which they are applied.

The final feature of Durkheim's positivism to be considered here is his use of logical methods of proof for relations of causality. Durkheim was convinced that the basis for all sociological explanation must be to show the causes of a given social fact. It is first necessary to discover the origins of social facts, and the conditions which make them possible, he concluded. Furthermore, Durkheim thought that we should take great care in the nature of sociological proofs for suggested causal explanations. He stated that: 'We have only one way to demonstrate that a given phenomenon is the cause of another, viz., to compare the cases in which they are simultaneously present or absent, to see if the variations they present in these different combinations of circumstances indicate that one depends on the other' (Durkheim, 1964a: 125).

Durkheim observed that when the data for a study can be artificially produced by the observer, then the study is a scientific experiment. However, this is not possible in sociology, where all we can do is bring data together in the way they have been produced in the social world. In sociology, therefore, we do not conduct experiments, but we demonstrate sociological proofs through the comparative method. We collect data, and compare whether a hypothesized cause occurs with a hypothesized effect, or not. Durkheim did not think that we should assume that a given cause is always followed by a given effect, as the cause might have been counteracted by some other factor in a particular situation. Therefore, we should look for a number of cases in which cause and effect coincide, even when one is present without the other in certain cases. Durkheim referred to this approach as the method of concomitant variations, or correlation. Durkheim claimed that: 'As soon as one has proved that, in a certain number of cases, two phenomena vary with one another, one is certain of being in the presence of a law' (1964a: 133).

Functionalism: Emile Durkheim, Robert Merton and Talcott Parsons

Emile Durkheim

Durkheim was not interested only in causal explanations, but he was also interested in functional explanations. In fact, he thought that the two types of explanations were both necessary in sociology. He stated that: 'When, then, the explanation of a social phenomenon is undertaken, we must seek separately the efficient cause which produces it and the function it fulfils' (Durkheim, 1964a: 95).

Functionalism is an approach that seeks to explain social patterns in terms of their effectiveness in meeting needs. As Durkheim put it, 'To ask what the function of the division of labor is, is to seek for the need which it supplies' (1964b: 49). This mode of explanation is linked to a way of looking at society known as 'organicism'. Society is conceived of as being like an organism that lives and dies, and which therefore has conditions that are necessary for its survival. Those conditions which are necessary for the survival of the social organism, and therefore for the maintenance of society over time, can be thought of as needs that have to be fulfilled. Any practice which has persisted over a reasonably long period of time is likely to have persisted because it fulfils some need which contributes to the survival of society.

Following the functionalist method, Durkheim claimed that the most common forms of social organization must be those which were most advantageous, at least on average. Any social practices which do not have beneficial effects would actually be harmful, Durkheim concluded, because they would cost time and effort and other resources without returning anything to society. If many social patterns had this 'parasitic character' then society could not survive and social life would be impossible. Durkheim therefore assumed that since existing societies must be those that have survived, then most existing practices must be functional for society. Based on this assumption, it is generally necessary for the sociologist to focus on a social pattern that is widespread, and to show its usefulness, and how it contributes to the maintenance of society and itself. This is what Durkheim did in his functional analysis of the division of labour.

Emile Durkheim thought that the true function of the division of labour is to create social solidarity. People who specialize in their work depend on each other because they have to exchange the things that they produce for the things that they need. Therefore, a positive attraction develops between exchange partners, and they are careful not to disrupt the relationship in order to keep the exchange going. It is in this way that social co-operation is ensured in modern societies, which is vital to the maintenance of society and to the division of labour itself.

Another example of Durkheim's functionalist logic is his analysis of the function of punishment. The true function of punishment, Durkheim claimed, was to maintain the strength of people's values and beliefs in the laws of society. If transgressions went unpunished, then people would quickly come to regard the difference between conformity and deviance as unimportant, with the result that there would be more deviance and less conformity. Punishment, on the other hand, serves to remind people of what are the moral and legal standards in their society. The process of conviction and punishment in court, for instance, dramatically enacts society's revulsion against the crime, and thus it re-affirms the existence of a moral consensus, and the essential correctness of the rules that have been broken. The publicity which a prominent case receives therefore incites the collective sentiments in support of society's laws. In this way, punishment helps to strengthen a society's collective conscience.

Durkheim's examples of the function of the division of labour and the function of punishment help to illustrate two important points about his approach to functionalist explanation. In the first place, Durkheim focused on the functions of social patterns for social order. As he put it, 'to explain a social fact it is not enough to show the cause on which it depends; we must also, at least in most cases, show its function in the establishment of social order' (Durkheim, 1964a: 97). The tendency is to see societies as requiring social order, and to see the most common patterns as maintaining that order. Durkheim's functionalist sociology is therefore socially conservative, as it takes the existing order for granted, and it favours co-operation over the conflict which might be needed to bring about radical change.

The second point to make about Durkheim's functionalist method is that he separated it from any analysis of conscious intentions. Social functions are beneficial effects of social patterns, but it is not necessary to assume that these effects are intended. Functions can emerge in an evolutionary manner, as the result of an unconscious adjustment of the parts of society. Furthermore, people may be unaware of the functions they perform, because the connections between events in society are too complicated for them to follow. Durkheim thought that in most cases it would be too difficult for anybody to see what the true functions of any social pattern are, except for the trained observer who has the time to devote to the study of social life. Therefore, it is the job of the sociologist to uncover the functions of social patterns, about which others may be unaware.

Durkheim thought that he had shown a social function that was not consciously intended in his study on *Suicide*. One of the patterns that Durkheim demonstrated in his statistical analyses is that family ties are associated with lower suicide rates. Durkheim concluded that the family group acts as a preservative against suicide, and therefore it has the social function of reducing the death rate. At the same time, Durkheim thought it would be ridiculous to suppose that the composition of the family existed because people anticipated that it would have this beneficial result. Durkheim therefore thought that he had shown a social function that the average person could not possibly have known in advance of sociological enquiry.

Another example of Durkheim's belief that conscious thoughts are often different from real social functions concerns the function of punishment discussed above. Durkheim pointed out that the common sense viewpoint on punishment holds that it exists either to correct the guilty by inducing them to change their ways or it serves as a warning that will prevent others from following the bad example of lawbreakers. However, Durkheim claimed that in both of these respects punishment is in fact relatively ineffective, and therefore these effects of punishment are mediocre. The real function of punishment, of which most people may be unaware, is to maintain social solidarity by strengthening the collective conscience.

Durkheim's logic of functional analysis has rarely been pursued in the manner that he intended. However, it was popular in the middle of the twentieth century, especially in the United States of America, in an approach known as structural functionalism.

Robert Merton

Structural functionalism was an approach which involved identifying the structures that constitute society, such as the family, and then describing the functions that those structures fulfil. One of the most prominent of the American structural functionalists was Robert Merton (1910–2003). Following in the Durkheimian tradition, Merton (1957) wanted to avoid confusion between motives for action and the functions of action. He therefore introduced the distinction between manifest functions and latent functions.

Manifest functions are objective consequences of action that have advantages for a social system, and which are intended and recognized by participants in the system. Latent functions, on the other hand, are positive consequences of action which are neither intended nor recognized. Merton thought that one of the important tasks of sociology was to uncover latent functions, thus contributing new knowledge that goes beyond common sense, everyday understandings. An example given by Merton concerns high levels of expenditure on costly consumer goods. The common-sense understanding of such behaviour is that it is undertaken in order that the consumer can enjoy all the benefits of the goods that have been purchased. However, the latent function of this expenditure, uncovered by the sociologist, is that purchasing expensive goods is making a symbolic claim about one's wealth, and it is therefore a way of making a claim for high social status.

Talcott Parsons

Presenting claims about functions that go beyond common sense was a prominent characteristic of another American structural functionalist, Talcott Parsons (1902–1979). In Parsons' case, the aim of functional analysis in revealing the unconscious bases for action was to outline very general principles of social organization. Parsons argued that it was possible to describe a set of abstract conditions for survival that must be satisfied by any system of action. He claimed that there are four functional prerequisites, or functional imperatives, in all social systems. They are: pattern-maintenance, integration, goal-attainment, and adaptation (Parsons, 1961).

Pattern-maintenance refers to the functional imperative of maintaining the culture of a system. In Parsons' opinion, it is culture that defines the structure of a system. It provides the values which are guides to action, and when they are internalized by many people it produces consensus on appropriate ways of behaving. In this way, the culture of a society produces definite patterns of behaviour that persist over time. Therefore, it is essential that the culture should be maintained if the system is to survive.

Parsons claimed that there are two problems which have to be solved if the culture is to be maintained. First, there is the potential problem that values can change as they are subject to various pressures in the dynamics of social systems. If the values are to be stabilized, he argued, then they must be integrated with the fundamental beliefs in the culture. These beliefs are found in religion and in ideologies. For example, if the value that competition is a good activity in sports, business and politics is to be maintained, then it must be integrated with the belief that competition leads to greater effort, productivity and attention to the needs of others. Such beliefs justify, or legitimate, the value of competition.

The second problem of pattern-maintenance is that of maintaining people's motivations so that they will want to continue following the rules laid down in their culture. To begin with, people must learn the culture, or at least a relevant part of it, in the process of socialization. In other words, they must internalize the values, beliefs and norms of their culture. However, people can lose the desire, or will, to follow the rules, for many different reasons. For example, when someone close to us dies we may lose the will to keep on going with the routines of daily life; indeed, we may even lose the will to go on living without the other person. Procedures of what Parsons called 'tension management' are therefore necessary to restore the individual's motivation. Funeral rituals, in particular, bring together a large number of people whose demonstrations of concern show the affected individual that he or she is not alone, and that there are others who will help the person to get back on their feet. Another example of tension management is institutionalized leisure time at the weekends or on holidays that provides us with temporary relief from work. The discipline of work is difficult to maintain, it can be stressful, and it can involve working with difficult people. Therefore, we need occasional relief from it, in order to 'recharge our batteries' so that we are ready to continue working again. In these ways we can see that the system provides ways of maintaining motivation, thereby fulfilling the functional imperative of pattern-maintenance.

The second functional imperative is that of integration. According to Parsons, one of the characteristics of a social system is that it tends to become differentiated, or divided up, into separate structures that fulfil different functions. For example, the family is concerned with socialization and tension management, whereas business organizations are concerned with production and distribution of goods and services. The functional imperative of integration is that these differentiated structures must be adjusted to each other so that they do not come into conflict and prevent each other from fulfilling their functions. To continue the example above, families and employers must reach agreement on how much time each of them can claim from particular individuals. Employers need their employees to spend time at work, but families need their members to spend time at home. The result of fulfilling the functional imperative of integration is a series of agreements, in law and in collective agreements, about such things as the maximum length of the working day, the working week and the availability of paid holidays and sick days. The potentially conflicting demands of families and employers are integrated through legal agreements.

Parsons claimed that among the four functional imperatives, it is the integrative function that has the major effect on the social system. Accordingly, he stated that 'the problems focusing about the integrative functions of social systems constitute the central core of the concerns of sociological theory' (Parsons, 1961: 41). This focus on integration is similar to Durkheim's focus on social order as the key problem for functional analysis.

Parsons' third functional imperative is goal-attainment. It is important to note here that in his discussion of functional imperatives, Parsons was not talking about the goals of individuals but about the goals of social systems. Social systems formulate goals, in Parsons' view, when some change in the environment produces a discrepancy between the actual situation and the tendencies of the system to remain the same. As we saw in his discussion of pattern-maintenance, Parsons assumed that social systems tend to follow the same pattern unless they are disturbed. The function of goal-attainment is to reduce the disturbance and restore the system to a state of equilibrium, by minimizing the discrepancy between the needs of the system and the condition of the external environment. A relevant example is when one country finds its exports to another country reduced following the introduction of an import quota, or some other restriction on trade. The country whose exports have fallen will formulate the goal of trying to get the exports back up to where they were before, by negotiating with the other country or exerting pressure through international agencies.

Finally, the fourth functional imperative is adaptation. The functional problem here is one of providing facilities, or resources, that are needed by the various specialized structures within a system. All action requires resources of some kind, whether it be food, machinery, electricity, and so on. Any system must therefore ensure that particular resources are available when and where they are needed. There are two functional problems here. One is the production of resources, for example, when electricity is generated in turbines driven by water power, or steam power, or wind power. The other functional problem is the distribution, or allocation, of facilities to the places where they are needed. Parsons was more concerned with this problem, as it involves making choices between alternative uses for resources. In a highly differentiated society this can be a complex process. For example, in a market economy different structures compete for resources and the ones with the most money, who are prepared to pay the highest prices, are the most likely to receive the resources that they need.

Interpretive Understanding: Max Weber

Contrary to functionalism, the next mode of explanation to be considered here takes seriously the meanings that actors give to their actions. This approach is exemplified here by the work of Max Weber (1864–1920). In fact, Weber's approach to sociology differed from both positivism and functionalism, as we can see in the contrasts between Durkheim and Weber. We will start with Weber's views on objectivity, in order to see how he differed from positivism.

Emile Durkheim thought that in order to have objective knowledge of the social world, all preconceived ideas must be eradicated. This was not Weber's position. Weber believed that a sociology without presuppositions was impossible. He recognized something that Durkheim had overlooked, that is the question of how topics for investigation are chosen in the first place. Weber thought that all sociologists should be concerned with the problem of what is worth knowing. There is potentially an infinite number of topics that could be investigated, but it is not possible to study all of them. The sociologist therefore has to choose what will be studied, and what will be ignored. Weber thought that since this is the case, the sociologist should study topics that are important. Importance is something that must be interpreted, based on some subjective understanding of the world. Important topics are topics that have some 'cultural significance', Weber concluded (1949). What he meant by this is that we select issues that have value-relevance for us because we are able to relate empirical reality to our own values. As a result, Weber claimed that there could be no such thing as absolutely objective knowledge in sociology. Data are always selected and analysed with some purpose in mind. Only a part of concrete reality is significant to us because it reveals relationships which are important to us due to their connection with our values.

This does not mean that Weber thought that sociologists should display their biases in their work. On the contrary, Weber thought that once the topic of investigation had been chosen it was important for sociologists to keep their value judgements out of their work as much as possible, in order to avoid making errors. It is important in any scientific work that the rules of logic and method in a particular field should be followed. Furthermore, Weber was concerned that work which was biased towards one particular point of view would make it impossible for people with opposing points of view to reach agreement on relevant conclusions (Gerth and Mills, 1948).

Turning now to Weber's relationship with functionalism, he believed that functional analysis does have a place in sociology, but only as a guideline to identifying sociological issues that are worth studying (Weber, 1947). It is sometimes a convenient way of thinking about the connections between social patterns, so that the sociologist becomes aware of what is important to understand. But functional analysis in itself is not an adequate mode of explanation, in Weber's view, and it should be used only as a starting point for enquiry. Weber thought there was a real danger that the contributions of functionalism would be overestimated, and that it would erroneously be taken as the final word on sociological topics. Weber argued that whereas functional analysis may be useful in natural sciences such as biology, the sociologist is able to do something that no natural scientist can ever do. As human beings we are capable of understanding how our fellow human beings think and feel, and why they act in the ways that they do. Weber believed that it is important for us to use the capacity for subjective understanding that we possess because it enables us to know the actual manner in which behaviour is produced. According to Weber, 'subjective understanding is the specific characteristic of sociological knowledge' (1947: 104).

For Weber, subjective understanding is essential at all stages of sociological enquiry, including the first steps that we take in theorizing. That is because the very concepts that we use in sociology are derived from the people whose lives we are studying. For example, if we are studying the political system of Canada we will need to use concepts such as Prime Minister, Member of Parliament and Queen, in order to describe the component parts of the system. These terms are not simply inventions of the social scientist, but they are, in the first place, terms that Canadian political actors use to describe their world. As such, these terms have a meaning in their world, which social scientific observers cannot ignore if we are to understand how that world actually works.

Weber sought to integrate understanding into sociology by combining it with causal analysis. This was such a fundamental point for Weber that he incorporated it into his definition of sociology. 'Sociology ... is a science which attempts the interpretive understanding of social action in order thereby to arrive at a causal explanation of its course and effects. In "action" is included all human behaviour when and in so far as the acting individual attaches a subjective meaning to it' (Weber, 1947: 88). Weber outlined two interconnected goals for sociology in this definition. In the first place, the sociologist must engage in the interpretive understanding of behaviour that is meaningful to the actor. Second, the sociologist uses this understanding in order to provide a causal explanation of the pattern that is under investigation. Weber insisted that a correct explanation of action must be both adequate with respect to the interpretation of motives and causally adequate.

According to Weber, causal explanation in sociology involves demonstrating what he referred to as 'empirical uniformities' in the behaviour of a number of people (1947: 120). This does not mean that everyone has to behave in the same way. Rather, it means there is a probability that they will behave in a certain way. A causal explanation involves determining that there is a probability that an event will be followed or accompanied by another event. Weber thought it is necessary to show that there is a certain pattern of action which is typical of a certain group of people, and also that there is a certain pattern of subjective meaning which is also typical of the group that causes them to act in the way that they do. Weber believed that describing typical patterns for a number of cases was so important to the sociological method that he made it the basis for his most famous contribution to methodology, namely the ideal type. Proof of a causal explanation is given by providing evidence that action normally takes a course which has been described as meaningful, and this involves showing its approximation to an ideal type.

An ideal type is a theoretical construct whose various elements have been abstracted from reality and combined in a logically integrated fashion, on the basis of some principle of subjective meaning. As Weber put it,

> An ideal type is formed by the one-sided accentuation of one or more points of view and by the synthesis of a great many diffuse, discrete, more

or less present and occasionally absent concrete individual phenomena, which are arranged according to those one-sidedly emphasized viewpoints into a unified analytical construct. (1949: 90)

Weber also referred to the ideal type as a 'pure type', to indicate that its elements have been carefully selected and they are freed from the admixture of other elements that are found in reality. Because of its selective nature and its logical integration by the observer, an ideal type may never be found in real life. For example, Weber did not think it was any criticism of his method that none of his ideal types of authority are usually found in pure form. An ideal type is a theorist's concept, to which actual events will correspond with different degrees of approximation. As such, it is not the end point of enquiry but only a means to help the sociological investigator understand the social world.

According to Weber, the concepts of economic theory are ideal types. They state what action would be like if it was purely rational and oriented only to the maximization of personal economic advantage. Economic concepts are therefore unrealistic to some extent, and we should not expect them to correspond with reality all of the time. However, they have the great advantage of clarifying the distinction between economic motives and non-economic motives so that both of them can be studied. Weber thought that this successful methodology should be extended to sociology.

Weber used ideal types in a variety of ways, and he thought they could be useful in several respects (Weber, 1949). To begin with, they help us to select the data that are to be used in our studies, by defining in practical terms what we take to be of cultural significance. Weber was very conscious of the fact that there is an enormous range of material waiting to be investigated, and we cannot possibly study all of it. An ideal type helps to distinguish which data are significant, and therefore worthy of careful attention, and which data are insignificant and can therefore be safely ignored. An ideal type therefore provides a scientific basis for selecting a manageable amount of material to be studied in a particular investigation.

Second, ideal types help the sociologist to clarify concepts by making them the focus of explicit attention and careful argument. In particular, it is possible for the sociologist to ensure that the ideal type is internally consistent and contains no logical contradictions. In order to be scientifically useful, concepts must be logical. But this makes them different from reality, which is often influenced by factors other than logic. Weber thought that the logical character of ideal types was very important for all theoretical work. He was therefore suspicious of studies that did not use ideal types because he thought they were likely to be vague and unclear. The advantages of ideal types are their precision and clarity, and thus their aid to sociological reasoning.

Third, ideal types help the observer to simplify and standardize a reality that is too complex to be conceptualized in any other way. The example that

Weber gave here was 'Christianity'. Empirically, Christianity exists in the minds of an indefinite number of individuals who believe their faith in a multitude of different ways. It would be impossible to include all the differences of belief in one definition, and even if we tried to do so the result would be chaotic since some of the different beliefs are contradictory. The only useful way of defining Christianity is to abstract certain selected elements of belief from reality, or in other words to construct an ideal type.

Fourth, ideal types help in the formulation of hypotheses to be tested against reality. An ideal type tells us what patterns to expect, if it is appropriate to a particular field of investigation. The role of the sociologist is therefore to construct ideal types that permit useful comparisons with reality in particular situations. In general, Weber thought that it was most useful to construct ideal types as pure patterns of rational action.

Fifth, ideal types are sometimes necessary for sociological explanation when the majority of actors are unable to provide conscious reasons for their actions, or when their conscious meanings are unclear. Weber believed that in most cases actual action goes on in a state of inarticulate half-consciousness or actual unconsciousness of its subjective meaning. Under such conditions it is the responsibility of the sociological investigator to try to clarify the actors' meanings, in order to permit systematic investigation in an area in which it would otherwise be very difficult. Here, the ideal type is a construct in which the observer attributes certain meanings to the actors who are being studied. Such attributions may be guided by the contributions of a few key individuals who are unusually conscious of their subjective meanings.

Finally, Weber emphasized what ideal types are not. They are not moral ideals which people strive to realize in their lives, or which they use in making value-judgements about other people. Weber drew a sharp distinction in principle between the logical analysis of reality by ideal types and value-judgements about reality on the basis of ideals.

Bureaucracy

Max Weber's most famous ideal type is his ideal type of bureaucracy. The phenomenon of bureaucracy had considerable cultural significance, Weber thought, because it was of growing importance in his own time, and he thought it would be even more important in the future. Weber drew the elements of bureaucracy from the leading forms of public administration and management of private businesses. The guiding principle that he used to logic-ally organize the elements of bureaucracy was that of rational administration. Weber believed that bureaucracy was a type of administration that was rationally organized to achieve the goal of long-term organizational survival. Bureaucracy is a rational means of control over everything of importance in the organization that effects its functioning. That control is exercised primarily through control over knowledge. Thus, Weber stated: 'Bureaucratic administration means fundamentally the exercise of control on the basis of knowledge. This is the feature of it which makes it specifically rational' (1947: 339). As a rational type of organization, Weber clearly thought that bureaucracy had distinct advantages which made it superior to any other type of organization.

Weber identified six main features of bureaucracy (Gerth and Mills, 1948).

1. The organization consists of a number of positions which have fixed duties defined by rules. This involves a systematic division of labour, in which the activities carried out in the organization are divided up in a rational manner. All the activities are distributed among the positions as official duties, thus ensuring that no activities are neglected. Each official holding a position has a specific sphere of competence and authority so that she or he is able to carry out their duties. This includes the authority to give commands that the work should be done. Arrangements are also made so that the duties will be carried out in an effective manner. For example, anyone holding an official position must have the regular qualifications for that position.

2. The positions in a bureaucracy are organized into a hierarchy of authority. A bureaucratic hierarchy consists of a series of levels of authority, so that each higher level has control over a broader range of decisions than the level below it. Every official in the organization, except the individual or group at the top, reports to someone above them in the hierarchy of authority. Therefore, each lower office is under the control and supervision of a higher one (Weber, 1947). Information and decisions can be passed down from higher to lower positions, and everyone is subject to supervision to ensure that they carry out their assigned duties.

3. All important decisions and actions are recorded in documents which are stored in files. In Weber's day, the affairs of the organization were recorded in writing. Today, they are more often recorded in typed documents or in electronic documents in computers and databanks. However, the principle remains the same. Everything that is of importance that needs to be known is recorded, so that the records can be consulted at a later date when new decisions need to be made. These records belong to the organization, and they are kept in the office where they are accessible. They are not stored in the home of the official, and business correspondence is separated from private correspondence.

4. Management of an office requires specialized training. As a result, offices are run by experts who possess the knowledge needed to carry out their duties. It is normally the case that a person must have demonstrated adequate technical training in order to be hired for a position in a bureaucracy. Candidates are appointed to positions on the basis of technical qualifications, by passing examinations or by possessing educational certificates or

diplomas. Weber thought that the role of technical qualifications in bureaucratic organizations is constantly increasing. As a result, the length of time that the average person spends in education is growing.

5. Official business demands the full working capacity of the official, and the office is treated as the sole, or at least the primary, occupation of the incumbent. Work is not conducted in a casual manner, or on an unsystematic part-time basis along with other activities. The organization is therefore able to call upon the services of the official as and when they are needed.

6. The organization is governed by a stable set of rules, which cover all, or almost all, of the activities carried out in the organization. The rules therefore provide most of the answers to the practical questions that arise in day-to-day activities. The holders of official positions are expected to know these rules, and they receive special training in them.

Although these six features are the main characteristics of bureaucracy, there are several other features which, though not essential, are often found associated with the pure type of bureaucracy (Weber, 1947). For instance, Weber claimed that the ideal official conducts himself or herself in an impersonal manner. Everyone is to be treated in the same way according to the rules of the organization, and therefore there is no room for likes or dislikes influencing the official's behaviour. As a result, Weber thought that bureaucracies tend to undermine class privileges and lead to a levelling of class differences. Another feature of bureaucracy is that officials are paid a fixed salary, usually in the form of money. As long as officials follow their organization's rules, they do not need to worry about where their income will come from, and they do not need to exploit their position for financial gain. The official who is paid a fixed salary is able to devote all of her or his undivided attention to working for the organization. Also, the position of the official is separated from ownership of the means of administration. The organization itself owns, and therefore controls, everything that is needed for the performance of official duties. Finally, working for a bureaucratic organization is a career, which is supported by a system of promotion based on the seniority or achievement. Faithful service to the organization is therefore rewarded, and long-term commitment to the organization is encouraged.

Weber was convinced that the advantages of bureaucracy made it superior to any other form of organization. He stated that the purely bureaucratic organization 'is, from a purely technical point of view, capable of attaining the highest degree of efficiency and is in this sense formally the most rational known means of carrying out imperative control over human beings' (Weber, 1947: 337). Weber compared bureaucracy to a machine which produces precise, predictable outcomes. If all organization members are following the rules, which they should be doing since there is effective supervision, then the result will be precise behaviour in all areas of performance. Weber also thought that bureaucratic organizations had faster response times than non-bureaucratic organizations, due to the fact that there is less delay. He attributed the main forms of delay in earlier types of organization to lack of attention from people who were only partly committed to the organization, and to frictions and conflicts between people who had competing claims to decide on a case. In contrast, Weber thought that having the full commitment of officials, and having unambiguous lines of authority in a single hierarchy, would make for faster reaction times when problems arose. Weber therefore identified as one of the factors causing bureaucratization, the demand for faster responses in public administration, owing to the speed with which issues arise in a society in which news was spread by the printing press. Weber was one of the first sociologists to consider the impact of the mass media in social life. He also thought that in private business the competitive nature of the market economy was one of the factors creating pressures for greater speed and precision, and therefore for more bureaucratization. Weber therefore argued that capitalism had played a major role in the development of bureaucracy. In fact, Weber claimed that bureaucratic administration was growing everywhere, not just in government departments and private businesses, but also in churches, armies, political parties, and private associations and clubs of all kinds.

Authority

Weber used ideal types in a variety of ways. In some cases he created only one ideal type in a specific area, but in other cases he created more than one ideal type, when he thought that was necessary in order to do justice to the richness of historical events. In general, Weber thought that additional ideal types would be necessary as a study progressed, in order to utilize the data which were not relevant to earlier ideal types. Weber's work on authority is an example of an area where he employed more than one ideal type. Weber identified three pure types of authority, but even so he did not think they would be able to describe all patterns of authority.

Authority, in Weber's view, is legitimate domination. It is the right to give a command, and to expect that it will be obeyed, because those who obey believe that it is right to do so. The critical factor in authority is the beliefs of the subordinates in the legitimacy of domination by their superiors. It is this basis of obedience which makes authority possible. Therefore, Weber set out to classify the types of authority according to the kind of claim to legitimacy typically made by each (Weber, 1947). The three types of authority identified by Weber are: traditional authority, legal authority (sometimes also called rational legal authority) and charismatic authority.

Traditional authority rests on a belief in the importance of continuity with the past, and the legitimacy of those who represent that continuity. The right to exercise domination is therefore believed to be handed down from the past.

Traditional beliefs define the scope and nature of authority, but within those limits traditional authority takes the form of personal obedience to the individual who occupies the traditionally sanctioned position of authority. This is therefore a personal form of authority, which takes the form of a diffuse personal loyalty. These obligations of personal loyalty are very broad in scope, and a person exercising traditional authority usually has considerable freedom of action. This may result in a degree of arbitrariness in decision-making. Whenever a traditional authority figure intervenes personally within the limits of tradition, all others give way to him. However, there may be resistance if he is thought to have acted outside of customary practice, or he has failed to follow established precedents. An example of traditional authority is a system of leadership by the elders. They are believed, on the basis of their age, to be most familiar with the sacred traditions of a group. Another example is a hereditary position. Here, the current authority figure is descended from earlier authority figures in a continuous line of authority, and authority is exercised in ways that are consistent with how things were done in the past.

Legal authority is the type that is most characteristic of the modern world. It rests on a belief in the importance of rules and regulations, and the legitimacy of those who exercise authority within a framework of rules. The rules are believed to be rationally created to serve specific purposes. In contrast to the other two types of authority, legal authority is therefore an impersonal system in which rules take precedence over persons. Rules define positions whose holders are entitled to exercise authority. Authority is thus a property of an official position, and it has no existence outside that position. It is therefore characteristic of legal authority that its possessors only exercise authority in certain circumscribed areas, and not in all aspects of their lives. Similarly, people who obey a person who has legal authority over them do so only within the terms of the law, and only with respect to their membership in a specific group. Therefore, people under legal authority are personally free and are subject to authority only with respect to their official obligations. The classic example of legal authority is authority in a bureaucracy. The rules of the organization define who has access to positions of authority, and what the terms and conditions of authority are.

Charismatic authority is an unusual type of authority. It rests on a belief in the exceptional personal qualities of a remarkable individual. These qualities may be so exceptional that they are regarded as superhuman, or supernatural. Charismatic authority is therefore often associated with strong emotions of enthusiasm and hope. The exercise of charismatic authority is entirely dependent upon the wishes of the charismatic person, as long as that person continues to inspire confidence in their exceptional qualities. Charismatic authority therefore exists only through a relationship with the leader. Followers of a charismatic leader are believed to have a duty to recognize his or her quality, and to offer complete personal devotion. Contrasting examples of people who had this capacity to inspire tremendous faith and devotion in others, and who established charismatic authority over them, are Jesus Christ and Adolf Hitler.

Charismatic authority tends to be associated with change, and it is sometimes a revolutionary force. In the pure type of charisma the leader reveals new beliefs and makes demands for new obligations of his followers, and he or she therefore repudiates the past. Charismatic authority is definitely outside of everyday routine, and it often takes the form of challenging the existing social order. In this respect, the pure type of charismatic authority contrasts with both traditional and legal authority.

Evolution of Capitalism

Weber thought that religion, in the form of charismatic authority, had the potential to bring about revolutionary transformations of the social world. He applied this point of view to an actual historical case in his account of the role that the Protestant Reformation played in the rise of capitalism. Here, Weber departed from the position of Karl Marx, who thought that capitalism had grown out of developments in material conditions, such as the expansion of world trade. Marx thought that ideas played a secondary role in history, and that religious ideas were a reflection of the material circumstances under which people live. Weber, on the other hand, thought that ideas (or, at least, certain ideas) played a formative role in history. Nevertheless, it is possible to exaggerate the difference between Marx and Weber. Weber, too, recognized the importance of material conditions for historical changes in economic activity. For example, he pointed out that there must be reliable means of transportation available before trade can develop on a large scale.

Weber was very interested in the historical evolution of capitalism. He identified six presuppositions of capitalism that were necessary for a completely capitalistic society to emerge (Weber, 1961). First, there was the development of what Weber referred to as 'rational capital accounting'. This involves the systematic calculation of the costs of private production, and the profits and losses to be expected from it, with a view to making profits and avoiding losses. Weber indicated that a condition for the emergence of rational capital accounting was the prior appropriation of the means of production as private property. Second, there was the development of a free market in which most restrictions on trade had been removed. This allowed producers to purchase the resources they need, and to find buyers for their products. Third, Weber said that capitalistic accounting presupposes rational technology that permits the precise calculation of the quantities of goods produced, in small or large amounts. This implies the use of machinery to produce goods. Fourth, Weber thought there must be what he called 'calculable law'. By this he meant that producers must be able to calculate the effects of laws upon their enterprises, and especially upon their costs. Such things as taxes must be predictable so that entrepreneurs can make investments knowing they have a reasonable expectation of making a profit. Fifth, there must be what Weber called 'free labour'. By this Weber did not mean that workers should work for nothing. Rather, he meant that workers should be available for employment because they possess the legal freedom to work for whomever they choose, and at the same time they do not own the means of subsistence and must work for someone else in order to live. Sixth, there is the commercialization of economic life, in which all forms of ownership become saleable in a general process of economic exchange that is mediated by paper documents such as share certificates.

Weber recognized the importance of material conditions for the emergence of capitalism, such as the appropriation of private property, as well as the emergence of a class of workers who are forced to offer themselves for hire 'under the compulsion of the whip of hunger', as he put it (1961: 209). But, in addition, Weber attached importance to the role of ideas in the history of capitalism. The restless pursuit of the accumulation of capital, which Marx had taken so much for granted as a feature of capitalism, was regarded by Weber as a historically peculiar motive. It was not found on a large scale in any previous historical period, Weber argued. He therefore thought it was important to understand the nature of this motive, and its origins. Underlying all of the specific developments leading to a capitalistic society, Weber thought there had been the growth of a certain spirit, or culture, of capitalism which had been essential for its emergence. This capitalistic culture had broken the hold of traditionalism on people's minds, and had encouraged a rational attitude to all aspects of economic activity. Weber attributed the emergence of the culture of capitalism to a specifically religious development whose original inspiration had been non-economic. He claimed that the Protestant reformation in northern Europe, and its adoption in the United States of America, had made those parts of the world the leading territories economically by the middle of the nineteenth century. He set out this thesis in his famous work on *The Protestant Ethic and the Spirit of Capitalism* (Weber, 1958).

Weber presented his thesis as a relationship between two ideal types. On one hand there was the spirit of capitalism, and on the other hand there was Protestant asceticism. Weber argued that the spirit of capitalism was a derivation from Protestant asceticism as it came into existence in Europe in the sixteenth century. The essential elements of the spirit of capitalism emerged in the inner-worldly asceticism of the Puritans in northern Europe, and later in the USA, though they subsequently became independent of this religious base as they were institutionalized in capitalist society.

For Weber, there were three essential features of the spirit of capitalism. First, there is the emphasis upon earning more and more money, without end. As Weber put it, 'Man is dominated by the making of money, by acquisition as the ultimate purpose of his life' (Weber, 1958: 53). It is this that gives capitalism its characteristic obsession with growth, and which has made it such a dynamic system.

Second, this emphasis upon earning more and more money is combined with asceticism, that is, self-denial and the strict avoidance of all spontaneous enjoyment of life. Money is not used to enjoy life in constant expenditure on pleasures, but it is saved and hoarded. The result is that there is a pool of money, capital, which is available for investment. Weber pointed out that this capitalistic principle reversed the natural relationship between money and life, that people make money in order to live, and replaces it with the idea that people live in order to make money. This is an idea that is not found among people who are not under capitalistic influence, but it is a leading principle of capitalism, Weber argued.

The third feature of the spirit of capitalism is an ethic of dedication to a calling. Originally a religious term, it referred to a calling by God to serve him in a special form of work. In the secular sense, a calling is a vocation with which one has an affinity, and which one feels an obligation to serve. Weber emphasized that the idea of a calling involved a strong sense of duty to work, no matter what kind of work the person might choose. This sense of duty was not natural, Weber argued, but it was a historically specific social construction.

The capitalistic culture outlined by Weber had two important economic consequences. In the first place, it produced a group of entrepreneurs who had capital to invest, because they earned much money but spent little of it on themselves. The continuous accumulation of capital supplied the investment that drove the expansion of the economy. The spirit of capitalism also produced a disciplined and hard-working labour force. It was this combination of capital and hard work that made capitalism so productive.

Weber traced the origin of the spirit of capitalism to Protestant asceticism. Protestant asceticism was a development of Roman Catholic asceticism, but removed from a separate group of religious specialists and applied to every member of the faith. After the Protestant Reformation, monks were not the only ones who had to lead ascetic lives, but in a sense everyone now had to be like a monk throughout his life. The Puritans were warned to avoid the enjoyment of wealth, because it increases the temptation to sin and distracts the individual from the proper pursuit of a righteous life. Wealth was not something to be squandered on personal pleasures, but it was something that was to be held in trust for God, to be used for God's purposes. The good Christian was a good steward for God, who looked after the resources he had been given and used them well.

The feature of Protestant asceticism that was of most interest to Weber was the rational acquisition of goods and money as part of one's calling in life. Weber insisted that although greed for gain had been present in some people in other societies, what made Protestant asceticism different was the moral basis that it supplied for acquisitiveness. This development of the concept of a calling gave the modern entrepreneur a clear conscience to gain wealth, and to exploit his workers in doing so.

The very concept of everyday working life as a calling was something that first came into western civilization with Protestantism, Weber claimed. Protestantism replaced the other-worldly asceticism of Catholic monasticism, which was oriented towards prayer to God, with an inner-worldly asceticism which was oriented towards serving God in the world. At least one thing was unquestionably new, Weber claimed, namely, 'the valuation of the fulfilment of duty in worldly affairs as the highest form which the moral activity of the individual could assume' (Weber, 1958: 80). It was this that gave everyday working life a religious significance, and supplied the moral basis for acquisition among the owners of capital. The rational pursuit of gain became a moral obligation. Not to make the most efficient use of one's resources and talents was not just foolishness, it was regarded as a moral failure.

Weber thought that this conception of religion and life was most evident in the Calvinist branch of Protestantism. He therefore attached a special importance to it. There were two features of Calvinism that made it remarkable. In the first place, there was the Calvinist interpretation of the Christian requirement to show 'brotherly love' towards one's fellow human beings. Among the Calvinists this took on an impersonal character. Rather than giving to the poor, brotherly love could be shown by serving in one's position in the world. That was so because it was thought that the world had been designed by God to serve the human race, so that it could glorify Him. The organization of work in the world, including the division of labour, therefore served one's fellow human beings, and God. Filling one's specialized role in life was part of God's plan for helping one's fellow human beings.

The second distinctive characteristic of Calvinism stressed by Weber was the peculiar development of the Calvinist belief in predestination. Belief in predestination means holding that God has pre-determined the spiritual fates of men and women before they are born. Some people are destined to spend everlasting life with Him, the 'chosen', and others are destined to spend everlasting life in hell, the 'damned'. Weber argued that for true believers there can have been no question more important than that of knowing where one was going to spend eternity. This must have pushed aside all other concerns, and become a matter of overwhelming interest. Insofar as belief in predestination was not toned down or abandoned, ministers provided their followers with two interconnected pieces of advice on how to handle this problem. First, the Calvinists were advised to have absolute confidence in themselves as being among the chosen, and to combat all doubts as temptations of the devil. Second, they were recommended to attain a sense of self-confidence and overcome religious anxiety by throwing themselves into intense worldly activity. By working in the world, and being successful, the Calvinist could believe that God was working through him, that he was a tool for the divine purpose. Good works were a sign of faith, and of God's grace. It was therefore essential to live a life of continuous good works, understood as fulfilling one's position in the social order that God has created for His own glory. Weber thought that this unusual religious psychology was a tremendously powerful force for the expansion of that attitude towards life which he called the spirit of capitalism.

It should be noted that Weber did not think that the spirit of capitalism, and the economic success that followed from it, was an intended consequence of Protestant asceticism. On the contrary, it was an unintended, and even unwanted, result of the efforts of the religious reformers. The obsession with economic activity and the inevitable temptations that followed from the accumulation of great wealth were often contrary to what the reformers themselves had striven for. Nevertheless, Weber claimed, the spirit of capitalism was born in religion, even though it later became independent of its religious origins.

Conclusion

In this chapter we have outlined key elements of three modes of explanation in sociology, namely positivism, functionalism and interpretive understanding. Positivism was represented by the work of Emile Durkheim, functionalism was represented by the works of Emile Durkheim, Robert Merton and Talcott Parsons, and interpretive understanding was represented by the work of Max Weber.

Durkheim's positivism was an early attempt to apply the methods of the natural sciences to sociology. Four general features of positivism have been illustrated from Durkheim's work. They were: (1) the goal of discovering scientific laws; (2) a belief in philosophical realism; (3) the practice of empirical research; and (4) the use of logical methods of proof for relations of causality.

Scientific laws are general statements about relationships between factors (e.g., causes and effects), which can be proven to be universally true under specified conditions, and that are usually independent of time and space. This was illustrated from Durkheim's law on the division of labour.

Philosophical realism is the belief that it is possible to have an exact understanding of how the world really works, and therefore that theories can (and should) correspond with reality. Durkheim was a strong advocate of this point of view, and he thought it had some important implications for sociology. The main problem was to avoid all subjective ideas that might interfere with an objective understanding of the social world. First, as far as the researcher's own subjective ideas are concerned, Durkheim recommended that all preconceived ideas should be ignored. Second, Durkheim recommended that the ideas of the subjects of research should also be ignored, in favour of studying their actual behaviour and circumstances.

Durkheim thought that empirical research was a necessary corrective to erroneous theories, and he thought that sociologists should begin by studying things rather than ideas. His practical recommendations for research included studying relatively stable phenomena rather than unstable phenomena, so that the sociologist could follow a systematic pattern of work.

In his research, Durkheim advocated the use of logical methods of proof for relations of causality. He tried to show how one social fact varied with another, as a way of demonstrating the dependence of an effect upon its cause.

Durkheim's work was also used to illustrate the mode of explanation known as functionalism. Functionalism is an approach that seeks to explain social patterns in terms of their effectiveness in meeting needs. Conditions which are necessary for the survival and maintenance of society over time can be thought of as needs that have to be fulfilled. Durkheim thought that any practice which has persisted over a reasonably long period of time is likely to have persisted because it fulfils some need which contributes to the survival of society. Therefore, it is necessary for the sociologist to show the usefulness of social patterns, and how they contribute to the maintenance of society and themselves.

Two important points were made about Durkheim's approach to functionalist explanation. First, Durkheim focused on the functions of social patterns for social order. For example, he claimed that the true function of the division of labour is to maintain social solidarity. Second, Durkheim stressed that functions are not necessarily consciously intended by the people who enact them. This point was later taken up by the structural functionalist Robert Merton, in his distinction between manifest and latent functions.

Structural functionalism is an approach which involves identifying the structures that constitute society, and then describing the functions that those structures fulfil. The best known structural functionalist, Talcott Parsons, outlined four general functional imperatives that he believed every social system had to fulfil. They are: pattern-maintenance, integration, goal-attainment and adaptation. Pattern-maintenance refers to the functional imperative of maintaining the culture of a system. The functional imperative of integration requires that differentiated structures must be adjusted to each other, so that they do not come into conflict and prevent each other from fulfilling their functions. The functional imperative of goal-attainment is to minimize any disturbance to a system and restore the system to a state of equilibrium. Finally, the functional imperative of adaptation involves providing facilities, or resources, that are needed by the various specialized structures within a system.

The last theorist discussed in this chapter was Max Weber, who represents the mode of explanation referred to here as interpretive understanding. Interpretive understanding involves understanding the meanings that actors give to the objects in their social world, and interpreting their relevance for the culture of the sociological investigator. As human beings, sociological researchers are capable of understanding how their fellow human beings think and feel, and why they act in the ways that they do. Weber believed it is important for sociologists to use the capacity for subjective understanding that they possess because it enables them to know the actual manner in which behaviour is produced. Sociologists must also interpret the cultural significance of social objects, as a guide to choosing important topics for enquiry. Only a part of concrete reality is significant to us because it reveals relationships which are important to us due to their connection with our values.

Weber sought to integrate understanding into sociology by combining it with causal analysis. He insisted that a correct explanation of action must be both adequate with respect to the interpretation of motives and causally adequate. Proof of a causal explanation is given by providing evidence that action normally takes a course which has been described as meaningful, and this involves showing its approximation to an ideal type.

The most characteristic feature of Weber's approach to explanation was his use of ideal types. An ideal type is a theoretical construct whose various elements have been abstracted from reality and combined in a logically integrated fashion, on the basis of some principle of subjective meaning. Weber used ideal types in a variety of ways, and he thought they could be useful in several respects. To begin with, they help the sociologist to select data that are to be used in sociological studies, by defining in practical terms what is taken to be of cultural significance. Second, ideal types help the sociologist to clarify concepts by making them the focus of explicit attention and careful argument. Third, ideal types help the observer to simplify and standardize a reality that is too complex to be conceptualized in any other way. Fourth, ideal types help in the formulation of hypotheses to be tested against reality. Fifth, ideal types are sometimes necessary for sociological explanation when the majority of actors are unable to provide conscious reasons for their actions, or when their conscious meanings are unclear. Several examples of Weber's use of ideal types were provided here, concerning bureaucracy, authority, and Protestant asceticism and the spirit of capitalism.

Further Reading

Crothers, Charles, 1987, *Robert K. Merton*, London: Tavistock.

Durkheim, Emile, 1964, *The Rules of Sociological Method*, trans. Sarah Solovay and John Mueller, ed. George E. G. Catlin, New York: Free Press.

Durkheim, Emile, 1966, *Suicide*, trans. John A. Spaulding and George Simpson, ed. George Simpson, New York: Free Press.

Gerth, H. H. and C. Wright Mills, eds, 1948, *From Max Weber: Essays in Sociology*, trans. H. H. Gerth and C. Wright Mills, London: Routledge & Kegan Paul.

Hamilton, Peter, 1983, *Talcott Parsons*, London: Tavistock.

Hamilton, Peter, 1991, *Max Weber: Critical Assessments*, 4 vols, London: Routledge.

Hamilton, Peter, 1992, *Talcott Parsons: Critical Assessments*, 4 vols, London: Routledge.

Johnson, Benton, 1975, *Functionalism in Modern Sociology: Understanding Talcott Parsons*, Morristown: General Learning Press.

Jones, Susan Stedman, 2001, *Durkheim Reconsidered*, Cambridge: Polity Press.

Kalberg, Stephen, 2000, 'Max Weber', in George Ritzer, ed., *The Blackwell Companion to Major Social Theorists*, Oxford: Blackwell, pp. 144–204.

Käsler, Dirk, 1988, *Max Weber: An Introduction to His Life and Work*, trans. Philippa Hurd, Chicago: University of Chicago Press.

Marshall, Gordon, 1982, *In Search of the Spirit of Capitalism: An Essay on Max Weber's Protestant Ethic Thesis*, London: Hutchinson.

Merton, Robert K., 1957, *Social Theory and Social Structure*, New York: Free Press.

Parkin, Frank, 1982, *Max Weber*, London: Tavistock.

Parsons, Talcott, 1961, 'An Outline of the Social System', in Talcott Parsons, Edward Shils, Kaspar D. Naegele and Jesse R. Pitts, eds, *Theories of Society: Foundations of Modern Sociological Theory*, Volume 1, New York: Free Press, pp. 30–79.

Poggi, Gianfranco, 2000, *Durkheim*, Oxford: Oxford University Press.

Ringer, Fritz, 1997, *Max Weber's Methodology: The Unification of the Cultural and Social Sciences*, Cambridge, MA: Harvard University Press.

Sztompka, Piotr, 1986, *Robert K. Merton: An Intellectual Profile*, New York: St Martin's Press.

Weber, Max, 1947, *Max Weber: The Theory of Social and Economic Organization*, trans. A. M. Henderson and Talcott Parsons, Glencoe: Free Press.

Weber, Max, 1949, *The Methodology of the Social Sciences*, trans. Edward A. Shils and Henry A. Finch, Glencoe: Free Press.

Weber, Max, 1958, *The Protestant Ethic and the Spirit of Capitalism*, trans. Talcott Parsons, New York: Charles Scribner's Sons.

Dimension Three

Key Factors

4

Key Factors of Social Evolution

In this chapter we will consider the question of which factors are believed to have the greatest explanatory value in developing a theory of social life. Every theory provides some conception of how certain factors are to be explained by other factors, and every theory recognizes that not all factors are equal. Some factors are believed to have a greater effect than others. But which ones are key? Sooner or later, every theorist is forced to consider this question, and the answers given to it have profound effects on the different directions that theories take. This issue has been especially important in theories of social evolution, that is to say, theories that seek to describe universal stages through which societies pass as they change over time. Marx is the classical theorist here, but his work has been engaged by later theorists who are also considered in this chapter. The theorists discussed here are Karl Marx, Talcott Parsons and Jürgen Habermas.

This chapter focuses especially on the classic confrontation between theories that stress economic factors as having the determining influence on social events, and those that stress culture as the dominant influence. On the one hand there are those, like Marx, who believe that it is ultimately the material conditions of existence which explain how human beings live, act and think. On the other hand, there are those, like Parsons, who believe that it is ultimately beliefs, values and ideas about social rules which are responsible for the patterns in social life. Finally, there are those like Jürgen Habermas who adopt complex approaches that try to avoid the polarization of economy versus culture.

Karl Marx

Karl Marx (1818–1883) adopted an approach to political, economic and social affairs known as historical materialism. This approach was profoundly original, and it provoked debate which has continued to this day. Marx's basic argument was that the way in which goods are produced affects everything else in society. People are compelled by necessity to engage in acts of production. As they do so, two things happen. First, they use resources such as energy, raw materials, tools and machines. Marx referred to these as the powers of production, or forces of production (Bottomore and Rubel, 1963; Marx, 1970). Second, people engage in economic relationships with one another as they co-operate to produce the goods that they need. Marx called these the relations of production. The forces of production and the relations of production are connected, and together they constitute the mode of production. The mode of production is the economic base for society. It is indispensable and independent of our will, and it determines everything else in society. Marx argued that out of the mode of production grow superstructures of law, politics, religion, art, and so on, and to these there correspond definite forms of consciousness. He therefore claimed that: 'It is not the consciousness of men that determines their existence, but their social existence that determines their consciousness' (Marx, 1970: 21).

One of the most influential applications of this approach was made by Marx to the phenomenon of religion. Marx's ideas on religion were formed partly under the influence of, and partly in reaction against, the work of Ludwig Feuerbach (1804–1872). Feuerbach claimed that religious knowledge of God is really human self-knowledge, but a self-knowledge that people do not recognize (Feuerbach, 1969). Religion is therefore an indirect form of self-knowledge. People project what they know about themselves onto God, and regard human nature as if it were outside of themselves, as belonging to something else, namely God. Their awareness of God is really their awareness of their own nature. To be more precise, Feuerbach thought that belief in God is belief in human nature purified of all its worst elements. God is the ideal, He is love, and goodness and truth, He is all-knowing and all-powerful. Religious belief in humanity consists of what is left over in real human nature once the believed characteristics of God have been subtracted from it. That is to say, the positive elements in human nature are believed to be true of God, and the negative elements in human nature are believed to be true of humanity. Humanity is seen as wicked, corrupt, incapable of good without God's intervention, ignorant and weak. In the religious worldview, God and humanity are mirror images of one another. According to Feuerbach, beliefs about God and humanity are split images from the same source in human nature. Therefore, the more emphasis that is placed on the divine nature, the greater the difference between God and humanity becomes. As Feuerbach put it, 'To enrich God, man must become poor; that God may be all, man must be nothing' (1969: 89).

Marx accepted Feuerbach's account of religion, but he felt that Feuerbach had not gone far enough (Marx, 1976a). In Marx's view, Feuerbach had correctly analysed the fact of religious self-estrangement, but he had left the analysis in the realm of ideas without tying it to material conditions. In particular, Marx felt that Feuerbach had failed to provide the basis for criticism of the existing conditions of life. Feuerbach had traced the origin of religion to humanity in the abstract, without connecting it to the lives of actual human beings. Marx made that connection by standing Feuerbach's analysis on its head. In Feuerbach's analysis, humanity is poor in spirit because God is rich in endowments. But in Marx's analysis God is rich because human beings are poor. People adopt the religious view of God and the world because they experience their lives as miserable. Marx argued that religion is a response to a society that has denied most people the opportunity to realize their full human nature. It provides consolation to those who experience a sense of loss, if not in this life then in the next life. Religion also provides a sense of meaning in conditions that would otherwise be meaningless, and it offers the promise of higher values than those that are realized in everyday life. In short, religion is 'the opium of the people', as Marx proclaimed (1971: 116). Because Marx believed that religion is an illusion which reflects the distorted conditions of the social world, it follows that religion is not an active force in history. Rather, it is a reactive factor that is determined by more basic factors in the mode of production. Marx argued that is necessary to replace religious fantasy production with an emphasis on the real production of the means of subsistence and of life itself (Marx and Engels, 1964b).

Mode of Production

Marx was convinced that all of human history had been shaped by the same basic condition, namely, that people must first be in a position to live before they can make history (Marx and Engels, 1964a). In other words, before they can act in ways that end up being recorded in history books, people must first be able to supply themselves with food and drink, clothing and habitation, in short with all the things that are necessary for survival. Marx therefore insisted that any analysis of history must first begin by studying the production of the means to satisfy these needs. This method of historical materialism offered Marx a path into a universal theory of the past, present and future because the same basic needs have always existed throughout history. Today, as in the past, the basic necessities of life must be continuously provided.

Marx claimed that the history of human societies could be divided up into different stages of the mode of production. He identified four stages as having brought about the progressive economic transformation of human society. They are: the Asiatic, the ancient, the feudal and the modern bourgeois, or capitalist, mode of production. Marx thought that capitalism must eventually be replaced by a new mode of production, namely communism. Marx was most interested in analysing capitalism, since it was the mode of production of his own time, and furthermore he believed that it had the capacity to bring about an enormous transformation that was far greater than anything that had happened before.

Marx defined the capitalist mode of production in the following way. He said that capitalist production only really begins when each individual capital simultaneously employs a comparatively large number of workers, and when, as a result, the labour-process is carried on on an extensive scale, and yields relatively large quantities of products. A large number of workers working together, at the same time, in one place (or, if you like, in the same field of labour), in order to produce the same sort of commodity under the command of the same capitalist, constitutes the starting-point of capitalist production. (Marx, 1977: 439)

The sociologically important feature of the capitalist mode of production is that it includes a relationship (a relation of production) between two classes of people, namely the workers and the capitalists who employ them. Marx referred to these two classes as the proletariat (the workers, or in other words the working class) and the bourgeoisie (the capitalists). It is the history of the relationship between these two classes which constitutes the social history of capitalism.

The relations of production in capitalism have two important features. In the first place, they involve a division of labour. For instance, the workers and the capitalists do different things. The capitalists supply capital and the things it can purchase, such as machines and raw materials, and they direct the labour process, while the workers supply the labour that turns raw materials into commodities. In addition, there is also a division of labour within each of the classes. One of the characteristics of capitalism is that the proletarians tend to work in highly specialized jobs. Marx was critical of this. He did not like the fact that workers are tied to a small part of the production process. Marx thought that extensive division of labour had the effect of diminishing the human capacities of workers, and turned them into a fraction of what they might have been. He talked about the crippling of body and mind that occurs when people do the same limited tasks over and over again, and he was especially concerned about the level of ignorance that he thought followed from having such a limited experience of the world (Marx, 1977: 482–485).

The second feature of the relations of production in capitalism is that they involve relations of domination, which is how Marx described the relationship between capitalists and workers in his definition of capitalism. The capitalist relation of domination is basically one in which the worker sells his labour power to the capitalist in return for a wage, and the capitalist controls the activities of the worker for however many hours in the day are agreed in the labour contract. The relationship between capital and labour is thus a power relationship, in which the bourgeoisie exercises power over the proletariat. This power is exercised in the workplace in the first instance, when employers tell their employees what to do. However, the power relationship extends beyond the workplace to all contexts in which the workers and the capitalists have definite interests. The bourgeoisie constitutes a ruling class which dominates the proletariat in all areas of life.

At work, the workers are subordinated to the capitalists because that is the only way in which capitalist production can be organized. For large numbers of people to work together to produce the same commodity, some individual capitalist or group of capitalists must possess the resources to buy the machinery and raw materials, and pay the wages of all the workers employed in the enterprise. The concentration of capital, and therefore of power, in the hands of a few people is a requirement of the capitalist mode of production. As production becomes organized on a larger scale, the exercise of power becomes extended since the individual capitalist is no longer able to direct everything himself. Specialized workers are hired as managers and supervisors. Their job is to control their fellow workers, and ensure that the wishes of the capitalists are carried out. A business organization therefore develops a hierarchy of power, with the capitalist at the top, the mass of workers at the bottom, and supervisors and managers in the middle.

Marx recognized that the capitalist form of domination was not the only historical basis for large-scale co-operation. In particular, he was aware that in pre-capitalist societies slavery had been used as a basis for carrying out large-scale projects under the direction of a handful of individuals. However, he insisted that the capitalist form of domination through wage-labour was the only one that was compatible with the capitalist mode of production. Slavery is an efficient form of domination, and it is also cheap, because the only expense to the slave-owner is what is needed to keep the slaves alive. Exploitation of labour is therefore high under slavery. However, slavery is incompatible with capitalism because it cannot generate capital. Slaves do not earn wages, and they therefore do not have the money with which to buy commodities. The production of commodities would therefore be severely restricted in a society based on slavery. Because the buying and selling of commodities is limited under slavery, the circulation of money is also limited, and opportunities to accumulate capital are small. The capitalist system of wage-labour is the only relation of production that is compatible with the large-scale production of commodities, as it is the only one that permits mass-produced commodities to be purchased and thereby permits the accumulation of money as capital.

Marx was very interested in the conceptual and historical circumstances that were necessary for the emergence and development of capitalism. One of these conditions was clearly the large-scale circulation of money, and therefore of commodities. According to Marx, the circulation of commodities is the starting point of capital. He dated the beginning of capitalism to the sixteenth century, when a world market and world-wide trade first emerged, which permitted the accumulation of capital by merchants. From that point onwards the history of capitalism has developed rapidly.

In Marx's view, the development of any mode of production is definitely a result of historical material conditions. For example, capitalist society has grown out of feudal society, and capitalism could only progress as feudalism was dissolved. At any given point in time, there are forces of production and relations of production that make some things possible, but not others. Marx therefore thought it was important to understand in these terms exactly how capitalism had emerged and developed. In addition to the history of the circulation of commodities, Marx analysed the process by which wage-labour had emerged as a type of relation of production. Marx pointed out that in a system of wage-labour, work has become a commodity which is bought and sold just like any other commodity. It is bought and sold in a market, which we refer to in fact as a labour market. Marx also pointed out that in historical terms there was nothing natural or inevitable about this state of affairs. It must, he concluded, be the result of special historical circumstances.

Marx began his analysis methodically by outlining the prerequisites for the emergence of wage-labour. For wage-labour to exist there must be people who put their work out for hire, and this means in the first place that they must be free to do so. They must, that is to say, possess the personal freedom to do what work they choose, whenever and wherever they choose to do so. For this to happen historically, it was necessary that people should have been granted certain basic liberties guaranteed in law. Part of the history of wage-labour is therefore a history of emancipation from slavery and other restrictive conditions. The second prerequisite for people putting their labour out for hire is that they must be driven to do so because they have nothing else to sell. They lack the tools, machinery and raw materials that would be necessary to produce commodities themselves. The history of this side of wage-labour is darker, and it is 'written in the annals of mankind in letters of blood and fire', as Marx angrily proclaimed (1977: 875). This history is a history of expropriation, whereby a growing segment of the population lost the means of subsistence that they once had. For example, Marx described how large numbers of English peasants had been removed from the land at the end of the fifteenth century and the beginning of the sixteenth century, in order to make way for less labour-intensive sheep farming. The result was a proletariat of wage-labourers, who, having no means of production, were forced to sell their labour power in order to live.

Marx was not only interested in past changes, of course, but he was also interested in the changes in his own day that he thought were leading to the transformation of capitalism, and its eventual dissolution. The capitalist mode of production dominates the modern world, in Marx's view, and in the pursuit of profit the bourgeoisie cannot help but revolutionize the whole of society. 'The bourgeoisie cannot exist without constantly revolutionising the instruments of production, and thereby the relations of production, and with them the whole relations of society', Marx claimed (Marx and Engels, 1973: 36). In a famous phrase, he stated that 'All that is solid melts into air' (Marx and Engels, 1973: 37). For example, Marx argued that capitalism is replacing social bonds with economic connections, as communities are replaced by markets. Naked self-interest is replacing all other motives, including in family life, he thought.

Marx was most interested in the economic transformations in capitalism, and their implications for social relationships. On the positive side, capitalism has unleashed enormous powers of production that permit goods to be manufactured on a previously undreamed of scale. Technological innovations enable construction projects that dwarf those of earlier times, and world trade provides consumers with a wealth of products from all corners of the globe. As national boundaries recede in economic life, so too do they recede in intellectual life. International communication occurs on a growing scale, and the intellectual creations of individual nations become widely shared. Marx also observed that capitalism was bringing about huge population changes, including massive urbanization and a shrinking proportion of the population living in rural isolation. He also anticipated that the concentration of capital would lead to increasing political centralization.

On the negative side, Marx thought that capitalism would not improve the economic conditions of the mass of the population, and he pointed out that economic progress was punctuated by economic crises. Here, he thought, was a crucial weakness in the capitalist system that would eventually bring about its demise. The bourgeoisie, he thought, would be unable to control the tendency of the system to result in crises of overproduction. That is to say, constant investment in new products, and in more efficient means of producing existing products, tends to outstrip the capacity of consumers to buy the products with their limited wages. In theoretical terms, the forces of production are no longer compatible with the narrow limits of property relations, which put most of the wealth in the hands of the few. In the long run, Marx thought that the main consequence of this would be intensified class conflict.

Class Conflict

Marx thought that modern society was more and more splitting up into two hostile classes, the bourgeoisie and the proletariat. The bourgeoisie owns property, whereas the proletariat is propertyless. Marx was convinced that the members of the proletariat could only be dissatisfied with their place in society, and they were likely to become increasingly dissatisfied as the history of capitalism unfolded. In the first place, the proletarians are subject to all the shifts in the labour market. In capitalism, labour power is a commodity, and like any other commodity there are times when demand for it is high, and times when demand is low. When demand is high, the number of people employed will increase and wages will tend to rise. But when demand is low, employment drops and wages tend to fall. Economic crises of overproduction followed by recession therefore result in personal financial difficulties for a number of workers. The greater the economic crisis, the larger the number of workers who are affected. Marx thought that as capitalism developed the tendency for economic crises would increase, and the fluctuation in wages would grow.

The second reason for dissatisfaction among the workers is that their wages would generally be low, according to Marx. Marx thought that in their efforts to gain a competitive advantage through lower prices, capitalists would tend to drive wages down as far as possible. He therefore believed that in general wages would not rise much above the subsistence level needed to maintain workers and their families.

The third reason why Marx thought that proletarians are likely to be dissatisfied with their place in society is because of the work that they do. Due to the extensive use of machinery and the division of labour, work is repetitive and boring, and it has lost all variety that would make it interesting. This dissatisfaction with work is part of a general condition that Marx referred to as alienated labour.

For Marx, alienated labour is work that is done for someone else, so that the person who does the work does not enjoy it but the fruits of labour are enjoyed by another person. Marx outlined four features of alienated labour in capitalism (Marx, 1963).

First, Marx says that workers are alienated from the products of their work. The things they produce belong to another who appropriates them. Workers are therefore separated from the things they produce, and they derive no satisfaction from them. Instead of the inner life of the worker being enriched by an accumulation of products which all have meaning to the individual because they are products of his or her own labour, the inner life of the worker is impoverished because effort is expended that leaves no lasting effect. In fact, the more he or she produces, and the greater the effort he or she expends, the more he or she is diminished. In particular, the more products that are produced with the aid of machinery, the more the worker's development is stunted as he or she becomes merely an adjunct to the machine. Marx was very critical of the effects of machine production upon workers, which he thought limited their intelligence and deformed them physically. Worse, Marx thought that the more time that is spent producing goods for another, the more impoverished the worker becomes in a material sense also because the less time is left over for subsistence activities.

Second, in capitalism the worker is alienated from the act of working. The human activity of making things belongs to another, who controls the worker's labour for the length of the working day. The worker therefore loses control over his or her own activity, and instead of being a self-directing person he or she becomes the means of realizing another's will. Here, work does not spring from the worker's inner nature, but it is imposed from the outside as an external activity. As a result, the worker does not enjoy working but he or she feels miserable. Furthermore, because the workers are compelled to work as hard as possible for another person, he or she is unable to take appropriate rests and becomes physically exhausted. Also, the workers are compelled to work in specific ways which prevents him from developing freely his mental abilities. Marx thought that the most obvious evidence for alienation from work is that people feel really free only in their non-working activities, and if they can avoid working they will do so in order to do things that they enjoy more.

Third, Marx claimed that workers are alienated from their species-being. This is their uniquely human capacity to produce things that are not required as material necessities, but that are produced for other reasons such as achieving a sense of beauty, or bringing about intellectual development. Marx thought that workers are unable to realize their species-being in the work they do for another person. Instead, work becomes reduced to a mere means of maintaining physical existence. It is a means of fulfilling a need, namely the need for physical survival, rather than being a path to free, unconstrained self-realization. Instead of setting conscious goals for ourselves to strive after, we simply work in order to live.

Fourth, alienated labour includes the alienation of workers from each other. Other workers are not seen as self-actualizing individuals, but they are seen as being in competition for the means of existence.

For all the reasons considered above, Marx was convinced that relations between capitalists and workers could only be hostile. Their relationship is one of oppressor and oppressed, against which the oppressed must rebel. Because of this, he thought that eventually the proletariat would rise up and throw off its chains, ushering in a new order of peace and prosperity for all. Marx argued that the ranks of the proletariat would swell as more and more people became dispossessed of the means of production. The proletariat would grow in size until it comprised almost all of the population, except for a handful of extremely wealthy individuals. Small manufacturers, tradespeople and small storekeepers would gradually sink into the proletariat because they cannot compete with large businesses which enjoy economies of scale, and because their specialized skills are rendered redundant by technological innovations.

As the proletariat grows in size, so too does it engage in more concerted action. Isolated groups band together and make common cause against their common enemy, and barriers between workers are gradually broken down as more of them are employed in large industrial establishments. Increased contact among the workers is facilitated by modern means of transportation and communication. Furthermore, the proletarians become more politically active as they are drawn into the conflicts between the bourgeoisie and the remnants of earlier classes. Eventually, the proletariat becomes a class for itself, that is to say a class that is aware of its own interests and its place in history, and that seeks to destroy existing society in the name of liberation. At this point, the struggles between the classes extend across the full range of possibilities, including ideological struggles over ideas.

Ideology

In Marx's view, ideas are shaped in the first instance by practical experiences of working in definite ways in a particular economic position within society. People think with the information that is at their disposal, and the information to which they have access depends on what they do and how they live. Since work is the most basic activity upon which life depends, it is clear that the activities of working constitute the fundamental basis for all ideas. Not all ideas are equal, however. Insofar as different work experiences are associated with the distinction between oppressor and oppressed, they produce a fundamental inequality in the social influence of different ideas. Marx thought that the dominant ideas in society are those of the dominant class. Or, as he put it, 'The ideas of the ruling class are in every epoch the ruling ideas' (Marx and Engels, 1964a: 61). In capitalism, this means that it is the bourgeoisie which has the greatest influence over ideas.

Marx presented a thoroughly materialist account of the ruling class's domination in the realm of ideas. The class which is the dominant material force in society is also its dominant intellectual force, for two fundamental reasons. First, the ruling class dominates the production of ideas. Ideas do not spring from nowhere. They are human constructions that require time to put together. In Marx's day, proletarians who worked very long hours under the direction of someone else simply in order to live did not have much time to devote to the production of ideas. On the other hand, members of the bourgeoisie had more leisure and more discretion in their work, and they could afford to spend more time on developing ideas. Also, to be effective ideas must be expressed, and expressed well. This requires literacy and skill in writing, which both depend upon education. In general, the higher the class position, the more education people receive. Here, too, the ruling class has a distinct advantage. Finally, the ruling class has the financial resources to hire speech writers and public relations experts to develop ideas and to communicate them effectively to the public. In all these ways the ruling class rules in the production of ideas.

The second fundamental reason why the class which is the dominant material force in society is also its dominant intellectual force is because it also rules in the distribution of ideas. Distributing ideas widely requires access to the mass media, and this is easiest for those who own and control them. In capitalist society the mass media are mainly privately owned by members of the bourgeoisie, and so once more the ruling class has an insurmountable advantage in making its ideas the dominant ideas.

According to Marx, the ideas of the ruling class are ideologies. An ideology is a distorted view of the world that serves to protect and advance the interests of the ruling class. In particular, the ruling class tries to represent its interests as being in the general interest. It claims that what it seeks as good for itself is really good for the whole society.

The instrument for expressing claims about the general interest is the state, or in other words the combined levels of government that administer a particular society. Ideally the state should represent the communal interest, or what is truly common to everyone. In practice, however, different groups make claims upon the state to further their particular interests. In order to gain the support of other groups, they need to persuade them that the particular interest of one group is really in the general interest of everyone. State policies, therefore, do not really reflect the communal interest, but they reflect claims about the general interest. Since the ruling class is the dominant force in society materially and intellectually, its claims about the general interest generally prevail and the state is a means by which the ruling class rules society. State policies are therefore ideological, and political struggles are also struggles over ideologies. In Marx's view political struggles occur between those whose particular interests are different due to their different positions in the division of labour. Above all, this means that political struggles occur between the classes, and political conflict is primarily class conflict. Ideological struggles are therefore above all forms of class struggle.

Marx illustrated this perspective on political issues in a speech that he gave to the Democratic Association of Brussels in 1848 (Marx, 1976b). This speech was on the question of Free Trade, which at that time was a lively political issue in Europe. The particular issue of greatest interest was the repeal of the Corn Laws in England two years prior, in 1846. This was a historic moment, since the Corn Laws had first been introduced in the fifteenth century. The Corn Laws had regulated the importation of wheat into England by imposing high tariffs and other restrictions on trade. Repealing these laws had not been easy, and there had been an intense conflict over the Corn Laws. Marx interpreted this struggle as a class conflict between the industrial bourgeoisie and the landed aristocracy. The landed aristocracy supported the Corn Laws because they had elevated the price of wheat, and this meant that the farmers could afford to pay higher rents to the landowners. The bourgeoisie, on the other hand, was in favour of repealing the Corn Laws and instituting Free Trade in wheat. In order to achieve this, however, the bourgeoisie needed the political support of the working class. It was with the relationship between these latter two groups that Marx was concerned in his speech on the question of Free Trade.

According to Marx, the English Free Traders claimed to be acting in the interests of the working class. They claimed that Free Trade in wheat would be of direct benefit to the workers because the price of wheat would fall and therefore also the price of bread would drop. Workers would therefore be better off. Furthermore, it was claimed there would be an indirect benefit to workers following from expanded economic production. The money saved buying cheaper bread would be spent on other goods, and this would lead to expanded production in the factories and therefore to a demand for more workers. The increased demand for workers, in turn, would lead to higher wages as employers competed for employees.

In contrast to this rosy picture of economic harmony between the interests of the proletariat and the bourgeoisie, Marx argued that the interests of the classes are really divergent because the eventual outcome will be different from what has been promised. To be specific, Marx claimed that the fall in the price of bread would be followed by a fall in wages as capitalists pushed wages down to a lower level of the costs of subsistence. Also, Marx thought that any economic expansion would not lead to more employment, because the expansion of capital means investment in more productive machinery, and hence a demand for fewer workers.

According to Marx, the harmony of class interests anticipated by the Free Traders is an illusion. Like all ideologies, the ideology of Free Trade makes illusory claims about the general interest. Marx's theory maintains instead that the underlying reality in all class societies is class conflict, whether overt or covert. This was a point of view that was not accepted by all sociologists.

Talcott Parsons

Talcott Parsons (1902–1979) adopted a position that was diametrically opposed to that of Marx. He rejected Marx's materialism, and he concluded that ideas can have a formative influence in social life. Parsons had little time for the work of Marx, despite his attempt to synthesize the contributions of all the major, and some minor, classical theorists. In his major work of synthesis, *The Structure of Social Action*, Parsons devoted only a few pages to Marx compared to much longer treatments given to Durkheim and Weber (Parsons, 1949). The reasons for this neglect became clear in his later criticisms.

Parsons argued that Marx had an inadequate theory of ideas (Parsons, 1954). In Parsons' view, the development of modern industry is based on technological change, and technological change is based on scientific knowledge. Science, according to Parsons, is an essentially autonomous sphere of activity. Therefore, ideas in the form of scientific knowledge have an independent influence in economic life. Parsons claimed that Marxists overlooked this because of the tendency to see all ideas as part of the superstructure, without making a distinction between different types of ideas. Some ideas, namely ideologies, are determined by material interests, whereas other ideas, such as science, are not, in Parsons' view.

Parsons claimed, in opposition to Marx, that ideas and the social rules derived from them can have basic significance in the determination of social processes (Parsons, 1967). He based this claim, in part, on the works of Durkheim and Weber. According to Parsons, Durkheim's account of the division of labour had shown that social norms in the form of contract law could regulate individuals' behaviour and force them to act in ways that were contrary to their immediate economic interests. At the same time, Weber had demonstrated in his account of the Protestant ethic and the spirit of capitalism that religious ideas could influence economic motives. Both of these achievements, in Parsons' view, give reason to question Marx's position that economic interests grounded in material conditions are the basic determinants of social action. Durkheim's contribution confirmed the independent influence of social norms, and Weber's contribution confirmed the independent influence of religious beliefs and values.

Parsons thought that Marx's failure to recognize the importance of ideas of certain kinds as a basis for social life led to him having an inadequate psychology and an inadequate sociology. Marx's inadequate psychology, according to Parsons, is fundamentally that of utilitarianism. That is to say, Marx took the ends of action for granted without explaining how motives are shaped by cultural movements. Marx's inadequate sociology, on the other hand, involved him misunderstanding the nature of social order. Parsons claimed that whereas Marx's view of social order was one of order being imposed by the powerful upon the powerless, in reality it is based on learned values from which practical standards are established in social life. Parsons identified this deficiency as the source of Marx's inability to understand what would happen in a post-revolutionary society, when the power of the ruling class is shattered.

Parsons summarized his objections to Marx by saying that his materialism had cut him off from the basic insight that action in all living systems, including social systems, is the result of organization through generalized codes that permit the programming of various actions. In human societies, these generalized codes take the form of cultural codes. Parsons therefore thought that culture had a determining influence in a system of action.

Cybernetic Hierarchy

Parsons envisaged society as a system of action, which consists of interdependent phenomena having definite patterning and stability over time. Any system contains differentiated sub-systems. The sub-systems differ in the amount of control that they have over the system. Sub-systems which are high in information but low in energy control sub-systems which are high in energy but low in information (Parsons, 1966). Parsons used the analogy of a programmable washing machine to illustrate this point. The timing switch which operates the sequence of actions uses little energy, but the information it contains directs the motor which uses a lot of energy. Parsons thought that society works in the same way.

Parsons ranked the sub-systems in society in terms of the amount of control that they exercise, with the one having the most control at the top and the one with the least control at the bottom. He referred to this ranking as a cybernetic hierarchy, or hierarchy of control. The first sub-system is the cultural system. This consists of the shared meanings that are communicated through symbols, and which can be transmitted and learned. Its core contains a cultural tradition that is shared by the members of a society, and that is transmitted from generation to generation through learning processes rather than biological inheritance. The cultural system is high in information but low in energy. The second sub-system is the social system. It is comprised of the patterns of interaction between people, and the groups that they form as they interact with one another. The third sub-system is the personality system. It involves all the individual mental processes, including cognitions, motivations and emotions. Finally, the last sub-system is the behavioural organism, or organic system. It consists of the human body, and it is high in energy but low in information. It is the least important in the cybernetic hierarchy.

Parsons thought that culture was the most important sub-system because it penetrated into the social system and personality system and controlled them. The relevant processes here are institutionalization and internalization. Institutionalization is the process whereby the culture of a society is established in the social system in formal and informal social practices. These practices are defined by the norms and rules of powerful social institutions, and reinforced by sanctions. A key part of the process of institutionalization is the specification of how values are to be applied in particular social situations. For example, the value of competition can be specified in competitive games or sports, competitive elections for decision-making positions, or in a market economy in which producers compete for the patronage of consumers. The different specifications of values in particular situations are referred to as value-orientations. Value-orientations are the selective standards used in making choices in concrete situations, based on values.

Internalization is the process of learning, and thereby incorporating into the personality, important elements of the culture of a society. In other words, it is socialization. However, Parsons did not want to emphasize personality development as much as he wanted to emphasize the way in which culture gets inside our heads. Although Parsons was aware of adult socialization, he thought that the incorporation of value-orientations into the personality was achieved mainly in learning in childhood, and was not changed much by adult experiences (Parsons, 1951). It therefore provides a fixed basis for social order, together with institutionalization. Parsons thought that the internalization of institutionalized values was essential for the stability of any social system.

As we have seen, Parsons assigned the greatest cybernetic importance to the cultural system, and in this sense he admitted to being a cultural determinist (Parsons, 1966: 113). As he put it: 'The core of a society, as a system, is the patterned normative order through which the life of a population is collectively organized. As an order, it contains values and differentiated and particularized norms and rules, all of which require cultural references in order to be meaningful and legitimate' (Parsons, 1966: 10).

Parsons also thought that the principle of a cybernetic hierarchy could be applied within each of the sub-systems of action. As a sociologist, Parsons was most interested in the social system. He thought that the social system could be divided into four sets of structures that fulfil the functions of the functional imperatives. The functional imperatives are requirements that must be fulfilled for any system to survive. These functional imperatives can be ranked in terms of their significance for cybernetic control (Parsons, 1961). The most important functional imperative from the perspective of cybernetic control is pattern-maintenance. Pattern-maintenance refers to the maintenance of cultural patterns, mainly by connecting values with belief systems such as religious beliefs and ideologies. The next functional imperative is integration. This refers to the necessity of adjusting differentiated structures to each other so that they do not come into conflict. The structure which fulfils this function is the societal community, for example through the laws that regulate the actions of different groups. The most important actors here are the courts and the legal profession, which manage the system of legal norms. Legal norms govern the allocation of rights and obligations, and resources and rewards, between different units of a complex system. The third functional imperative is goal-attainment. This is the necessity to reduce disturbances to the system and restore a state of equilibrium. The structure that fulfils this function is the polity. From this perspective, politics is the process of mobilizing significant numbers of socially important people in the system, in order to carry out an effective response to some threat to the stability of the system. Finally, the least important functional imperative from the perspective of cybernetic control is that of adaptation. Adaptation refers to providing the resources that are needed for all the structures in a system to function. This functional imperative is fulfilled by the economy, consisting of producers who make the goods that are needed, and markets that distribute them to the places where they are needed.

Clearly, Talcott Parsons adopted a very different approach to the question of key factors from that of Karl Marx . The two theorists have opposite ideas about which explanatory factors have the greatest weight in sociological theory. Whereas Marx put the mode of production first in his model of economic base and superstructure, Parsons put the economy last in his model of cybernetic control in the social system. On the other hand, whereas Marx thought that religious beliefs and ideologies are illusions that merely serve to obscure the real economic relations in society, Parsons thought that religious beliefs and ideologies are essential reference points for the legitimation of the values that are the core of a society. It is not surprising, then, that Parsons had little time for Marx's sociology.

Social Stratification

Parsons and Marx also differed in their accounts of social stratification. Whereas Marx perceived social stratification as a cause of conflict and ultimately of radical change, Parsons thought of social stratification as a cause of integration that contributes to the smooth functioning of a social system. Parsons argued from the position of a structural functionalist that some system of stratification is functionally necessary in every society. People have to be recognized and rewarded for their performances, if they are to be motivated to carry out their tasks well. According to Parsons, 'Some set of norms governing relations of superiority and inferiority is an inherent need of every stable social system' (1954: 325). Evaluations of superiority and inferiority, or in other words prestige, are at the heart of any system of stratification. Among the symbols of prestige, money is particularly effective because of its simplicity and lack of ambiguity (Parsons, 1951).

Parsons identified two universal imperatives as producing hierarchies of prestige, or status. First, in any society there are bound to be evaluations of people according to their skill and performance. If there were not, then there would be no standards of performance, and no reason to achieve them. Differences in skill and competence, and therefore in status, are accentuated by the division of labour into many different functional roles. Thus the division of labour produces a hierarchical ranking of prestige. Second, organization of the activities of many individuals requires leadership and authority, and people who occupy these positions must have a different status from those who simply carry out orders. The larger the scale of organization, the greater the differentiation of positions, and the more extensive the status rankings become.

Parsons thought that these fundamental functional requirements necessitated some stratification in any society, including communist societies. Parsons was sceptical about whether communist ideals of equality could be realized in an industrial society, which has extensive division of labour and large-scale organization. He therefore thought that the Soviet Union and capitalist societies like the United States were basically societies of the same type, with similar stratification characteristics, rather than representing different stages of social evolution.

Social Evolution

Because they emphasized different key factors, Parsons and Marx had different theories of social evolution. There are two factors to consider here. One is the mechanisms by which change occurs, and the other is the set of evolutionary stages that they identified.

Marx thought that change occurred due to developments within the mode of production, punctuated by violent conflicts when the contradictions between the forces of production and the relations of production become too great. Parsons, on the other hand described change as a non-violent process due to the inherent dynamics of social systems. According to Parsons, change occurs in a four-step process (Parsons, 1966, 1971). The first step is differentiation. This occurs when a unit in society divides into two or more units, each having a specialized structure and distinctive functional significance for the society. For example, with industrialization the subsistence household of peasant society became divided into specialized units of production in factories and offices, and a new, more specialized type of household that focused on socialization and tension management. Second, there is adaptive upgrading, as each new, specialized structure is better able to perform its primary function. Thus, production is much more efficient in factories than it is in households. Third, there is integration. The new, specialized structures must be related so that they do not come into conflict. For example, arrangements must be worked out for the management of time so that individuals are able to meet both the needs of their employers and their families. And fourth, there is value generalization. New values must be articulated that legitimize the diverse functions of the new units. For instance, the new values of the consumer society serve to legitimize both the expanded level of production in factories and the new roles of household members as consumers.

Turning now to evolutionary stages, Parsons did not see history as a succession of stages in the mode of production, as Marx did, but he saw history as consisting of stages of cultural and social innovation. Parsons stated his position as follows:

> In the sense, and *only* that sense, of emphasizing the importance of the cybernetically highest elements in patterning action systems, I am a cultural determinist, rather than a social determinist. Similarly, I believe that, within the social system, the normative elements are more important for social change than the 'material interests' of constitutive units. (Parsons, 1966: 113)

He concluded that the longer the time perspective, the greater is the relative importance of the cybernetically higher elements.

Viewed on the longest timescale, Parsons divided human societies into three evolutionary stages that he called primitive, intermediate and modern. These three stages represent different levels of adaptive capacity, in Parsons' view. That is to say, each successive stage has an enhanced capacity to control a greater variety of situations. The more advanced the society, the more it can free itself from particular circumstances for its maintenance.

Primitive societies, in Parsons' schema, are pre-literate societies. Their capacities to record and transmit information are very limited, and this restricts their development in many ways. The transition from primitive to intermediate societies involves the invention of written language. This facilitates the spatial transmission of information to a larger population, and it facilitates the transmission of information over time. Societies with written language can record their activities, and consult their recorded history of past events as an aid to decision-making in the present. With writing, human societies are freed from the limitations of the memories of living persons, and vague hearsay about things that happened to their predecessors. Written documents permit the careful analysis of issues, which enhances critical understanding and hence cultural innovation.

The transition from intermediate to modern systems involves the invention of a rationalized legal system. Such a system protects legal decision-making from interference by individuals and groups representing political and economic interests. It also emphasizes universal standards, so that all groups in society are treated equally. Finally, a modern legal system emphasizes procedural flexibility, so that decisions can be made about new conditions and the society can adapt to social change. Modern societies are societies that use their legal systems as instruments of social development, rather than simply emphasizing past precedents.

Jürgen Habermas

Jürgen Habermas (1929–) was influenced by both Marx and Parsons, but he is thought of mainly as a contemporary representative of the school of thought known as Critical Theory. Critical Theory is an approach developed in Germany, initially through the Frankfurt School, founded in Frankfurt in 1923. It is characteristic of Critical Theory that it is based on a critical engagement with the work of Karl Marx. Critical Theory presents a critique of modern, capitalist society, from a perspective that begins in the work of Marx but departs from it by bringing in elements of other theoretical perspectives. Jürgen Habermas is the most important contemporary representative of Critical Theory. He has drawn on a wide range of ideas from a variety of sources in addition to Marx, but especially from the work of Max Weber.

Habermas finds that Marx's distinction between economic base and superstructure is no longer valid (Habermas, 1970). First, echoing Parsons, he claims that it is no longer possible to separate science from industry. In the early stages of capitalism, innovations depended on sporadic inventions. This situation changed with the advent of large-scale industrial research. Now, science, technology and industrial utilization are fused into one system, and science and technology constitute a leading productive force. Second, Habermas argues that it is no longer possible to separate politics from the economy. That is because governments are now actively involved in directing the economy. Problems in the capitalist market economy, such as the tendency to overproduction and the resulting business cycle of booms and busts, can only be solved through government intervention. Governments try to restrain economic growth at the height of a boom, and they try to stimulate the level of economic activity during a recession. Furthermore, governments encourage technological innovation in industry by helping to fund major research and development costs. In these ways, the state is no longer part of the superstructure that is determined by an independent economic base. Rather, state and economy are interconnected in relations of mutual dependence.

Although Habermas rejects Marx's version of historical materialism, he does not abandon materialism entirely. Rather, he retains the model of base and superstructure, but he argues that the domain which constitutes the base has varied from one historical stage to another (Habermas, 1979). It is still the case, in Habermas's opinion, that one part of society determines another. But the economy is no longer identified as the universal base which determines everything else, including social evolution.

Social Evolution

Habermas has identified three main stages of social evolution, for which he has used different terminology at different times. The earliest societies he refers to as primitive, or tribal, societies; The next stage he refers to as traditional societies, or civilizations; And contemporary societies he refers to as modern societies, or capitalism. Habermas envisages evolution from one social formation to another as occurring when innovative solutions are produced to problems generated within the earlier social formation. These solutions are learned and passed on from one generation to the next within a cultural tradition. Thus, social evolution takes place through a social learning process that is comparable to the genetic basis for biological evolution.

It is important to note that Habermas does not think of evolutionary solutions as involving only technically useful innovations, but they can also involve moral innovations that contribute to social integration. In fact, Habermas attaches greater importance to the latter, as moral-practical innovation creates the potential to revise a wide range of social practices including the technical-organizational. Habermas therefore presents his theory of evolutionary stages as one of institutional cores that determine the dominant form of social integration. In primitive societies (i.e., tribal societies) kinship was the basic domain of social integration. In traditional societies (i.e., civilizations), systems of domination, especially through the state, were the basic domain. And in modern societies (i.e., capitalism), the dominant form of social integration is the complementary relation between the state and the economy. The state guarantees private property and maintains an orderly system of trade mediated by a stable currency, and through taxation the economy provides the financial resources with which the state is maintained.

The problems that create the opportunity for new social solutions are understood by Habermas as arising out of the basic social institutions in particular social formations. According to Habermas, we may 'speak of evolutionary learning processes on the part of societies insofar as they solve system problems that represent evolutionary challenges. These are problems that overload the adaptive capacities available within the limits of a given social formation' (Habermas, 1979: 160). It is in this context that Habermas interprets the distinction between base and superstructure as relating to the conditions that favour social evolution. The base of society is that domain which creates the problems that can be solved only by evolving a new social formation. For example, the transition from tribal societies to civilizations may have occurred in response to problems of land scarcity and population density, or an unequal distribution of wealth. These are problems that arose within the kinship domain of society. In modern societies, the basic domain in the base/ superstructure relationship has been the market economy, because the market was freed from social restrictions and became the most dynamic force for change.

Communicative Action

In his reformulation of historical materialism, Habermas conceptualizes two types of action, namely, work or purposive-rational action, and interaction, also referred to as symbolic interaction or communicative action. Purposive-rational action is action directed towards achieving goals. Communicative action, on the other hand, is co-operative interaction based on linguistic communication. 'It is governed by binding consensual norms, which define reciprocal expectations about behavior and which must be understood and recognized by at least two acting subjects' (Habermas, 1970: 92).

In practice, Habermas assigns more importance to communicative action than he does to purposive-rational action. He defends this position by arguing that the development of normative structures derived from communicative action is the leading factor in social evolution. New normative structures produce new forms of social integration, and the latter makes it possible to deploy existing productive forces or to create new ones.

An important aspect of communicative action discussed by Habermas is legitimation. Habermas uses this concept in Max Weber's sense, to refer to the justification of domination that converts power into authority. Unlike Weber, however, Habermas is not so much concerned with legitimation of the authority exercised by individuals. Rather, he is concerned with the legitimacy of political regimes. In Habermas's usage, legitimacy refers to a political order's worthiness to be recognized as right and just. He says that: 'Legitimations...show how and why existing (or recommended) institutions are fit to employ political power in such a way that the values constitutive for the identity of the society will be realized' (Habermas, 1979: 183).

In Habermas's view, the stability of an order of domination depends on its legitimation. An order which is not perceived as just and right will be subject to loss of legitimation that renders it unstable. He argues that this is a problem for advanced capitalist societies, which tend to fall into legitimation difficulties (Habermas, 1975). In contemporary capitalism, governments are expected to manage economic crises so that they do not lead to serious disruptions and loss of income. Failure to do so would generate a legitimation crisis. The modern state in capitalist society is also vulnerable to legitimation crises because its activities have expanded, and extend to planning all kinds of social arrangements. Such planning disrupts traditional beliefs. In the absence of traditional legitimations, it may not be clear what source of legitimacy will stabilize the system. Legitimation will therefore have to be reconstituted through discourse, or it will have to be replaced by the provision of rewards for conformity.

In practice, it seems that capitalist societies have been able to overcome their tendencies to legitimation crisis, in two stages. First, Habermas calls the form of legitimation in early capitalism the 'bourgeois ideology of justice' (1970: 97). It is based on the dominant form of rational-purposive action in capitalist society, namely, the market economy. The key concept in this ideology is reciprocity between buyers and sellers, who reach agreements on fair exchange. The bourgeois ideology assumes a formal equality between buyers and sellers, who are therefore both able to realize their wants. However, this ideology broke down as capitalism progressed. This was partly because of critics like Karl Marx, who pointed out that in the labour market the buyers and sellers of labour power are not equal. The bourgeois ideology of justice was also undermined by the fact that the market economy ceased to be based entirely on free exchange, as it was increasingly regulated by government action. Public intervention to stabilize the economy meant that governments rather than private individuals were increasingly responsible for the outcomes of economic relations. With the collapse of the old ideology, political power required a new legitimation.

In advanced capitalism, legitimation for political power is provided by a programme of action designed to compensate for the imperfections of the market. This includes promises of a guaranteed minimum level of welfare, secure employment, stable income, leisure time and opportunities for upward mobility. Government policy therefore becomes oriented towards guarding against risks to growth, and guaranteeing social security.

Technocratic Consciousness

Habermas has concluded that as government intervention in society has grown, government policy making has become increasingly important and it has increasingly relied on scientific research. This has consequences for people's political consciousness. As research of all kinds is more and more utilized by governments, people lose sight of the fact that government policies are ultimately decided by individuals who occupy specific positions in the social order, and who have definite social, economic and political interests. Government policy seems to be the result of scientific information, which is presented as the key to the most important system goal, namely economic growth. Politics as a process of debate between competing interest groups therefore comes to be replaced by administration based on technical information. Accordingly, the possibility of participatory democracy is undercut by the demand for technical administration, and a weakened version of democracy is legitimated that involves periodic elections of the leaders of administrative personnel (Habermas, 1970).

Habermas's view of modern mass democracy is that it consists of electing alternate ruling groups who govern, but it does not extend to involving most of the citizens in discussion of issues or actual political decision-making. Habermas is clearly critical of this outcome, in which communicative action is replaced by purposive-rational action. He is committed to the idea of progress through open interaction, which he feels is betrayed by the ideological power of technocratic consciousness. This ideology enters into the consciousness of the mass of the population, which becomes depoliticized.

The effect of the depoliticization of the masses in state-regulated capitalism is that class conflict is suspended. Wage-earners now have an interest in economic growth and thus in avoiding dangers to the system, and therefore in keeping conflict to a minimum. Nevertheless, Habermas believes that class remains a relevant sociological factor. Economic inequalities persist between wage-earners and other groups, and the wage-earners are generally hit hardest by any rise in unemployment. Class distinctions therefore persist in standard of living and life style, and these affect political attitudes. In Habermas's view, the potential for class conflict remains latent in capitalism.

Class conflict is only latent in capitalism, however, because of the powerful ideological effect of technocratic consciousness. According to Habermas, technocratic consciousness becomes the new ideology in capitalism. It is different from the old ideologies, in that it does not take the form of an illusion that conceals repression and exploitation. Instead, it promises a system of rewards for private needs. These needs are met by allowing those with superior technical information to govern without interference.

Habermas's response to this situation is to argue for removing all the restrictions on communication that have been imposed by advanced capitalism. Since capitalism is structurally dependent upon a depoliticized public realm, the mass media have no incentive to engage people's political interests. It is only through unrestricted communication that people can become aware of their situation, and that of others, so that they want to become politically active.

Lifeworld and System

Habermas has pursued his interest in unrestricted communication in his discussions of the lifeworld (Habermas, 1987). In Habermas's theory, the lifeworld is the world of lived experience of a social group whose members have reached agreement on how to live. This agreement takes place on the basis of an intersubjective understanding. That is to say, each person grasps the meaning of the other's actions.

Viewed from an evolutionary perspective, Habermas sees the lifeworld as first of all being constituted by religious symbolism. Religious symbolism is a pre-linguistic root of communicative action. Religious symbols have the same meaning for the members of a group of fellow believers, and therefore they make possible a kind of intersubjectivity. Habermas hypothesizes that in early societies normative consensus was expressed through religious rituals, which precede communicative action. Building on Durkheim's discussion of the distinction between sacred and profane objects, Habermas identifies sacred objects as a common focus of attention in ritual. They arouse collective feelings that create a normative consensus, and ritual actions have therefore served to establish and maintain collective identities.

In a later evolutionary development, Habermas proposes that the creation and maintenance of normative consensus shifted from ritual to communicative action involving language. The authority of the sacred is replaced by the authority of an achieved consensus. Language fulfils the functions of reaching understanding, co-ordinating actions and socializing individuals. It thereby becomes a medium through which cultural reproduction, social integration and socialization take place.

Habermas's concept of the lifeworld, and the related concept of communicative action, is only one part of his analysis of society. He argues that we should conceive of societies as consisting simultaneously of lifeworlds and systems. A system is a set of actions, in which each action has a functional significance according to its contribution to the maintenance of the system. A good example of a system is bureaucracy. Each feature of bureaucracy helps to maintain the bureaucratic system. For instance, maintaining written records makes it easy to replace people who quit, or who die, or who must be fired. Whenever someone leaves the organization, their replacement can be shown the appropriate manuals and files, so that they quickly learn what work needs to be done and how to do it. The bureaucracy goes on and maintains itself, even though the individual members come and go. Bureaucracy is a system that has become increasingly dominant in modern societies.

Habermas attributes a number of the characteristic problems of modern societies to changing relations between system and lifeworld. These changes occur in three dimensions. First, system and lifeworld, which were originally coextensive, become increasingly differentiated from each other. That is to say, they tend more and more to be separated out into distinct social structures. Second, systems become increasingly differentiated into autonomous subsystems. And third, the dominant subsystems are increasingly those in which linguistic communication is replaced by other media of interaction, mainly money and power. Habermas is especially concerned with the role of money, as he thinks that power tends to be assimilated to money in capitalism.

For example, the state raises money from the economy through taxation, and government policies tend to be shaped by how much money is allocated to their implementation, who gets it and under what conditions they receive it. Habermas therefore refers to money as a 'steering medium'. It is used to direct a multitude of affairs in capitalist societies. Interchange between subsystems, such as the state and the economy, or the economy and the household, are mediated mainly by money.

Habermas's sociology is especially concerned with the boundaries between system and lifeworld in modern societies. He describes these boundaries in the following way. On one side (system), there are the subsystems of the economy and bureaucratic administration. On the other side (lifeworld), there are the private spheres of family, neighbourhood and voluntary associations, and the public spheres of cultural activities and political debate. The private sphere is focused on the nuclear family, and the public spheres are focused on the mass media which circulate information and opinions about cultural events as well as providing for political discourse.

Habermas's conceptualization of the relationship between system and lifeworld is that system has become dominant over lifeworld. This development has grown to the extent that the system now penetrates into the lifeworld in a process that he refers to as the 'colonization of the lifeworld'. The colonization of the lifeworld is a process in which the previously differentiated structures of system and lifeworld become dedifferentiated, but under the control of the system. According to Habermas, 'The thesis of internal colonization states that the subsystems of the economy and state become more and more complex as a consequence of capitalist growth, and penetrate ever deeper into the symbolic reproduction of the lifeworld' (Habermas, 1987: 367). As a result, money and power tend to replace spontaneous meanings as the foci of concern in private and public spheres. For example, the mass media do not so much respond to the needs of people for information as they respond to the needs of advertisers who expect to make money from selling their products.

Habermas sees the colonization of the lifeworld as a pathological state that results in threats to subjective identity. This is an especial problem as a result of bureaucratization. Bureaucratic organizations are self-regulating social systems, and as such they do not take account of the meanings of the members of the organization. In bureaucracies, personal meanings and motivations become uncoupled from the meanings of action necessary to maintain the system. Individuals follow orders, regardless of their own dispositions and goals. Thus, the inner workings of bureaucracy are independent of elements of the lifeworld. The consequence of this is that the social relations of actors in bureaucracies are separated off from their identities.

More insidiously, Habermas claims that the private sphere is undermined and eroded by the economic system. The effects include consumerism and possessive individualism, as people respond to the constant pressure to buy more goods. At the same time, the private sphere and public sphere are undermined and eroded by bureaucratic administration. For example, Habermas criticizes the effects of growing legal regulation, or juridification, on family life and education. In Habermas's view, family and school are properly formed by communicative action since they involve primarily socialization and teaching, but they have been colonized by the system. Interaction comes to be formally regulated, and this produces functional disturbances.

For example, Habermas thinks that over-regulation of the curriculum in the German educational system leads to depersonalization, the inhibition of innovation and the breakdown of responsibility. Decision-making procedures should treat those involved in the learning process as having the capacity to represent their own interests and to regulate their affairs themselves. Habermas therefore calls for a move away from juridification and towards consensus-oriented procedures for resolving different points of view. In a similar vein, Habermas proposes to reduce the impact of legal regulation on family life. The impact of juridification on family life is visible in child custody decisions following divorce. Judges have little time or capacity to communicate with parents or children, and so the parents and children become subordinated subjects of court proceedings rather than participants in them. Habermas calls for reducing the role of law in family disputes. Instead, he emphasizes efforts to reach mutual understanding through discussion and negotiation.

Finally, Habermas thinks that his thesis of the evolution of capitalism and the colonization of the lifeworld helps us to understand the changing nature of contemporary social conflicts. He proposes that conflicts between labour and capital have been rendered less explosive by being channelled into consumerism on the one hand, and into the growth of the welfare state on the other hand. Capitalist dynamics of growth are protected by state intervention, and a constantly growing volume of resources is redistributed to the mass of the population through the welfare state. However, the tensions existing within capitalism are not removed, but only displaced into tensions between system and lifeworld. Conflicts today no longer take the form primarily of class conflicts over the distribution of economic rewards, but they take the form of a multitude of conflicts over lifestyles and ways of living. The effects of money and power on the lifeworld are resisted, for example their effects on the environment, and protest movements emerge that attempt to roll back the encroachments of the system.

Conclusion

This chapter has taken up the question of what are the key factors in sociological explanation, and especially in theories of social evolution. The three theorists considered here were Karl Marx, Talcott Parsons and Jürgen Habermas. Each of these theorists takes a different approach, but beneath their differences they all have one thing in common. They are all concerned with the question: What is the nature of modern society, and how is it to be explained?

Marx's answer to this question is clear. Modern society is capitalist society, and it is to be explained by changes in the forces of production and relations of production. Ideas do not exert a strong influence on the development of capitalist society because they are part of the superstructure that is determined by the economic base.

Capitalist society is based on a mode of production that consists of the mass production of commodities by workers who are under the control of a capitalist. The relationship between workers and capitalists is a relation of domination, in which the capitalists have all the power. Marx was very interested in how this relationship had come about, and he explained how the capitalists and workers had emerged as distinct groups as a result of definite historical processes. Capitalists are people who have accumulated money for investment due to the circulation of commodities mediated by monetary exchange. The workers, or proletarians, on the other hand, are people who are legally free to sell their labour power for a wage, and who are forced to do so because they do not own the means of production themselves. In both cases, a combination of historical circumstances were needed to bring about the emergence of these groups.

The history of the relationship between capitalists and workers, or in other words between capital and labour, is a history of class conflict, Marx concluded. Workers will never be satisfied with their conditions, he thought, because they are alienated, their wages are low and they are subject to the labour market. Conflict will intensify in capitalism, Marx thought, as the proletariat grows in size and it becomes more politically active.

Part of the conflict between classes involves struggles over ideas. This is a difficult struggle because the ruling class dominates the production and distribution of ideas. It promotes ideologies that serve its interests, by convincing other classes that the policies favoured by the ruling class are really in the general interest of everyone. Marx believed that this was an illusion. He therefore thought that it was his job to uncover the ideologies of the ruling class.

Talcott Parsons disagreed with Marx. He thought that Marx's theories were seriously flawed, and that this had led him into specific errors. In particular, Parsons disagreed with Marx's relegation of ideas to a marginal role in social evolution. According to Parsons, Marx had failed to understand that ideas such as science play a major role in modern economic development. Parsons therefore took a different approach. He argued that cultural codes are the basis for action, and they establish the patterns that are followed in the social system. Cultural codes are institutionalized in social norms, and they are internalized in the personalities of individuals.

Parsons summarized his approach in the idea of a cybernetic hierarchy, which is a hierarchy of control. Elements high in information but low in energy control elements that are low in information but high in energy. Parsons ranked the cultural system at the top of the cybernetic hierarchy, followed by the social system, the personality system and finally the behavioural organism. Within the social system, Parsons thought that the structures which fulfil functional imperatives could also be ranked in order of cybernetic importance. The most important functional imperative within the social system is pattern-maintenance. It is concerned with the maintenance of cultural patterns, mainly by connecting values with belief systems such as religious beliefs and ideologies. The second most important functional imperative is integration. It involves adjusting differentiated structures to each other, mainly through the legal system. The third most important functional imperative is goal-attainment. It consists of reducing disturbances to the system, and is fulfilled mainly by the polity. The least important functional imperative is adaptation. It involves providing resources, and is fulfilled mainly by the economy.

Parsons differed from Marx not only in the degree of importance attached to the economy, but also in the significance of social stratification. In Parsons' view, social inequality is functional for society and it is an unavoidable feature of any social system. Social stratification is a result of the unequal rewards given to people with different positions in the division of labour, and who occupy different positions in hierarchies of authority.

Finally, Parsons has a different conceptualization of modern society than that of Marx. For Parsons, a modern society is one that has a rationalized legal system. This emphasizes autonomy of the legal system, universality and procedural flexibility. According to Parsons, the evolutionary advantage of this system is that it gives society an enhanced capacity to control a greater variety of situations. Parsons sees social evolution as a result of the inherent dynamics of social systems, involving differentiation, adaptive upgrading, integration and value generalization.

Jürgen Habermas identifies modern society as capitalist society, like Marx, but he does not accept Marx's position that ideas are part of a superstructure that is always determined by an economic base. Like Parsons, Habermas believes that scientific ideas now play an important role in the economy. He therefore developed a theory of social evolution which does not attribute ultimate importance to the economy.

In Habermas's theory, evolution is seen as solving problems that were insoluble within an earlier social formation. The basic social institutions within which problems arise depend upon the stage of development. Only in modern society does this turn around developments in the economy because the market was freed from social restrictions and became the most dynamic force for change. Yet, even here the economy is not a completely autonomous force for change. The basis for social integration is the complementary relation between polity and economy, and Habermas thinks that politics plays an important role in today's economy. Political developments can therefore have economic consequences.

For Habermas, political debate is part of a process that he refers to as communicative action. One of the most important features of communicative action is legitimation of the existing system. Habermas thinks that there is a tendency to legitimation crises in capitalism. However, advanced capitalism has stabilized itself by successfully stressing economic growth and social security. These involve increased government intervention in economy and society.

In Habermas's view, increased government intervention has been associated with the growth of a technocratic consciousness, which sees political issues as technical problems to be solved by administrative technocrats. Habermas is critical of this development, which he thinks leads to a depoliticized populace. The end result of this is that class conflict is suspended.

However, this does not mean that all conflict has ceased in capitalism. In addition to the latent class conflict, new forms of conflict have emerged along the boundaries between lifeworld and system. The expansion of capitalism has led to new forms of differentiation between system and lifeworld, and to the growing importance of subsystems that utilize media such as money and power. Money, in particular, has become the steering medium for society. It colonizes the lifeworld, and undercuts the human process of meaning creation.

Further Reading

Antonio, Robert J., 2000, 'Karl Marx', in George Ritzer, ed., *The Blackwell Companion to Major Social Theorists*, Oxford: Blackwell, pp. 105–143.

Bernstein, Richard J., 1985, *Habermas and Modernity*, Cambridge, MA: MIT Press.

Habermas, Jürgen, 1975, *Legitimation Crisis*, trans. Thomas McCarthy, Boston: Beacon Press.

Habermas, Jürgen, 1979, *Communication and the Evolution of Society*, trans. Thomas McCarthy, Boston: Beacon Press.

Habermas, Jürgen, 1987, *The Theory of Communicative Action, Volume 2: Lifeworld and System: A Critique of Functionalist Reason*, trans. Thomas McCarthy, Boston: Beacon Press.

Howe, Leslie A, 2000, *On Habermas*, Belmont: Wadsworth.

Lidz, Victor, 2000, 'Talcott Parsons', in George Ritzer, ed., *The Blackwell Companion to Major Social Theorists*, Oxford: Blackwell, pp. 388–431.

Marx, Karl, 1977, *Capital: A Critique of Political Economy*, Volume 1, trans. Ben Fowkes, New York: Vintage Books.

Marx, Karl and Frederick Engels, 1964, *The German Ideology*, ed., S. Ryazanskaya, Moscow: Progress Publishers.

Marx, Karl and Frederick Engels, 1973, *Manifesto of the Communist Party*, Peking: Foreign Languages Press.

Mayhew, Leon H., 1982, *Talcott Parsons: On Institutions and Social Evolution*, Chicago: University of Chicago Press.

McLellan, David, 1995, *The Thought of Karl Marx: An Introduction*, 3rd edn, London: Papermac.

Outhwaite, William, 1994, *Habermas: A Critical Introduction*, Stanford: Stanford University Press.

Parsons, Talcott, 1951, *The Social System*, Glencoe: Free Press.

Parsons, Talcott, 1966, *Societies: Evolutionary and Comparative Perspectives*, Englewood Cliffs: Prentice-Hall.

Parsons, Talcott, 1971, *The System of Modern Societies*, Englewood Cliffs: Prentice-Hall.

Pusey, Michael, 1987, *Jürgen Habermas*, London: Tavistock.

Robertson, Roland and Bryan S. Turner, eds, 1991, *Talcott Parsons: Theorist of Modernity*, London: Sage.

Rocher, Guy, 1975, *Talcott Parsons and American Sociology*, New York: Barnes & Noble.

Sitton, John F., 2003, *Habermas and Contemporary Society*, New York: Palgrave Macmillan.

Suchting, W. A., 1983, *Marx: An Introduction*, New York: New York University Press.

Wolff, Jonathan, 2002, *Why Read Marx Today?* Oxford: Oxford University Press.

Dimension Four

Sociological Knowledge

5

Sociology and Ideology

An important issue for sociological theory is the nature of the relationship between sociology, considered as a system of ideas, and the ideologies which exist in any society. That is because ideologies have a profound influence upon the expression of ideas. This issue has been important ever since Marx wrote about ideology, because he raised in a fundamental way the question of the social basis of social knowledge. Marx, it will be recalled, pointed out that we always need to take into account the conditions for the production and distribution of ideas. Who produces ideas, and what interests do they have in doing so? What is their position in society, and how does it affect the ideas that they advance? Marx, as we know, argued that the dominant ideas are those of the ruling class. These are distorted ideas, he claimed, because they reflect the interests and biases of that class. Therefore, Marx thought that it was necessary to analyse the ideological nature of existing ideas.

The questions that Marx has left for sociology are: Is sociology ideological? Does sociology advance a distorted view of the world, which is shaped by a particular perspective that reflects a specific social position in the world? Or, more accurately perhaps, does sociology advance a number of competing views of the world, all of which are distorted in different ways because they reflect a variety of social positions?

These are not trivial questions. They affect how sociology presents itself as a purveyor of truth, and they raise a number of questions about sociological practice. If sociology is ideological, how is valid sociological knowledge possible, if indeed it is possible at all? If all ideas are conditioned by social experiences, and different groups in a complex society inevitably have different ideas, how do we choose which ideas are correct? How do we know which ideas are true?

These are difficult questions, indeed, but they are also very important. Some answer is needed to them in any theoretical approach. The classical Marxist answer was to claim that all ideas are ideological, except for Marxism, which is true because of its exceptional position in history. History is seen as the history of class struggles, and with each successive struggle the ideas of the revolutionary class reflect increasingly more basic issues about social

organization. Eventually, there will be an end to all class struggle since capitalism will be replaced by communism. The proletariat is the last revolutionary
class. Its natural ideas are those of Marxism, which is a true understanding of
history because it is the ultimate product of class society and it alone is able to
understand the end of history.

The classical Marxist answer to the question of ideology and truth is what is
known as a realist position. Realism is the belief that it is possible to comprehend the nature of reality, through scientific methods that replace myths and
errors with truths, and that probe beneath the surface appearances to reveal
the underlying structures of the real world. It considers pre-scientific beliefs to
be in need of correction, and therefore it is the job of the realist to uncover
mistakes and falsehoods. Opposed to realism is a contrasting approach
known as relativism. Relativism is the belief that all understandings, including
scientific knowledge, are relative to some point of view, and that there is no
position from which absolute truth can be discovered.

In this chapter, we are going to consider the debates between relativism
and realism in sociology. First to be considered here is the work of Karl
Mannheim, who skirted the difficulties of relativism with an appeal to the
intellectuals as those who could work towards a greater understanding of the
truth. Next to be considered is Michel Foucault's analysis of knowledge and
power. Foucault's approach is both more profoundly relativistic than that of
Mannheim and also more ambiguous concerning his own position. Finally,
the chapter investigates a contemporary attempt to return to a realist position
in grounding feminist sociological work in the standpoint of women. This
section focuses on the work of Dorothy Smith.

Karl Mannheim

Karl Mannheim (1893–1947) originated the sociology of knowledge as a distinct
field in sociology. This sub-discipline is concerned with the scientific study of
the nature of social influences on ideas. Mannheim pointed out that just as it
is possible for Marxists to analyse the ideas of others as ideological, so it is
possible for non-Marxists to analyse Marxism as ideological. Marxism, too, has
taken on diverse forms in different places at different times, and the nature of
the social influences upon the various branches of Marxism is capable of being
analysed sociologically (Mannheim, 1960).

In order to take account of this insight, Mannheim introduced the distinction
between the particular theory of ideology and the total theory of ideology.
The particular theory of ideology identifies the thoughts of particular social
groups as ideologies, but presumes that other social groups, such as one's own
group, can have direct access to the truth. Classical Marxism adopted a particular theory of ideology. On the other hand, the total theory of ideology
identifies the thoughts of all groups as ideological, that is, as influenced by

their social location, historical experiences, economic interests, etc. This was Mannheim's position. He thought that the ideas of all groups in all epochs were of an ideological character, and that Marxism was no exception to this rule.

Mannheim's adoption of the total theory of ideology left him with a problem. If all ideas are ideological, then surely that must include his own ideas. And, if his ideas are ideological, why should we believe them as claims to the truth? This is a very uncomfortable position, intellectually speaking, to which Mannheim needed some solution. His solution was to advocate the sociology of knowledge as a way of understanding all ideas, including sociology itself.

Mannheim began by arguing that a modern theory of knowledge must drop any claim to the absolute truth of ideas which exists independently of the values and social position of their author. As Mannheim put it, 'the vain hope of discovering truth in a form which is independent of an historically and socially determined set of meanings will have to be given up' (Mannheim, 1960: 71). However, this does not mean that Mannheim gave up all claim to the truth. On the contrary, he thought that it would still be necessary to face the task of discriminating between what is true and what is false.

Mannheim therefore advocated searching for approximations to the truth. He thought that this could be done by studying the historical process of the development of ideas. By uncovering the social origins of different ideas about a particular issue we can move towards a more balanced and realistic point of view, albeit a tentative one.

Mannheim thought that contemporary observers were likely to move closer towards approximations to the truth because of the social structures of modern societies. He thought this was so because the limitations of particular points of view are revealed in the clash of opposing ideas. Each side in a conflict of ideas is quick to point out the weaknesses and biases in the claims made by the other side. The result is that the deficiencies in the approaches of both sides are uncovered. Furthermore, the experience of encountering a diversity of points of view creates uncertainty, Mannheim thought, and this encourages an open search for the truth instead of clinging to absolute matters of faith. Mannheim thought that this situation was increasingly common in the modern, western societies, due to their historical development. A rapidly and profoundly changing intellectual world had led to increased questioning of all kinds of ideas, with the result that no single position could be regarded as having the absolute truth. According to Mannheim, 'Only this socially disorganized intellectual situation makes possible the insight, hidden until now by a generally stable social structure and the practicability of certain traditional norms, that every point of view is particular to a social situation' (1960: 75).

If approximations to the truth are most likely to be found in modern societies, Mannheim also thought that they are most likely to be found in a particular group within those societies, namely, the intellectuals. There are three reasons why Mannheim thought that the intellectuals were likely to come closest to the truth. First, he described them as a relatively classless group that is not firmly situated in the social order. Influenced by Marx's theory of class, Mannheim identified the intellectuals as being neither workers nor entrepreneurs and therefore as not being influenced directly by any position in the economic process of society. Intellectuals stand outside the two main classes, and they are not committed to the worldview of either of them. As a group, they are therefore capable of embracing a number of points of view, and of debating them with equal interest.

The second reason why Mannheim thought that the intellectuals were likely to come closest to the truth is because he claimed they are being recruited from a wide range of social backgrounds. This is important because people's ideas tend to be influenced to some extent by their social background. Therefore, due to their broad recruitment, a wide range of ideas comes to be represented among the intellectuals, and their debates become increasingly inclusive. As a result, the individual intellectual who is engaged in discussions with his fellow intellectuals takes part in a mass of mutually conflicting points of view.

Third, Mannheim was convinced that among the intellectuals the influence of social background upon their ideas was moderated to some degree by their education. He thought that education was important because it exposed the intellectuals to a variety of ideas, and it provided the intellectual context for discussing different points of view. Mannheim stated that: 'Participation in a common educational heritage progressively tends to suppress differences of birth, status, profession, and wealth, and to unite the individual educated people on the basis of the education they have received' (1960: 138). Mannheim thought that modern education exposes students to opposing points of view, and that it provides an open forum for debate. Educated people therefore contain within themselves conflicting tendencies, and they are more likely to take an open-minded approach to issues.

Mannheim's position has been very influential in sociology. For example, it is the basis for courses in sociological theory that deliberately expose students to a number of different theories, and which encourage students to debate their strengths and weaknesses. However, it is not the only point of view on the question of the relationship between sociology and ideology. We turn next to the work of Michel Foucault.

Michel Foucault

Michel Foucault (1926–1984) analysed in a serious way the relationship between social scientific ideas and the social contexts in which they are produced. Foucault's position is that all scientific ideas (in the natural sciences as well as the social sciences) are profoundly enmeshed in social structures. However, he rejected the concept of ideology as a way of describing this situation (Foucault, 1980).

Like Mannheim, Foucault held that the claims made by Marxists could not simply be assumed to be more true than the claims made by people from other political positions. For example, he thought that the attack on capitalist society from the Left (i.e., that it is class domination) is the same as the attack on communist society from the Right (i.e., that it is totalitarian). Neither claim is any more true, or any less true, than the other, Foucault thought. Each claim merely attacks the abuses of power by the other side, and ignores the abuses of power on their own side. However, whereas Mannheim merely modified the Marxist theory of ideology to describe this kind of situation by turning it from a particular theory of ideology into a total theory of ideology, Foucault completely rejected the concept of ideology itself.

Foucault rejected the Marxist concept of ideology as difficult to use for three reasons. First, Foucault was critical of the idea, which he identified with the theory of ideology, that ideas are determined by the economic structure of society. Here, Foucault drew on the well-known objection to economic determinism in Marxism, namely, that it is an unrealistic one-factor theory. However, Foucault did not swing to the opposite extreme of cultural determinism, as Parsons did. Rather, Foucault emphasized that there are many social structures which influence the forms that ideas take, and all of them must be seen as instances of power. Foucault insisted that power does not reside only in the economic structures of society, although that is one source of power. Instead, he claimed that power is everywhere. For example, the exercise of power over thought is to be found in the mental normalization of individuals, as well as in such places as mental hospitals and prisons.

Foucault illustrated his approach to power in his discussion of the Panopticon. This was an imaginary penal institution invented in the eighteenth century, whose key feature was the relationship between the observer at the centre and the prisoners who are observed (Foucault, 1979). Foucault used this invention as a metaphor to describe the emergence in the seventeenth and eighteenth centuries of a distinctively new type of society based on discipline, which he referred to as the disciplinary society. Discipline is a type of social control which produces regular and constant effects through the continuous application of controls.

The disciplinary society is an effective means of social control for three reasons. First, control is exercised through surveillance. Everyone in the system of control is open to observation, at all times, without limits. Second, those who are observed cannot see their observers, and therefore they do not know when they are being watched and when they are not. The result is a psychological form of control, in which people control their own conduct rather than having to be physically restrained. Third, each person who is subject to the system is individualized. They are isolated, which means that they cannot combine against those who exercise the discipline, and therefore they cannot effectively resist.

Foucault claimed that this system of discipline can be applied in many different situations, for many different purposes, with equal effectiveness. For example, it can be applied to the control of prisoners, or the mentally ill, or schoolchildren. Wherever it is applied, however, it has one important feature in common. Discipline is related to knowledge. The Panopticon, and all the systems related to it, involve the collection of detailed knowledge about the individuals in the system, which can become the basis for many specific kinds of interventions.

Foucault's second criticism of the concept of ideology is that it places too much emphasis on the role of individuals in ideological struggles. For example, in the cruder versions of Marxism, the members of the capitalist ruling class are seen as deliberately promoting false ideas, in order to create confusion about their real intentions and the consequences of their actions. On the other side, the intellectual leaders of the proletarian revolution saw themselves as engaged in a heroic struggle to penetrate illusions and to throw off false ideas, through their individual intellectual efforts. Foucault thought that this view of ideologies and counter-ideologies overstated the control that individuals have over the expression of their own ideas. For Foucault, ideas are not the products of individual thought, but they are the result of a social conversation that he called a discourse.

A discourse is a way of talking (or writing) about a topic. It defines what the topic is, and it identifies themes that are important subjects of discussion. For example, sociological theory is a kind of discourse. It is a way of identifying topics of common interest in sociology, and of making claims about them. In Foucault's view, the ideas of individuals are never entirely original, but they are always developments in some discourse or other. Before developing their ideas, people read the works of others. And as they articulate their ideas, they discuss them with other people in an ongoing conversation. The discourse therefore shapes how people think in profound ways, and individuals are less important than the discourse which speaks through them.

In particular, Foucault was very critical of the romantic view of the intellectual, and especially of the writer, which he found in France under the influence of Marxism. The intellectual was expected to express a correct understanding of history on behalf of the proletariat, which was unable to articulate its own position. As such, the intellectual was seen as having a position of great importance as the bearer of universal truths. In opposition to this view of the intellectual, Foucault claimed that in reality intellectuals today do not work with grand theories but with specific theories that are conditioned by their locations in the social order. He claimed there had been a shift from the 'universal intellectual' to the 'specific intellectual' (Foucault, 1980: 126). Specific intellectuals such as magistrates and psychiatrists, doctors and social workers, laboratory technicians and sociologists, work in specific sectors of society.

They work on problems which are particular to their own field. However, their work acquires a general significance due to their collaboration in social networks that are often connected through the universities. Foucault sees the modern university as a point of intersection for the intellectuals, where information is exchanged and power is exercised through control over knowledge.

Foucault was very concerned with the close connections between power and knowledge, which he symbolized with the conceptual pairing of power/ knowledge. Knowledge of human functioning is the basis for defining standards of normality and pathology, and thus of gaining power over the body and mind. At the same time, the will to acquire knowledge may derive from the desire to dominate others, in which case knowledge may be considered as a strategy of power.

The third, and most fundamental, criticism of the Marxist concept of ideology advanced by Foucault is that it misunderstands the nature of truth. In the theory of ideology, an ideology is thought to be an illusion, and it therefore stands in opposition to something else that is thought to count as truth. Foucault disagreed with this position. He did not find the opposition between truth and illusion useful because all ideas are believed to be true by someone. The important question for Foucault is how the sense of the truthfulness of ideas is produced. As Foucault put it,

'the problem does not consist in drawing the line between that in a discourse which falls under the category of scientificity or truth, and that which comes under some other category, but in seeing historically how effects of truth are produced within discourses which in themselves are neither true nor false' (Foucault, 1980: 118)

That is to say, Foucault was not concerned with the question of true versus false, but with the question of how beliefs about the truth are produced within every discourse.

Foucault had an interesting definition of the truth. According to him it is not a set of accurate statements which are to be discovered and accepted, but it is the set of rules according to which true and false are separated, and the ways in which true statements are distributed and acted upon. Foucault claimed that each society has its regime of truth. A regime of truth consists of discourses that are accepted as producing the truth. These discourses contain procedures for distinguishing true and false statements, and sanctions that are attached to seeking the truth and avoiding false statements. They also identify the statuses of those who are given the right to say what counts as true. For Foucault, questions of truth are ultimately political questions. They are decided by those who have the power to make their ideas the 'true' ideas. Once again, power and knowledge are intimately connected in a system of power/knowledge.

Foucault was very clear about his understanding of the concept of ideology and how it is related to systems of power/knowledge. However, he was not very clear about where he thought that he himself stood in relation to systems of power/knowledge and questions about what counts as true knowledge. The same cannot be said of Dorothy Smith, who has provided a cogent account of her standpoint as a feminist sociologist.

Dorothy Smith

Dorothy Smith (1926–) is a feminist sociologist, who is an exponent of what is sometimes referred to as women's standpoint theory. This is an approach which claims to speak from the standpoint of women. Dorothy Smith does not think that all women have a common viewpoint, but she does think that all women have in common the experience of a set of social relationships which have excluded them from positions of power or influence.

Smith articulates a point of view that encourages women to speak for themselves, based on their everyday experiences of the world. In particular, she has outlined a position from which it is possible for women to criticize existing institutions as failing to meet their needs. In doing so, she has avoided any kind of relativism associated with the works of Mannheim or Foucault. Smith adopts a realist position that enables her to lay the foundations for women to say what is definitely true. This is necessary in order for her to have an intellectual basis for arguing that claims made by men about women have been false.

The heart of Dorothy Smith's approach to sociology and ideology is a critique of ideology and its relation to women, especially women in sociology. Women have two relationships to sociology. They are subjects of sociological theorizing and some of them are also sociological practitioners who work as sociologists. Dorothy Smith is concerned with both of these aspects of women's experiences in sociology.

Dorothy Smith's position on the sociology of ideology is a modified version of Marxist realism. It is from Marx and Engels that she draws her concept of ideology. She defines ideology as: 'those ideas and images through which the class which rules the society by virtue of its domination of the means of production, orders, organizes and sanctions the social relations which sustain its domination' (Smith, 1979: 140). Ideologies are produced by specialists who are part of the apparatus through which the ruling class maintains its control over society. In her later work, Dorothy Smith has referred to this apparatus as the relations of ruling, or ruling relations (Smith, 1987, 1999a). The ruling relations are found within government, law, business, education and the professions, as well as in the discourses that go on between these sites of power. Within the ruling relations, ideologies serve to organize the work of ruling, as well as to order and legitimize relationships of domination.

Dorothy Smith says that she makes use of the Marxist concept of ideology because it encourages us to examine what are the sources of ideas (1987). She identifies two different kinds of sources, whose relationship has profound effects on women. First, there is the source of ideas in people's own immediate experiences of the world. In particular, since we spend so much of our lives working, there are the direct experiences of working with and for others. Second, ideas may also be received from external sources who communicate their ideas to us. These ideas are conceptualized by Dorothy Smith as a set of imposed categories of thought, which do not necessarily fit the direct experiences of everyday life. She believes that in women's lives there has been a rupture, or line of fault, between these two sources of ideas. The external ideas have generally not been consistent with women's direct experiences. For example, women in the 1950s and early 1960s were all expected to be happy and fulfilled by a life consisting of housework and child rearing, but many women found this depressing.

The Marxist theory of ideology is important for Smith because it enables her to describe the bifurcated consciousness experienced by women like herself, whose experiences as wives and mothers do not fit the categories of thought that are external to them because they are formed in men's ideas and imposed upon them. This formulation of ideology allows her to conceptualize the contrast between the social forms of thought which are expressive of a world that is known directly and shared by women and the social forms of thought which are made for women by men.

According to Dorothy Smith, the external ideas which are imposed upon women are ideologies which have their origins in the ruling relations. The relations of ruling are power relationships on behalf of the capitalist ruling class in the first instance, but secondly they are also relations of patriarchal rule. Men dominate within the ruling relations, and their ideas are therefore imposed upon women.

The ideas that are found within the relations of ruling are impersonal and abstract, because they are used to cover a multitude of situations, and many different people. Dorothy Smith locates the historical origins of this abstract mode of ruling in capitalism (Smith, 1987). Capitalism has created a sphere of social relationships that involves anonymous buyers and sellers who are dispersed in space. The particular, local experiences of these people are irrelevant to their roles in economic transactions. Subsequently, they are also irrelevant to the agencies which attempt to benefit from and to regulate market activities. Governments have entered into increasing relationships with the capitalist market economy. As they have done so, they too have developed increasingly abstract modes of ruling. This differentiation of the market economy and the state from local contexts of action has had different consequences for women and men. Men have been more active in the market economy and the state, and women were confined to a local sphere of action involving personal relationships.

The growth of the market economy and the state have created a separation of public and private spheres. The public sphere consists of business and government, and related professional organizations. The private sphere consists of family, neighbourhood and friendship ties. The private sphere has become a lesser sphere, with less power and influence. It has been reserved for women. Most of the power is located in the public sphere, which has been occupied mainly by men.

The public sphere dominated by men has expanded, and it increasingly regulates the private sphere. For example, governments produce laws regulating family life, reproduction and childhood. Dorothy Smith therefore argues that 'Skills and knowledge embedded in relations among particular persons have been displaced by externalized forms of formal organization or discourse mediated by texts' (Smith, 1987: 5). The external sources of ideas become dominant over immediate experience, which has three important consequences. First, women's experiences in the private sphere are rendered subservient to men's interests in the public sphere. There is a dimension of gender stratification in the relations of ruling in which women are dominated by men. Second, the dominant ideas that originate in external sources are abstract ideas into which particular, local experiences must be forced. That is because ruling requires objectified, impersonal principles of management which are intended to cover all possible situations. Third, sociology is a discourse that is located in the relations of ruling in the public sphere, and as such it is both abstract and dominated by men.

Sociology

According to Dorothy Smith, sociology as a discipline is engaged in the process of transcribing the local meanings of action into general forms of knowledge that are appropriate to the ruling relations. It provides the abstract and impersonal principles of social organization required by the ruling apparatus in a modern society. For example, sociology transcribes particular dissatisfactions with work into an abstract sociology of alienation from work which may be of use to business managers. In Dorothy Smith's view, sociology is an ideology that is situated in the relations of ruling. In this context, she disputes Karl Mannheim's theory of ideology and the sociology of knowledge (Smith, 1979). Smith claims that Mannheim's goal was to create an impersonal and disinterested sociology that would be a synthesis of the best elements in all the existing ideologies. It would be a point of view that contrasted the broad, social scientific perspective of the sociologist with the biases of specific ideologies. As such, it would be an abstract point of view that is removed from the particular, local experiences of time and place.

In one sense, Mannheim's viewpoint has been successful. It has been widely adopted, and the result is that sociology has indeed taken on the form of an abstract system of knowledge in which people's particular, local experiences are discarded in favour of general concepts. Hence, when we enter into sociology we encounter it as a discipline which is outside of any individual point of view. The problem with this impersonal sociology, in Smith's opinion, is that although it attempts to be objective in the sense of getting rid of subjective influences, it is not able to tell the truth about the world. That is because in practice the particular experiences of women tend to be overlooked and ignored in favour of the experiences of men acting within the relations of ruling.

In Dorothy Smith's view, the established sociology that seeks to account for the social world from a standpoint which is independent of particular positions is nevertheless a particular point of view, because it is part of the ruling relations. The ruling relations require abstract, general principles of thought as a means of controlling the many localized contexts of action beneath them. Sociology provides the general concepts that are needed by people who are active in the relations of ruling. This means, importantly, that sociology views society and social relations 'in terms of the perspectives, interests, and relevances of men active in relations of ruling' (Smith, 1987: 3). For example, Max Weber's ideal type of bureaucracy, or his ideal types of authority, may be considered as illustrations of this point of view. They deal with abstract concepts having to do with relations of ruling, from the perspective of men who are responsible for such relations.

Dorothy Smith does not mean that male sociologists are necessarily involved in relations of ruling themselves. Rather, she thinks that they participate in social networks with those who rule, and they are thereby influenced by them. For example, sociologists seek funding for their research and access to data from a variety of sources, including business and government. They are influenced by these interactions, and come to take on some of the perspectives of those upon whom they depend. Smith insists that she does not mean by this some sort of conspiracy theory by upper class males to manipulate ideas to their advantage (Smith, 1979). Rather, she thinks it is simply that people who interact on the basis of shared interests develop common perspectives. They participate in circles of discourse in which they influence others, but are also influenced by them. Some of these circles of discourse are formally organized, and others are informal. Also, some of them are located within the discipline of sociology, and other circles of discourse link sociologists to individuals located within other institutions in the relations of ruling.

In sociology, ideologies are constructed in circles of discourse that are shaped by interaction practices within social structures. Dorothy Smith is especially concerned with those features of social structures in sociology which have led to the exclusion of the ideas of women (Smith, 1987). This means paying attention to inequalities in the production of social knowledge and control over what is admitted as genuine additions to knowledge.

In the first place, Smith is concerned with the exclusion of women themselves from important positions in the production and distribution of knowledge, especially in educational institutions. Using data from the 1970s, she notes that as we go up the Canadian educational hierarchy from elementary to secondary school to community college to university, we find a lower proportion of women teachers at each step. The proportion of women teachers is lowest in the universities, which are most involved in the production as well as the distribution of ideas. Also, within the universities women are more highly represented in the lower status ranks than they are in the upper status ranks. Since it is the members of upper status ranks who are most likely to act as gatekeepers controlling access to publication and other means of recognition, men have an advantage over women in access to the means of distributing their ideas.

Second, Dorothy Smith claims that men have a greater influence over the decisions that are made within educational institutions, because their voices carry more authority. According to Smith, authority is a form of power that is a capacity to get things done in words. Some people's words count for more than the words of others, and their words are more likely to be acted upon. In general, Smith thinks that men are those whose words carry the most weight. That is because men have a dominant position in society, and people are accustomed to following what men say. 'They are those whose words count', as Smith puts it (1987: 30).

It follows from the above two points, Smith thinks, that sociology is shaped in many invisible ways by the assumptions of men. Although sociology presents itself as impersonal, objective and value-neutral, in reality it is ideological. The relevances of men creep into their discourses, and they become fixed in the standards and criteria of sociological knowledge. Established sociology is therefore a predominantly masculine sociology. This bias is manifested in the concepts and examples that are used, and it is perpetuated by the way in which new entrants into sociology are required to learn the existing theories and to study the established texts. Professors require their students to cite the existing literature, and they punish them with low marks if the students do not do so. In these ways, which are quite normal to the operation of a discipline, the ideas of the dominant group are perpetuated in the ongoing practices of sociology.

An example provided by Smith (1979) is the division between the sociology of work and the sociology of leisure. This division is based on the distinction between being at work and not being at work, which makes sense from the perspective of men's experiences with paid employment outside the home and leisure time at home. However, from the perspective of a housewife, it is a distinction that makes no sense at all, Smith argues. If sociology had begun with the experience of housework, separate categories of work and leisure would never have emerged, she claims. In a similar vein, Smith argues that theories of rational choice that begin with individuals forming projects and choosing the means to pursue them, do not reflect the experiences of women. That is because women are expected to respond to the projects of others, mainly their husbands and children, and to be available when called on to assist in others' lines of action. Sociology has ignored women's experiences, in Smith's opinion, and it therefore needs to be changed.

Dorothy Smith's solution to the neglect of women's issues in sociology is to urge women to construct a sociology for women. In this approach, women will speak from the base of their own experiences. In doing so, women must claim authority for themselves, Smith claims. They must delve into their own experiences in everyday life, and present them as worthwhile objects of attention against professional opinion and the traditions of academic disciplines, which they must be prepared to repudiate.

There is inevitably an argument to be made against this approach, of which Smith is aware. It can be argued that the result of a sociology for women will merely be another particularizing ideology, just as Mannheim argued that Marxism had become another ideology. Dorothy Smith's counter to this argument is to claim that a sociology for women will not only be a different sociology, but it will also be a better sociology. That is because in some areas, such as family life, women have a more extensive and more accurate knowledge than do men. As subordinate members of families and other groups, women have to pay more attention to the needs and activities of others than men do. They therefore have insights into how things work that are denied to men.

In defence of Marxism, as well as the standpoint of women, Smith claims that both approaches can be considered as valid because they speak from the position of the servant (Smith, 1979). That is to say, they speak from the position of the working class and of women, which are subordinate groups whose task is to serve others. The working class, and women, have a broad perspective on their work because they have to interpret the wishes of others as well as carrying out the practical tasks through which things actually get done. The ruling class, and men, on the other hand, do not see the full range of human activities because they merely ask for things to be done and wait for the results. In particular, it is women who must negotiate the line of fault between the abstract, conceptual mode of working in the ruling relations and the local and particular mode of working through which tasks are actually accomplished. Managerial work of all kinds depends upon a large number of mundane tasks, which are mainly carried out by women. Women's work has been both necessary to the relations of ruling and unrecognized by it. In marriage as wives, in the office as secretaries, in the hospital as nurses and social workers, and in many other ways, women mediate for men the relation between the abstract, conceptual mode of working and the actual concrete forms of action on which it depends. According to Dorothy Smith, 'women's standpoint locates a subject in the fundamental "item" of the twofold basis of knowing the world. The organization which divides the two becomes visible from this base. It is not visible from within the other' (Smith, 1979: 169).

In order to encourage women to make the twofold basis of the world visible, Dorothy Smith has outlined an approach to sociological research that she refers to as 'institutional ethnography' (Smith, 1987). This approach begins with experiences from everyday life, in the details of day-to-day practices that are enacted in particular situations, under particular conditions. It asks questions such as, how do practices and relations actually work? The aim of this stage of the enquiry is to take issues and problems not as they have been defined in the discipline, but as they appear from a standpoint within the everyday world. Subsequently, enquiry into the practices and relations is then broadened to include the institutional contexts of action that are beyond the scope of any one individual's experience. This means, especially, studying how everyday practices are connected to the relations of ruling. It is Dorothy Smith's belief that a sociology beginning from the standpoint of women should take up the connection to the ruling relations of people whose work is necessary to it but is unrecognized by it. It is her hope that by following the method of institutional ethnography, women can arrive at a deeper understanding of themselves and of the world within which they are situated.

Her method is no doubt intended partly as a corrective to the tendency that she sees for universities to become disconnected from those who are exploited, marginalized or subordinated by the relations of contemporary capitalism (Smith, 1999b). In particular, she argues that there is an increasing disconnection between academic feminism and women's groups outside the universities. Feminism has become professionalized, and it has become hooked onto the ruling relations of the professions, public service, scholarly careers, etc. In the latter context, women's academic careers depend upon publication. In order to get their work published, they must conform to procedural and methodological standards that have no relationship to the relevances of women activists. For Dorothy Smith, the method of institutional ethnography provides a way of cutting through the established criteria of the discipline of sociology, and of connecting directly with the lives and problems of women outside the universities.

Conclusion

This chapter has considered a theme extending from Chapter 4, namely the implications of the Marxist theory of ideology for sociology. Three theorists were discussed here: Karl Mannheim, Michel Foucault and Dorothy Smith. Mannheim corrected Marx, by arguing that the particular theory of ideology should be replaced by the total theory of ideology. Foucault rejected Marx's theory of ideology as difficult to make use of. And Dorothy Smith extended Marx's theory, by using it to analyse the line of fault in women's experiences of the world.

Karl Mannheim introduced the distinction between the particular theory of ideology and the total theory of ideology. The particular theory of ideology identifies the thoughts of particular social groups as ideologies, but presumes that other social groups are capable of telling the truth about the world. The total theory of ideology identifies the thoughts of all groups as ideological. Mannheim adopted the total theory of ideology. This left him in the difficult position of claiming truth for his own ideas while acknowledging that all ideas, including his own, are biased and distorted by social influences. Mannheim's answer to this dilemma was to hold that it is possible to move closer to approximations to the truth under certain conditions and for certain groups. Under conditions of social change and cultural pluralism, competition between conflicting ideas reveals the ideological element in all thinking. This is especially the case for the intellectuals, who preserve the diversity of ideas and engage in debates about them.

Michel Foucault rejected the concept of ideology for three reasons. First, he was critical of the principle that ideas are determined by the economic structure of society. In contrast, he claimed that power is everywhere and ideas are influenced by many factors. Second, Foucault thought that too much emphasis had been placed on the role of individuals in ideological struggles. Instead, he argued that ideas are shaped by discourses that circulate in social networks. Third, Foucault thought that the contrast between ideology and truth was not useful. All ideas are effects of truth, understood as a set of procedures for separating true claims from false claims. The ability to make effective distinctions between true and false is a form of power. Power and knowledge are therefore connected in systems of power/knowledge.

Dorothy Smith utilizes the theory of ideology of Marx and Engels to describe the rupture, or line of fault, in women's experiences of the world. On the one hand, there are the immediate experiences of everyday life in local and particular situations. On the other hand, there are abstract ideas that are imposed from external sources. The latter ideas are ideological. They do not fit women's everyday experiences, and they distort women's understanding of themselves and the world in which they live.

Ideologies are distorted because they reflect the relations of ruling, or ruling relations. The ruling relations is a system of power which is based on both capitalism and patriarchy. Men dominate women through the relations of ruling, and the dominant ideas are therefore men's ideas. Dorothy Smith encourages women to speak for themselves, from the standpoint of women. Women's standpoint can make claims to truth because women's experiences give them insights that are denied to men working within the relations of ruling. This involves challenging the established theories and practices of sociology, and developing methods of enquiry that enable women to understand themselves and how they are affected by the ruling relations. Dorothy Smith's recommended method is institutional ethnography.

Further Reading

Brown, Alison Leigh, 2000, *On Foucault: A Critical Introduction*, Belmont: Wadsworth.

Campbell, Marie and Ann Manicom, eds, 1995, *Knowledge, Experience, and Ruling Relations: Studies in the Social Organization of Knowledge*, Toronto: University of Toronto Press.

Danaher, Geoff, Tony Schirato and Jen Webb, 2000, *Understanding Foucault*, London: Sage.

Foucault, Michel, 1979, *Discipline and Punish: The Birth of the Prison*, trans. Alan Sheridan, New York: Vintage Books.

Foucault, Michel, 1980, *Power/Knowledge: Selected Interviews and Other Writings 1972–1977*, trans. Colin Gordon, Leo Marshall, John Mepham and Kate Soper. New York: Pantheon Books.

Gutting, Gary, ed., 1994, *The Cambridge Companion to Foucault*, Cambridge: Cambridge University Press.

Kettler, David, Volker Meja and Nico Stehr, 1984, *Karl Mannheim*, London: Tavistock.

Longhurst, Brian, 1989, *Karl Mannheim and the Contemporary Sociology of Knowledge*, New York: St Martin's Press.

Mannheim, Karl, 1960, *Ideology and Utopia*, London: Routledge & Kegan Paul.

McHoul, Alec and Wendy Grace, 1997, *A Foucault Primer: Discourse, Power and the Subject*, New York: New York University Press.

Meja, Volker and Nico Stehr, 1990, *Knowledge and Politics: The Sociology of Knowledge Dispute*, London: Routledge.

Simonds, A. P., 1978, *Karl Mannheim's Sociology of Knowledge*, Oxford: Clarendon Press.

Smart, Barry, 2000, 'Michel Foucault', in George Ritzer, ed., *The Blackwell Companion to Major Social Theorists*, Oxford: Blackwell, pp. 630–650.

Smart, Barry, 2002, *Michel Foucault*, Revised Edition, London: Routledge.

Smith, Dorothy E., 1987, *The Everyday World as Problematic: A Feminist Sociology*, Boston: Northeastern University Press.

Smith, Dorothy E., 1999a, 'From Women's Standpoint to a Sociology for People', in Janet L. Abu-Lughod, ed., *Sociology for the Twenty-first Century: Continuities and Cutting Edges*, Chicago: University of Chicago Press, pp. 65–82.

Smith, Dorothy E., 1999b, *Writing the Social: Critique, Theory, and Investigations*, Toronto: University of Toronto Press.

Dimension Five

Structure and Agency

6

Social Structure and
its Alternatives

In this book we have been considering sociological theory from the perspective of the process of theory construction. We have outlined the steps that go into developing a theory, and for each one we have examined the options that are open and the major alternatives that exist in the literature. In this chapter, and in the following chapter, we consider the issue of the concepts that are used in sociological theories.

Concepts are terms and their related meanings. They are the building blocks in theoretical arguments. They define what the theory is about, and they identify objects in society to which the theory refers. The stress put on one concept or another is also a way of identifying the emphasis of the author, and of telling the lines along which the theory is likely to be developed.

There are many concepts in use in sociology. However, one in particular has been both widely used and widely debated. That is the concept of 'structure'. Social structures can be conceptualized initially as fixed arrangements of the parts of a social system that constrain the actions of actors in that system. They constitute the framework of society, around which the society is built. This is an imagery of social structure that we have inherited from structural functionalism. It is worth recalling that structural functionalism was first referred to by its early exponents as 'structure-function' theory. In an earlier chapter we have already encountered the concept of function and its uses. It is now time to take up the concept of structure. One of the clearest exponents of this concept in sociology was Robin Williams.

Robin Williams

Robin Williams (1914–) claimed that to demonstrate structure we need to be able to show a set of patterned activities that recur over time, and that are related to other patterns (Williams, 1951). There are three criteria of structure, according to Williams. First, there must be complexes of action, thought and

137

emotion that are shared by many individuals. Second, these patterns are repeated in many situations. And third, the patterns are related to other patterns in the same society.

Structure, as defined, is easy to observe in human affairs. For example, every day of the working week enormous numbers of children get up and go off to school. They repeat this action every day, for many weeks of the year, year after year until they finally leave school. This pattern of behaviour is also related to other patterns in the society. It is related to the arrangements that are made for transporting children to school, whether in parents' cars or in school buses. And this in turn is related to the time that parents leave for work, or perhaps whether they are employed outside the home at all. Also, this pattern is related to the arrangements that must be made to pay for schools, by levying taxes so that teachers can receive their salaries. In short, going to school is repeated by many children, and it is definitely related to other social patterns. It is an example of social structure.

Williams claims that social structure is the product of social rules. From his perspective, society consists of a vast network of rules that approve or require some behaviours, and disapprove or forbid others. Some of these rules are unique to particular individuals or small groups. On the other hand, other rules, such as the rule against killing human beings, are held in common by large numbers of people. According to Williams, the most important rules are cultural norms that are widely shared by the members of a particular society. Some of these cultural norms have a special importance, and they are strongly established, or institutionalized. These are the institutional norms. Institutional norms, such as the rule that parents should support and care for their children, are effectively compulsory by social agreement. There is a broad consensus in support of such norms. They are typically regarded as moral imperatives, and they are binding upon the occupants of certain social positions, such as parents. Institutional norms also have severe penalties attached to them for norm breaking, and the penalties are often enforced by specialized social agencies.

Sets of institutional norms are referred to as institutions. They occur in those areas of social life which are of vital importance to society. As defined by Williams, the term 'institution' refers to 'a set of institutional norms that cohere around a relatively distinct and socially important complex of values' (Williams, 1951: 29). These values are connected to the major needs of the society. They regulate important recurring situations, such as birth and death, raising the young, providing the necessities of life, managing power relations, etc. Accordingly, there are economic institutions, political institutions, educational institutions, etc.

As a structural theorist, Williams believes that social behaviour is conditioned by institutional norms. For example, he insists that there is no such thing as the pure play of economic forces. He points out, for instance, that in contemporary society no one can sell themselves into slavery. There is a fundamental restriction here on economic transactions, in the name of personal liberty. Furthermore, there are special provisions that prevent the equivalent of slavery occurring through permanent, crushing indebtedness. People who stand no chance of paying off their debts are allowed to go into bankruptcy in order to receive protection from their creditors. Economic transactions that were entered into in good faith are set aside by the courts even though the creditors will receive only a fraction of what they are owed, in order to maintain the independence of the individual.

It is characteristic of Williams' strong emphasis on institutions that both social order and social disorder are seen as the results of institutional norms. Social disorder is seen as the result of problems in the norms, either because the norms are unclear or because there are conflicts between different norms. For example, struggles between adolescent children in America and their parents are not seen as the inevitable result of human nature, but they are seen as due to the institutional character of the American family. The problem is one of an erratic and inconsistent transition from the dependent status of childhood to the independent status of adulthood. There is no clearly marked onset of adulthood in America, as it begins at different times in different ways. Getting a driver's licence, being able to drink in a pub, being able to vote, leaving school and getting full-time employment are all signs of social adulthood. But they occur at different times, with the result that neither parents nor children know at what point the child should be treated as an adult. The result is that the exact nature and timing of adult privileges and responsibilities are handled through negotiation and conflict.

Despite his strong emphasis on institutions, Williams recognizes that not everything can be explained by institutional norms. A realistic picture of society should also take account of variation, violation and evasion. First, there are variations in behaviour because norms do not prescribe just one action but they permit a range of behaviours. Some norms are particularly vague, because they state religious or ethical ideals that people are expected to aspire to. Also, there are variations in norms between subcultures, especially in societies that are composed of different ethnic groups. Second, there is violation of norms as conformity to norms is never absolute and some norms are deliberately broken. For example, some people may be tempted to achieve the goal of economic success through illegitimate means. Third, there is evasion of norms when norms are given public lip service but are widely ignored in practice.

Williams' discussion of behavioural variation, and norm violation and evasion, points to the difficulties that can arise with the structural conception of society. Not all behaviour can be explained in structural terms. Another difficulty is that an approach which begins with the idea of structure as recurring patterns of behaviour implies an image of society in which things remain much the same over time. This may also be taken as implying a social or political conservatism, in which it is preferred that things *should* remain the same. However, it is not necessarily the case that a structural view of society is socially and politically conservative. A structural view of society can be combined with a radicalism in which the existing structures are seen as obstacles to progress. This is the case with feminism and the concept of patriarchy, as illustrated by the work of Mary O'Brien.

Mary O'Brien

The concept of patriarchy is arguably the most distinctive and the most valuable contribution that feminism has made to sociological theory. As used in feminist theory, patriarchy refers to the domination of women by men. It is presumed to be a universal structure that affects women everywhere, in both the private and public spheres. Private patriarchy consists of the personal relations of domination that individual men exercise over individual women in their private relationships, mainly in the family. Public patriarchy consists of the impersonal relations of domination that men exercise collectively over all women, through the power that men wield within public institutions such as governments, schools and businesses.

Mary O'Brien (1926–1998) claimed that structures of patriarchal ideology and practice exist in almost all societies (O'Brien, 1989). She asked who needs patriarchal structures, and she answered that men appear to need them and they are therefore engaged in the defence of patriarchal structures. O'Brien traced the origin of patriarchy to men's position in the process of reproduction, and their response to it. The crucial factor in men's position in the process of reproduction is what O'Brien referred to as 'the alienation of the male seed' (O'Brien, 1981). A man ejaculates his sperm in copulation, and it enters a woman where it may fertilize her. As a result, men do not bear children, but it is women who engage in the reproductive labour of childbirth.

In order to have a relationship with a child, a man must appropriate the child of a woman. However, it is not obvious which child should be appropriated, because there is no way of knowing which children were fathered by a particular man and which were fathered by other men. Paternity is uncertain, and as a result there is no natural relationship between particular children and particular men. The relationship between particular children and particular men must be established on social and ideological grounds. Men appropriate particular children by appropriating particular women, and they enter into agreements with other men to do so. Paternity, then, is not a natural relationship to a child, but it is a right to a child that is mediated by a right to a woman. These rights have to be supported by a social process of co-operation among men. According to O'Brien, 'It is the historical movement to provide this support system which transforms the individual uncertainties of paternity into the triumphant universality of patriarchy' (1981: 54).

Patriarchy is manifest first of all in marriage, in which men have exclusive sexual access to women. Second, it is manifest in the isolation of women away from other men, in the private sphere of family and home. The public sphere then becomes reserved for men, as a sphere within which the laws defining and regulating patriarchy are made. According to O'Brien, 'A huge and oppressive structure of law and custom and ideology is erected by the brotherhood of Man to affirm and protect their potency' (1981: 60). O'Brien believed that women now have the potential to oppose and transform this structure, in part because of the revolution in contraceptive and reproductive technologies which have given women greater control over their fertility.

Herbert Blumer

The structural approach to the study of society, whether in its conservative or radical versions, is open to the criticism that structures do not really exist because there is too much variation in behaviour, or, if they do exist, they are not pre-determined by underlying forces in the way that structural theorists presume. This was the position of Herbert Blumer, who adopted an anti-structural approach to sociology (Smelser, 1988).

Herbert Blumer (1900–1987) was a founding figure of a school of thought that he called Symbolic Interactionism. He traced the origin of his approach mainly to the influence of George Herbert Mead (1863–1931). Mead was concerned with the analysis of acts by individuals, which he proposed were instrumental in satisfying some interest or impulse. How these interests are satisfied depends upon the meanings that are attached to objects in the environment, including the self. Human beings are conscious of themselves, Mead pointed out, and they act with reference to themselves as well as to others. Meanings, including the meanings assigned to the self, are social because we require the co-operation of others in formulating our lines of action, and we therefore engage in communication with other people.

Following this approach, Blumer criticized what he called 'the structural conception of human society' (Blumer, 1969). Blumer did not question the existence of structure in human society, as he noted that there are recurrent patterns of behaviour in many areas and he acknowledged that there are such structural features as roles, norms, bureaucratic organizations and so on. What he did question was the idea that these structural elements have a determining influence on behaviour. He did not think that regularity of behaviour can be automatically explained by adherence to rules which specify how individuals are to behave in particular situations. Rather, regularity of behaviour is to be explained as the outcome of individuals having shared meanings which they give to situations, and on the basis of which they act. In Blumer's view, people form their meanings through a process of interpretation and definition of the objects in their environment. Social objects such as norms or roles do not produce behaviour, but they are taken into account by individuals as they form their lines of action in the practical conditions of their lives. Blumer was especially critical of the idea found in structural functionalism that action is the result of an individual's position in a self-operating social system. He claimed that actions are pursued to serve the purposes of individuals, not the requirements of a system. According to Blumer, 'from the standpoint of symbolic interaction the organization of a human society is the framework inside of which social action takes place and is not the determinant of that action' (Blumer, 1962: 189).

Principles

Blumer thought that the explanation of action in symbolic interactionism rested on three principles. First, human beings act towards things on the basis of the meanings that things have for them. Blumer complained that this simple principle was constantly broken by social scientists, who substitute their meanings for the meanings of the people whose actions they are describing.

Sociologists who formulate hypotheses to be tested often do so by drawing upon their own opinions, or upon the theory of some other sociologist, without finding out how the people being studied actually see their own worlds. The result, Blumer thought, is the setting up of fictitious worlds that tell us more about the sociologist than they do about the people being analysed. Blumer was therefore opposed to the divorce between theory and research that he saw in sociology. Theory is of value in social science, he concluded, only if it is closely connected to empirical research. Blumer's answer to this problem was to urge sociologists to acquire a detailed knowledge of the people being described, through a first-hand acquaintance with their way of life. This means getting close to the people involved, participating in their conversations, observing how they handle the problems that arise in their daily lives and watching how their lives unfold.

The second principle of symbolic interactionism is that the meanings which people assign to the objects in their environment are drawn from the social interactions in which they engage. As Blumer put it, 'The meaning of a thing for a person grows out of the ways in which other persons act toward the person with regard to the thing' (1969: 4). That is to say, we do not simply form our meanings as a result of psychological elements in our personalities, but other people's actions define the meanings for us. In interacting with one another, human beings have to take account of what the other is doing and adjust their behaviour accordingly. As a result, sociologists must pay special attention to social interaction as a formative process. That is to say, interaction is not simply a medium within which behaviour occurs, but it forms human action. In particular, sociologists must study the interactions through which joint actions are formed.

Blumer used the term 'joint action', to refer to 'the larger collective form of action that is constituted by the fitting together of the lines of behavior of the separate participants' (Blumer, 1969: 70). Examples are abundant and include a marriage ceremony, a war, a conversation, a trading transaction and a church service. In all these cases the participants have had to adjust their behaviour to that of the other participants in order for the collective form of action to be created. They do this by ascertaining what the others are doing or intend to do, and then aligning their own actions on the basis of their inter- pretations of the others' acts (Blumer, 1962). According to Blumer, social life consists of the fitting together of lines of action in joint actions. He claimed that: 'It is evident that the domain of the social scientist is constituted precisely by the study of joint action and of the collectivities that engage in joint action' (Blumer, 1969: 17).

The third principle of symbolic interactionism is that the meanings of things are handled in, and modified through, an interpretative process. There is a process of interaction that goes on within the individual, as people engage in an internal conversation about what things mean and how they should respond. They indicate to themselves how objects are defined, and they may consider several possibilities before finally deciding on one of them. Choices of how to act may be weighed before one is selected, or the decision may be made not to act at all. The significance of this is that people do not simply respond to external stimuli, but they engage in a process of interpretation of how to respond whose outcome is not pre-determined.

Blumer was critical of sociological approaches that do not include the inter- pretative process in the investigation of human behaviour. These approaches, such as the use of variable analysis in sociology, do not account for what really happens, in Blumer's view. The analysis of independent variables and dependent variables, and even intervening variables, does not take account of the shifting process of interpretation whereby meanings are assigned to things. The conventional procedure is to take some factor which affects behaviour and to consider it as an independent variable. The behaviour which is presumed to be affected is identified as a dependent variable. The process of interpretation that goes on between independent variable and dependent variable tends to be ignored. That is because there is an implicit assumption in most variable analysis that the independent variable automatically exercises its influence upon the dependent variable. This cannot be the case because objects do not determine their meanings, and meanings that are assigned to objects are not permanently fixed.

Blumer concluded that variable analysis can be useful in sociology where common meanings have become stabilized, and a fixed relationship exists between independent and dependent variables for practical purposes. How- ever, we should never forget, Blumer reminds us, that such relationships are likely to be temporary and they probably apply only to some groups but not to others. Blumer thought that in general the utility of variable analysis would be limited by the fact that there are many areas in which common, stabilized meanings do not exist. These areas are increasing in contemporary society, he claimed, and this means that it is becoming more important to pay attention to how meanings are constructed through the process of interpretation.

Anti-Structure

Blumer used his three principles of symbolic interactionism to advance the symbolic interactionist view of social life, and also to criticize the structural conception of society which he found in the sociology of his day. What is wrong with the structural approach from a symbolic interactionist point of view is that it does not pay enough attention to individual meanings in particular situations; it tends to overlook or downplay the importance of interaction in the formation of conduct; and it ignores the process of inter- pretation through which people shape their responses to events. As a result of these failures, the structural approach cannot easily account for some very important features of social life, Blumer claimed.

The main problem with the structural approach is its tendency to see behaviour as a result of individuals responding to forces which play upon them. In particular, Blumer criticized the view that sees behaviour as being due to people following rules, as a result of which they go on acting in the same way. In the first place, Blumer asserts that it is not the case that human life in any society is only the result of established forms of joint action. New situations are constantly arising that the established meanings do not fit, and for which the existing rules are inadequate. As a result, people must invent their lines of action as they cope with new demands. Such behaviour is just as common as rule-governed behaviour, in Blumer's view. In modern societies, especially, many new situations arise and old situations become unstable.

Second, Blumer stated that even where joint actions are repeated, they are formed by a process of interpreting the meanings of events. 'Repetitive and stable joint action is just as much a result of an interpretative process as is a new form of joint action that is being developed for the first time', Blumer claimed (1969: 18). For example, people have to decide whether or not certain rules are still appropriate to certain situations, or whether they should be discarded. If it is decided that the rules are still appropriate, people then have to decide whether the rules will be given only minimal recognition or whether they will be followed with enthusiasm. Blumer pointed out that the meanings which underlie joint actions can be handled in a variety of ways. They can be treated with indifference, or they can be invested with new vigour; they can be subject to pressures to tone them down, or they can be subject to pressures to reinforce their application. These varying uses of the rules depend upon the interactions that go on among the participants as they influence each other's definition of the situation. According to Blumer, 'It is the social process in group life that creates and upholds the rules, not the rules that create and uphold group life' (1969: 19).

Third, Blumer thought that it was only by studying the underlying processes of social interaction and self-interaction that we can understand many of the things that go on in organizations. Such factors as morale, or its lack, the functioning of bureaucracy, exploiting the system, and favouritism and cliquishness cannot be ascertained from studying the structure of an organization but only from studying its interactional dynamics.

Blumer consistently attacked the tendency to over-generalization in sociology as a result of assuming fixed, determinate relationships between social factors. He continually stressed the shifting nature of interpretations, and the immense variety of social life due to the complexity of the ways in which people define their social worlds. A prominent example of this is Blumer's analysis of the effects of industrialization (Blumer, 1960, 1964, 1990). He argued that industrialization does not necessarily have the effects that are attributed to it. Industrialization is frequently seen as producing the disintegration of an earlier family system, the appearance of discontent, political radicalism, etc. Blumer claimed that such patterns are not always associated with industrialization, and when they do occur in conjunction with industrialization they do not necessarily have industrialization as their cause. Rather, Blumer argued that industrialization provides a neutral framework within which many other factors have their effects. Industrialization has no definite social effect, he asserted, and it is a mistake to believe otherwise. Industrialization lays the groundwork for extensive social change, but it does not determine or explain the particular forms of social change that take place. That is because there are extensive variations in the process of industrialization, and because there are variations in the responses to it.

Method

Blumer presented a flexible approach to sociology, which allowed him to describe a wide range of variations in human behaviour. First, he insisted that behaviour is constructed by individuals, it is not simply released in response to some stimulus. Individuals note the events in their environment, they interpret their meaning, and they engage in a process of interaction with themselves as they work out an appropriate line of action. Second, individuals' interpretations of the meanings of events depend crucially upon how they define the situation they are in. In order to understand why an individual acts in the way that she or he does, it is essential to get inside the defining process and discover how situations are identified as being of certain kinds. This means seeing the situation as it is seen by the acting individual. Third, separate acts by individuals are fitted together into joint actions. This is done by individuals identifying the act in which they are about to engage, and by defining and interpreting each other's ongoing actions. In the case of repetitive joint action, people fit their lines of action together by using the same recurrent meanings. These common definitions provide guidance to the individual in constructing his or her own acts to fit into the acts of others. Fourth, individuals take account of each others' actions through the symbols that they communicate. In communication, people indicate to each other what their intentions are and how they define their situation. According to Blumer, 'Human group life is a vast process of such defining to others what to do and of interpreting their definitions' (Blumer, 1969: 10). Interaction is thus symbolic interaction. This was also the approach taken by Erving Goffman.

Erving Goffman

Erving Goffman (1922–1982) has sometimes been referred to as an exponent of 'dramaturgical sociology'. That is to say, he conceived of each individual as being literally an actor who puts on performances in order to communicate to others a certain kind of impression of himself or herself. Goffman's approach to the study of action was that he was concerned with 'the participant's dramaturgical problems of presenting the activity before others' (Goffman, 1959: 15). He likened these problems to the issues of stage-craft and stage management in the theatre. Part of the impact of Goffman's work has therefore come from his view of human beings, namely, that we are all continuously engaged in constructing performances in order to make other people think about us in a certain way. We want people to think about us in ways that enable us to achieve our purposes in life. For example, if students want to get an extension on the due date for an essay, it is normally necessary for them to present an impression of themselves as serious students who have run into unexpected difficulties, rather than of slack students who are belatedly trying to catch up on their responsibilities.

Goffman's importance as a sociologist does not depend entirely upon his views on the presentation of self. His work is also noteworthy for its unique relationship to the concept of structure. Goffman did not think it worthwhile to study societal structures, such as organizations, and he shifted emphasis to study face-to-face interaction. However, he did not abandon the concept of structure entirely. Rather, he set as his goal the study of the structure of inter-action. Even though it may not be useful to study society as a framework of rules that govern people's behaviour, it may still be useful to study the rules that people follow in their interactions, Goffman concluded. He said, 'In fact, to describe the rules regulating a social interaction is to describe its structure' (Goffman, 1967: 144).

Goffman's underlying interest was in social order. He wanted to know what factors make for orderly, co-operative relations and the absence of conflict in most of social life. He did not attribute this to culture and socialization, nor to agencies of social control, but to the structure of social interaction. Like the symbolic interactionists, Goffman saw social life as a vast network of interactions which are shaped by the actions that individuals take. People influence each other through their actions, and we therefore have to look at the ways in which individuals' actions are constructed. It is in the structure of everyday face-to-face interaction that we must look for the factors which produce the experience of an orderly social world.

In the first place, and most fundamentally, there are the rules that govern the manner in which people interact with one another. Goffman referred to these as 'ground rules', indicating their basic nature in the formation of action (Goffman, 1971). Ground rules are social norms that do not specify the objectives that the participants are to seek or the consequences of their actions, but they specify the means that people are to follow in pursuing their goals. Goffman gave as an example the traffic rules that regulate trans-portation (Goffman, 1963). People obey the traffic signals because they know that by doing so they can avoid crashing into one another, and everyone can get to where they want to go with the minimum of inconvenience. The destinations to which people are travelling, and their reasons for going there, are irrelevant to the orderly flow of traffic. What matters is that people follow the rules regulating their relations with one another while they are on the road.

Goffman drew a direct parallel between the rules governing the flow of traffic on the highways and the rules that govern the flow of communications in face-to-face interaction. There is a kind of communication traffic order, he claimed. This order arises from the fact that when people are presented to one another in some situation there is always the possibility of communication between them. The possibility of communication is fateful, because it can lead to a variety of unwanted outcomes. As a result, it comes under normative regulation in every society. Goffman called these particular ground rules the 'situational proprieties'. They regulate when and where it will be permissible to initiate talk, among whom, and what the topics of conversation will be. As such, they guide and organize the flow of messages. For example, there are rules concerning the significant gestures through which conversations are opened and closed. These 'openings' and 'closings' are equivalent to the traffic lights that turn the flow of traffic on and off. Standard greetings and farewells signify that the person is now available, or no longer available, for interaction. Greetings show that a relationship is still where it was when the parties last met, and that they can now pick up where they left off. Farewells show that the interaction which is ending was pleasurable for both parties and that they are open to further interaction in the future.

Another situational propriety is the rule for 'civil inattention'. This rule requires that when people who are not known to each other are in each other's presence in a public place, they should pay just enough attention to the other to signify awareness of the other's presence, but not so much attention that it would be taken as an attempt to initiate interaction. On the street, for example, people approaching each other will look fully at the other while they are still some distance apart, but then as they draw closer they will either look away or they will drop their gaze and look at the ground.

One of Goffman's most important ground rules is what he referred to as the 'maintenance of face' (Goffman, 1967). This is the requirement that an actor, and usually those with whom he or she is interacting, must work to sustain a particular impression of the individual. It is expected that the individual will present an internally consistent image of the self, and one that projects socially desirable characteristics. This is done by acting out a 'line'. A line is a pattern of acts by which individuals express their view of the situation, and through their actions their evaluation of the participants, including themselves. Every line has implications for the face that the individual is attempting to present in the situation. A face is a positive social value that an individual claims for herself or himself. It can be sustained, or undermined, but usually the individual can expect that it will be maintained and that others will co-operate to do so.

Faces in a situation are treated as sacred things, which are to be respected and protected. In the first place, an individual is expected to maintain an attitude of self-respect. He or she will be expected to live up to the face that they have claimed for themselves. This will mean being careful to maintain an expressive order of significant acts that are consistent with the face that is claimed. Second, individuals are expected to assist others in maintaining their faces. They accept each other's faces, and they are expected to go to some lengths to save the faces of others when they are threatened by apparently inconsistent events. For example, they may refuse to acknowledge events that would destroy another's face. In short, all of the participants in a situation will act to prevent lines from being discredited, and thus they avoid loss of face for everyone. As a result, the line taken by each participant is usually allowed to prevail, and each participant is able to carry off the role that he or she has chosen for himself or herself.

Lines become known to others by the individual communicating them through symbols. One way of doing this is by presenting a certain kind of 'front'. A front is an aspect of a performance which regularly defines the situation for those who observe it (Goffman, 1959). It includes the setting for a performance, as well as the personal fronts that individuals put on when they prepare themselves for a performance. Examples of settings include the furniture and décor in a lawyer's office, or the blackboard and podium in a lecture hall. Examples of personal fronts include military uniforms, make-up or a white lab coat. The white lab coat, for instance, symbolizes cleanliness, and clinical, professional efficiency. It is an example of a standardized personal front that has the advantage of simplifying the process of recognizing what type of role the person is playing. Because of this advantage, the same front can be used for a variety of lines of action, ranging from medical technician to scientific researcher, or pharmacist or cosmetics consultant. Standardized fronts become widely shared ways of enhancing the impression created by a performance.

Goffman pointed out that the front is an area of social life that frequently receives a great deal of attention. Prior to a performance, settings and personal fronts frequently undergo elaborate preparation in places that Goffman referred to as 'back regions'. By comparison, the place where a performance is enacted he referred to as a 'front region'. In the front region, a performer has to work to maintain a front of a certain kind in order to impress an audience. On the other hand, in the back region the front can be dropped and the person can relax since no members of the audience are present. While in the back region, people knowingly act in ways that contradict their performance, and they use the back region to construct their expressive equipment. As a result, the back region is usually kept hidden from the audience and it is closed to intruders. According to Goffman, this is a widely practiced technique of impression management.

Social Order

Goffman's goal in analysing all these features of interaction was to study the ground rules which people follow when carrying through their lines of action in situations which they share with others. As a result of following the ground rules, most social life is orderly and shows a minimum of conflict. Goffman's conception of social order is as a set of ground rules which facilitate the pursuit of individual purposes in social situations, with the minimum of trouble for all concerned. It is characteristic of Goffman's approach that he assumes most people seek an easy solution to interaction problems, and that they are willing to co-operate with others to allow them the same. People stay away from situations where they are not wanted, and they co-operate to save each other's faces.

Most social life proceeds smoothly because people who are present in the same situation arrive at a working consensus on the definition of the situation. When an individual is in the presence of others, his or her actions influence the definition of the situation that the others have. And the others, too, project a definition of the situation through their response to the individual, and through any lines of action they initiate towards the individual. Goffman implied that the normal situation is one of relatively equal and co-operative treatment of the definitions of the situation projected by the different partici-pants. This does not mean that Goffman thought people reach agreement on their real feelings and beliefs. Rather, they suppress their real feelings and beliefs and express only those to which others are likely to agree. In this way the participants reach a surface agreement, which lasts only as long as the specific encounter. In particular, temporary agreement is reached on those aspects of the situation which are especially important to the individuals involved. Each individual is allowed to define matters that are important to him or her but not to others, such as the accounts he or she gives of his or her own activity. In return, he or she remains silent on matters that are important to others but not to himself or herself. This division of definitional labour enables the participants to negotiate their respective claims without coming into conflict.

Goffman was aware that not all social life has this co-operative and egalitarian character. Definitions of the situation can also be used in contexts where they are used to control others. The ability to carry off a particular definition of the situation is the ability to control the lines of action occurring within a particular occasion. It is therefore a form of power. A classic illustration of this occurs in 'total institutions'. Total institutions are institutions such as prisons and mental hospitals, in which the institution controls all, or almost all, of an individual's life. Goffman was especially interested in the implications for the individual of being committed to a mental hospital (Goffman, 1961).

In mental hospitals, unlike everyday life, the patients do not have the moral right to expect that their own definitions of themselves will be allowed to prevail. Rather, the self that they project is likely to be discredited by others. In engaging in lines of action, each individual simultaneously performs a self that others are encouraged to accept. Usually, the performed self is accepted at face value, but that is not always the case. Sometimes, as in mental hospitals, the individual's performed self is discredited and it is challenged by others who advance an alternative definition of the self.

In Goffman's view, the self 'is not a property of the person to whom it is attributed, but dwells rather in the pattern of social control that is exerted in connection with the person by himself and those around him' (Goffman, 1961: 168). Each self is the product of an institutional arrangement of performances. These self-defining aspects of institutions are taken to an extreme in total institutions, where a profound difference is performed between staff and inmates. To be an inmate in a mental hospital is to be a person whose own claims about himself or herself are suspect. In the mental hospital, the patient is confronted with claims that his or her past life has been a failure. He or she is encouraged to believe that the only way to progress towards personal freedom is to acknowledge that fact, and to follow the rules of the institution which have been established for his or her benefit.

In everyday life there is likely to be less emphasis on adherence to rules, Goffman concluded. There, social order is maintained not only by rule following, but also by various forms of interaction about breaking the rules which Goffman called 'remedial interchanges' (Goffman, 1971).

In Goffman's view, the breaking of rules is not just an occasional and strictly controlled feature of social life. It is a pervasive feature of social life, and so are its consequences. This is so, Goffman thought, because social interaction is organized primarily in order to achieve the easy adjustment of individuals, in order that each can pursue her or his private goals with the minimum of stress. It may be less troublesome to overlook someone's rule infraction than it is to enforce rule-following behaviour. In that case, breaking of the rules is not likely to be followed by a punitive cycle.

Goffman was critical of social control theories of social order, which maintain a firm distinction between conformity and deviance, and which hold that deviance is punished. This image may be true of some areas of social life, such as major crimes, but in face-to-face interaction much of the breaking of ground rules goes unpunished, Goffman argued. This does not mean that the rules are abandoned or neglected. On the contrary, the rules and their breaking are acknowledged in ways that enable the participants to confirm their commitments to the rules while avoiding the necessity to punish infractions. The main concern with rule infractions in face-to-face encounters is 'to get traffic moving again' (Goffman, 1971: 108). If all rule infractions had to go through the punitive cycle of investigation, trial and punishment, then everyday life would be hopelessly clogged with time-consuming tasks. Instead, the participants engage in remedial work that enables them to repair a damaged situation so that everyone can get on with their pursuits.

An example of a remedial interchange is when two people approaching a blind corner from different directions turn the corner at the same time and bump into each other. Neither one feels that he or she is to blame for having physical contact with the other, but each apologizes so that the mishap can be smoothed over. They are then able to continue about their business after a momentary interruption. The traffic is moving again.

This simple example illustrates that social order in Goffman's view is not just a result of the rules that govern behaviour. It is also a result of communication about behaviour and the relationship between behaviour and the rules. Goffman thought that there are three kinds of communication involved in remedial work. They are: accounts, apologies and requests. In accounts, the actor who is suspected of committing an offence provides a story that deflects responsibility for the incident. He or she may claim that it was not him or her who committed the offence, or that if he or she did he or she was not himself or herself at the time due to illness or some other disturbance. Or, she or he may claim that the offence was just a temporary oversight, or that she or he faced an unusual situation and did what any reasonable person would have done under the circumstances. In apologies, the actor accepts responsibility for his or her actions, and expresses regret that the incident occurred. He or she makes clear that he or she acknowledges the force of the rule, and he or she laments the fact that he or she has broken it. Finally, in requests the actor seeks to regain the approval of the person who has been offended. She or he asks for forgiveness, and seeks to restore the positive feelings that were previously held towards her or him.

Finally, Goffman maintained that although remedial interchanges show that there is a great deal of behavioural variability concerning the rules, they also illustrate a common awareness of the rules and concern for them. There are core moral traditions of western culture, he claimed, that tell all of us what we must be alive to in situations of face-to-face interaction.

Conclusion

In this chapter we introduced the concept of structure, and we began our discussion of the issue that has been referred to as the structure-agency problem. That is to say, there is a choice to be made in sociology between those approaches which emphasize the constraint exercised by structures and those approaches which emphasize the active participation of individuals in constructing the social world. In this chapter we studied the structural approaches of Robin Williams and Mary O'Brien, and the stark alternative to them posed by the work of Herbert Blumer. In Blumer's work, the point of departure is the individual attribution of meaning to objects in the environment, and the responses to it. Lastly, we considered the complex approach of Erving Goffman. Goffman focused on the activities of individuals as they construct face-to-face encounters, but he did so by analysing the rules that structure interaction.

Robin Williams' account of structure is as a set of related practices that persist over time. He explains structure as a result of people's tendency to follow rules that regulate their behaviour. The most important of these rules are institutional norms. These norms establish how a society handles recurring problems, and as a result they are strongly supported. Institutional norms are morally binding on the occupants of certain social positions, and they are reinforced by sanctions.

Mary O'Brien was concerned with structures of patriarchy, which she claimed exist in almost all societies. These structures exist to advance men's interests in children, by giving them control over women's fertility through control over women themselves. Patriarchy thus exists to meet the needs of men. However, it can, and should, be opposed by women.

Herbert Blumer argued against the structural conception of society. In particular, he was opposed to the idea that social life could be explained as the result of people following norms. He argued that it is not the rules that create and maintain group life, but it is the social process in group life that creates and maintains the rules. Blumer therefore proposed an alternative approach that he called symbolic interactionism.

According to Blumer, social life can be explained by three simple principles of symbolic interactionism. First, human beings act towards things on the basis of the meanings that things have for them. Second, the meanings which people assign to the objects in their environment are drawn from the social interactions in which they engage. Third, the meanings of things are handled in, and modified through, an interpretative process.

Following these principles, Blumer claimed that the study of human society is the study of joint actions. These are social interactions in which the participants define each other's actions, and they adjust their own actions to fit what the other person is doing.

Erving Goffman studied face-to-face interactions, but he did not reject the concept of structure. Rather, he adapted the concept of structure to refer to the rules that are followed in encounters. These rules produce an orderly flow of interactions which enable the participants to pursue their individual goals. At the same time, Goffman did not see slavish commitment to rules as a constant feature of interaction. Rules are frequently broken, and when they are individuals restore their relationships with each other, and with the rules, through remedial interchanges.

Further Reading

Baugh, Kenneth, 1990, *The Methodology of Herbert Blumer: Critical Interpretation and Repair*, Cambridge: Cambridge University Press.

Blumer, Herbert, 1962, 'Society as Symbolic Interaction', in Arnold M. Rose, ed., *Human Behavior and Social Processes*, London: Routledge & Kegan Paul, pp. 179–192.

Blumer, Herbert, 1969, *Symbolic Interactionism: Perspective and Method*, Englewood Cliffs: Prentice-Hall.

Burns, Tom, 1992, *Erving Goffman*, London: Routledge.

Drew, Paul and Anthony Wootton, eds, 1988, *Erving Goffman: Exploring the Interaction Order*, Boston: Northeastern University Press.

Fine, Gary Alan and Philip Manning, 2000, 'Erving Goffman', in George Ritzer, ed., *The Blackwell Companion to Major Social Theorists*, Oxford: Blackwell, pp. 457–485.

Goffman, Erving, 1959, *The Presentation of Self in Everyday Life*, Garden City: Doubleday.

Goffman, Erving, 1963, *Behavior in Public Places: Notes on the Social Organization of Gatherings*, New York: Free Press.

Goffman, Erving, 1967, *Interaction Ritual: Essays on Face-to-Face Behavior*, Garden City: Doubleday.

Hammersley, Martyn, 1989, *The Dilemma of Qualitative Method: Herbert Blumer and the Chicago Tradition*, London: Routledge.

Lyman, Stanford M. and Arthur J. Vidich, 1988, *Social Order and the Public Philosophy: An Analysis and Interpretation of the Work of Herbert Blumer*, Fayetteville: University of Arkansas Press.

Manning, Philip, 1992, *Erving Goffman and Modern Sociology*, Stanford: Stanford University Press.

O'Brien, Mary, 1981, *The Politics of Reproduction*, London: Routledge & Kegan Paul.

O'Brien, Mary, 1989, *Reproducing the World: Essays in Feminist Theory*, Boulder: Westview Press.

Williams, Robin M., Jr., 1951, *American Society: A Sociological Interpretation*, New York: Knopf.

7

New Ideas on Structure and Agency

This chapter continues the examination of issues of structure and agency by examining the work of three theorists: Pierre Bourdieu, Anthony Giddens and Zygmunt Bauman. These three theorists take very different approaches to the problem of structure-agency. To begin with, Pierre Bourdieu worked out an original approach that attempted to combine aspects of structure and agency within the same theory. Bourdieu did this through use of the key concepts of 'field', 'habitus' and 'capital'. Together these concepts gave Bourdieu a flexible means of analysing a variety of empirical situations.

Our second theorist is Anthony Giddens. Giddens attempts a redefinition of the concept of structure, which he refers to as 'structuration'. In contrast to the static concept of structure, structuration is a dynamic concept which is adapted to a theoretical approach that is intended to deal with social change.

Lastly, the work of Zygmunt Bauman rejects the concept of structure in favour of an approach that emphasizes the fluid character of contemporary social life. He sees the world in which we live today as a melting pot of ideas, practices and resources, in which individuals struggle to make their way without the supports provided in earlier, and simpler, times.

Pierre Bourdieu

Pierre Bourdieu (1930–2002) attempted to resolve the tension between structure and agency in sociological theory by incorporating both of them within the same theoretical approach. He did this by introducing three concepts as the foundation stones for his theory. The first concept is 'field', which is Bourdieu's structural concept. The second concept is 'habitus', which refers to the impetus to agency. And the third concept is 'capital'. This is the means of agency and the form of structure.

Field

In highly differentiated societies, a society consists of a number of specific, autonomous fields. For example, there is the artistic field, the religious field, the economic field, etc. Bourdieu's approach is complex, as he rejected the idea of reducing other fields to the economic field but he thought that the economic field was dominant. Bourdieu adopted an approach which stressed the relative autonomy of fields. That is to say, he argued that the economic field influences the other fields more than it is influenced in return, yet it does not determine what happens in the other fields. As Bourdieu put it, 'In reality, the social space is a multi-dimensional space, an open set of relatively autonomous fields, fields which are more or less strongly and directly subordinate, in their functioning and their transformations, to the field of economic production' (1991: 245).

A field is a structure of relationships between positions (Bourdieu and Wacquant, 1992). These positions are defined objectively, and they have definite effects upon their occupants. In particular, the positions are subject to a certain distribution of unequal amounts of capital of various kinds. Any field therefore consists of relations of superiority and inferiority, of domination and subordination. It is the distribution of capital, and the relations of superiority and inferiority, that most interested Bourdieu.

Bourdieu used the analogy of a game to describe how the relationships in a field are structured. People co-operate in following the rules of the game, and this therefore constitutes their relationships as a game. Of course, this assumes that people are allowed to play. An important distinction, then, is between those who are allowed into the field to play the game, and those who are excluded.

The principal dynamic of a field is that there is competition. People compete with one another for 'stakes' of various kinds, which can become the capital that enables them to play the game. In playing the game, people follow strategies of various kinds. For example, they can play to increase or conserve their capital. Or, they can work to change the rules of the game. One way of changing the rules of the game is to change the value of particular species, or types, of capital. Bourdieu assumed that people will usually work to increase the value of the species of capital that they possess, and devalue the species of capital possessed by their opponents. For example, Bourdieu argued that those people who more or less completely monopolize the specific capital associated with power in a certain field will tend to favour strategies that conserve their capital (Bourdieu, 1993). They will therefore tend to be socially and politically conservative, and they will defend orthodoxy. On the other hand, those who are least endowed with specific capital (who are often also the newcomers, and therefore generally the youngest) are inclined towards strategies that devalue the capital of those who are well endowed. They will therefore tend towards subversion, and they will advocate heresy. Bourdieu also argued that there is a constant symbolic struggle between the different classes and class fractions in society, who compete to impose the definition of the social world that is best suited to their interests (Bourdieu, 1991).

Capital

The concept of capital, as used by Bourdieu, refers to a possession that gives individuals the ability to do certain things, such as exercising domination over others. It represents power over a field at a given moment in time (Bourdieu, 1991). Capital can be accumulated, and once accumulated it tends to persist. Some people accumulate more capital than others. Bourdieu found the concept of capital useful because it shows that everything is not possible for everyone. It shows the fundamental inequalities that exist between individuals.

There can be various types of capital, such as economic capital, or cultural capital, or social capital, or symbolic capital. Each species of capital is a store of value. Like money, which is a store of value for economic capital, it can be drawn on when desired and converted into other things. The unifying feature of all the species of capital is that they require time and effort to accumulate. The essence of all capital is therefore accumulated labour time. Because of this, one species of capital can be converted into another species of capital. Cultural capital, for instance, can be converted into economic capital. For example, educational qualifications (a form of cultural capital) have an economic value on the labour market. Similarly, economic capital can be converted into cultural capital through the time that is spent in socialization and education. The wealthier a family is, the more likely they are to be able to afford for the mother to stay home and attend to the socialization of the children so that they are prepared for school. Also, the wealthier a family is, the more they can afford to prolong the schooling of their children so that they acquire higher educational qualifications.

Although the different species of capital can be converted into one another, at any given moment in time each individual has different amounts of the different types of capital. For example, one person may have a lot of economic capital and little cultural capital, whereas another person may have a lot of cultural capital and little economic capital. This affects the individual's ability to play the game within a particular field, because each field requires more of one type of capital than it does the other types. The force of a player in the game in a certain field depends upon the total amount of capital possessed, and the composition of the capital, that is, how much of each species of capital the individual possesses.

The four species of capital (economic, social, cultural and symbolic) can be found in all fields. However, in any given field there is a certain hierarchy of the types of capital which differs from that in other fields. The value of a species of capital hinges upon the nature of the field in which it is employed.

As Bourdieu put it, 'A capital does not exist and function except in relation to a field' (Bourdieu and Wacquant, 1992: 101). A species of capital is what works in a given field, both as a resource to be used in struggles with others and as a stake to be struggled over. It is what allows the individual to play the game, and therefore to be part of a certain field.

Bourdieu saw individuals as engaged in a struggle over capital, in which they are all trying to increase the amount of their personal stock of capital. Bourdieu's analysis of capital is therefore 'economic' in one sense, in that he sees people as motivated by interests to accumulate capital. But it is not economic in the sense that he does not see all action as a direct or indirect result of the pursuit of material wealth. It is therefore necessary to analyse each type of capital separately.

Economic Capital

Economic capital exists as material wealth in the form of money or things that can be converted into money, such as stocks and shares, or property. Economic capital is the dominant type of capital in the sense that it is at the root of all the other types of capital (Bourdieu, 1986). Every type of capital is reducible in the last analysis to economic capital. However, Bourdieu rejected economism. That is to say, he rejected the tendency to explain everything in economic terms. He claimed that it is necessary to recognize the specific effects of the other types of capital, and to give them their due importance in social analysis.

Social Capital

According to Bourdieu, 'Social capital is the sum of the resources, actual or virtual, that accrue to an individual or a group by virtue of possessing a durable network of more or less institutionalized relationships of mutual acquaintance and recognition' (Bourdieu and Wacquant, 1992: 119). In other words, social capital is all the resources that are gained through social ties with other people. The volume of a person's social capital depends on the number of people to whom she or he is connected, and on the amount of economic, cultural or symbolic capital possessed by each of those persons (Bourdieu, 1986).

It is through the concept of social capital that Bourdieu draws our attention to the importance of membership in a group or social network. Social capital arises out of contexts for meeting people, such as neighbourhood, workplace or kinship. For these potential relationships to become actual relationships, however, they must be recognized and practiced through material and symbolic exchanges. Only in this way will the relationships come to be experienced as necessary relationships that involve mutual obligations as a result of subjective feelings such as gratitude, respect or friendship.

Bourdieu emphasized that social ties require work to sustain them. In order to maintain the availability of other people's resources, it is necessary to maintain the relationships through a constant round of sociability. Social invitations received must be returned, and every effort must be made to ensure that opportunities for interaction are pleasurable. This takes time, and it is also a drain on resources to meet the economic costs of sociability. Economic capital is therefore an asset in acquiring social capital, together with social skills and knowledge of social relationships.

Cultural Capital

Cultural capital is the knowledge and tastes that are transmitted within families and in schools, and that mark those who possess them as socially superior to those who do not. It also includes such things as educational qualifications which signify the acquisition of knowledge and tastes. Cultural capital is important, in Bourdieu's view, because of its relationship to social stratification. Bourdieu argued that knowledge and tastes are markers of social class. They are used by individuals to distinguish the members of one class from another class. Since knowledge and tastes are shaped by socialization and education, they are often related to family and class background. When they are passed from one generation to the next in childhood socialization, they constitute cultural capital which serves to maintain class membership (Bourdieu and Passeron, 1977).

Bourdieu stressed the transmission of cultural capital in the family through socialization and financial support for prolonged education. He referred to this as a process of the hereditary transmission of capital. Bourdieu argued that as other means for the inheritance of privilege have been restricted, the inheritance of cultural capital has become more important (Bourdieu, 1986). The transmission of cultural capital is a hidden means for reproducing class position in families, that is to say of ensuring that class position is passed on from one generation to the next. This is so because there is a link here between economic capital and cultural capital, through the time needed for the acquisition of cultural capital. The length of time available for the acquisition of cultural capital depends on the capacity of the family to afford the necessary free time from work.

Cultural capital works as a means of passing on class position because of the way in which knowledge and tastes are stratified. Bourdieu claimed that in France in the 1960s it was possible to identify statistically a stratification of tastes covering many different areas – painting and music, but also clothing, cookery, cars, and so on. (Bourdieu, 1984). There is a hierarchy of taste, he argued, between genres such as classical music and popular music, and also between specific items within genres. For example, classical music has higher status than popular music. Based on survey research, Bourdieu distinguished three zones of taste which roughly correspond to different educational levels and social classes. First, there is the zone of 'legitimate taste'. This is the taste for legitimate works of art. Interest in these items increases with educational level, and it is highest in those fractions of the dominant class that are richest in educational capital. Second, there is the zone of 'middle-brow taste'. This is the taste for minor works of the major arts. Interest in these is more common in the middle classes. Third, there is the zone of 'popular taste'. This is the taste for devalued works of art which belong to an inferior genre or which have been popularized. Popular taste varies in inverse ratio to educational capital, and it is most frequent among the working classes.

Symbolic Capital

Symbolic capital is the 'power of constructing reality' (Bourdieu, 1991: 166). In other words, it is the capacity to construct beliefs about the world and to make them seem real. Through symbols, people define what is real for themselves and for other people. More precisely, symbolic capital is the ability to define what is perceived to be the reality of the other three forms of capital (i.e., economic, social and cultural) through the use of symbols.

The forms of symbolic capital include reputation, prestige and fame. These can be manipulated even when the underlying reality of economic, social and cultural capital remains unchanged. Bourdieu gave the example from an agrarian society of a peasant family which purchased a second yoke of oxen after the harvest, on the grounds that they were needed for treading out the abundant grain, only to sell them again for lack of fodder in the fall, before the ploughing when they would technically be most useful (Bourdieu, 1990). The reason for this seemingly irrational set of transactions was to create the (fictitious) impression of the family's affluence and success during the season when marriages are negotiated. To have the reputation for success and affluence makes it easier to attract desirable partners, and thus it contributes to the family's long-term strength.

According to Bourdieu, political capital is a form of symbolic capital (Bourdieu, 1991). It is based on trust in the reputation of the leader. The leader who is able to project an image of invincibility can attract many followers and will therefore be successful. This image is sustained by symbols of power and majesty, such as thrones, sceptres and crowns. Or, it may be sustained by the symbols of popularity, such as public opinion polls. In either case, the leader is known and recognized as having the legitimate right to lead. In some cases this recognition is formally bestowed by a political party that transmits its political capital to the incumbent of a position.

Habitus

Bourdieu's third major concept, after field and capital, is habitus. Habitus is a set of dispositions which incline individuals to act and react in certain ways.

The dispositions generate perceptions, attitudes and practices which are predictable without being consciously articulated or governed by any rule. The important point about habitus is that it is not innate, but it is socially conditioned. The concept of habitus refers to the system of dispositions that individuals internalize by virtue of having a certain social and economic condition. As conditions change under new circumstances, the habitus is affected by them in ways that either reinforce or modify it (Bourdieu and Wacquant, 1992).

There are several points to keep in mind about habitus. First, habitus is acquired in practice, in the activities of everyday life. Because different individuals have different practices, it follows that different individuals within the same field will have different habitus. Second, at any given moment in time the habitus will have a structure that is the result of previous experiences. New experiences are filtered through the habitus, and in that sense early experiences take priority over later experiences. Therefore, individuals are profoundly influenced by patterns of dispositions developed early in life, including the results of socialization. Third, if individuals have not modified their dispositions through practice, then the dispositions they acquired earlier may cause them to act inappropriately in the present.

Power

Bourdieu's approach can be illustrated by considering what he has to say about power. Power over others, or in other words domination, was a consistent interest in Bourdieu's sociology. In particular, Bourdieu was interested in class relationships. Bourdieu conceived of the relation between classes and class fractions as one of competition and struggle. In these struggles, one class or class fraction is likely to be dominant. Bourdieu's general assumption was that the dominant class or class fraction was likely to be the one possessing the most economic capital, and the dominated class or class fraction is the one with the least economic capital. Thus, Bourdieu wrote of the captains of industry and commerce as being dominant and the industrial workers being dominated (Bourdieu, 1991). However, Bourdieu's approach is complex, as other forms of capital such as cultural capital also enter into relations of domination. Thus, Bourdieu wrote of the intellectuals as being 'the dominated among the dominant' (Bourdieu, 1991: 245).

Symbolic power is one alternative to economic power, and Bourdieu attached some importance to it. Symbolic power exists when people voluntarily give up power over themselves to another, because they believe that the particular person has the power to do things. 'It is a power which exists because the person who submits to it believes that it exists', Bourdieu said (1991: 192). For example, symbolic power comes into play when a person agrees to follow a politician because she believes that he represents her interests, and she also believes that he is actually able to pursue her interests. In this case, the belief in the other person as an effective politician is what makes them an effective politician. The fact that the politician is believed to be effective attracts supporters, and their support in the form of votes, party subscriptions and work in elections gives the politician the power to get things done. The belief in the politician therefore becomes a self-fulfilling prophecy, and it is the basis for the power which the politician exercises over his followers and over others.

Bourdieu is careful to point out that the 'magical' power exercised by the politician requires work on her part, and it is not simply the result of her position in the field of power. Because the symbolic power of the politician rests on faith, she must do everything she can to maintain the faith of her followers. For example, she must try to minimize any pronouncements that would show inconsistency between present and past positions, and she must try to keep secret anything that would tend to discredit her. Politicians are vulnerable to suspicions and scandals that would undermine trust in them, and they must either take precautions to avoid these things or they must try to disguise their role in them so that they are not held responsible for problems.

In addition to symbolic power, another form of power that interested Bourdieu was symbolic violence. Symbolic violence is domination which is exercised upon social agents with their complicity because they misrecognize the conditions of their existence. Misrecognition is the failure to perceive correctly important social, economic, cultural and symbolic conditions. It includes the failure to perceive violence as such. By violence Bourdieu meant the use of excessive or unjustifiable force. In symbolic violence people recognize, or tacitly acknowledge, the legitimacy of the hierarchical relations of power in which they are embedded. They therefore fail to see that the hierarchy is, in the last analysis, an arbitrary social construction which serves the interests of some groups more than others.

Bourdieu gave as an example of symbolic violence the use of gift strategies in pre-capitalist societies. Bourdieu claimed that in such societies there are only two ways of getting and keeping a lasting hold over someone, either through the overt violence of indebtedness or through the symbolic violence of the gift (Bourdieu, 1990). In the latter, the individual is bound by emotional attachments of gratitude and the moral obligation to make a return gift. A gift that is not returned can become a lasting obligation. The violence of the gift, as a deliberate way of gaining control over someone, is not recognized as such. Instead, the gift is regarded as an act of generosity. In gift transactions the obligation to make a return gift is disguised in that each gift must be different from the gift that preceded it, and because there is a time gap between the gift and the return gift. The inherent reciprocity between gift and return gift is hidden, even though each gift is really one moment in a series of gift exchanges.

In modern society, Bourdieu gave as an example of symbolic violence the effect of the educational system upon students from the subordinate classes (Bourdieu and Passeron, 1977). The educational system exercises violence, in Bourdieu's view, because it imposes an arbitrary set of cultural standards upon such students which do not reflect their own way of life. The standards that are imposed in education reflect the culture of the dominant classes. Working-class students are not taught the practical knowledge of their own class, such as home medicine, folk art, craft techniques and customary law. In their place they are taught the value of the symbolic products of the dominant classes, such as clinical diagnoses, the importance of legal advice and the products of cultural specialists. This violence against lower class culture is disguised by the way in which educational knowledge is imparted, and as a result it is misrecognized. The arbitrary imposition of cultural standards is concealed by a 'soft' approach to education, which emphasizes human relations and, especially in elementary school, overwhelming students with affection. This technique gives educators possession of that subtle instrument of repression, the withdrawal of affection. Students, and teachers themselves, are unaware of the symbolic violence that is practiced in schools on behalf of the dominant classes.

Anthony Giddens

Anthony Giddens (1938–) opposed himself to the theorists he called 'structural sociologists', who he says were interested only in making generalizations about circumstances of which people are unaware and which act upon them (Giddens, 1984). In place of structural sociology, he argues for an approach that takes seriously people's own knowledge of the world and the use that they make of it. Giddens' objection was part of a larger critique of social theory, which he has attempted to reformulate. He calls this reformulation 'structuration theory'.

In structuration theory, the concept of structure means something quite different from what it means in structural sociology. Giddens understands by structure the rules and resources that individuals draw on in constructing their lines of action. Because rules and resources are available over time, they produce tendencies for individuals to act in the same way on more than one occasion. Giddens refers to this as the reproduction of conduct. Structuration refers to the conditions governing the continuity or transformation of structures, and therefore the reproduction of systems (Giddens, 1979).

Structuration theory is an attempt to recast individuals as active agents who construct their own lives, but not always under conditions of their own choosing. It does two things. First, it provides a theory of the acting subject, and second, it situates action in time and space (Giddens, 1979). Taking the first of these points, Giddens believes that there are unconscious as well as conscious grounds for action. However, it is the conscious grounds which interest him most. Giddens envisages people as engaged in a process of monitoring their conduct, and of using the knowledge that they gain from monitoring to revise their behaviour. According to Giddens, 'All human beings are knowledgeable agents. That is to say, all social actors know a great deal about the conditions and consequences of what they do in their day-to-day lives' (Giddens, 1984: 281). This process of gaining and using knowledge about the self, which Giddens refers to as reflexivity, is of fundamental importance in human social life. He believes that reflexivity is an especial characteristic of modern societies. It is one of the ways by which modern societies bring about progress, which is a defining characteristic of modernity. For example, Giddens cites research into sexuality as an instance of the reflexive monitoring of behaviour which had profound implications for sexual attitudes and for later shifts in behaviour (Giddens, 1992). Giddens also notes that sociology and the social sciences more generally are elements of the institutional reflexivity of modernity. They provide information that people draw on in improving their lives.

The importance of reflexivity in human conduct does not mean that individuals can articulate the reasons for all of their conscious actions. Most day-to-day life goes on in a state of 'practical consciousness', in which people are aware of what they are doing as they do it but without paying special attention and without being able to explain their actions. 'Discursive consciousness', on the other hand, involves holding something as an object of conscious attention where it can be examined and discussed.

Turning now to Giddens' ideas about time and space, he has emphasized that all social life must be studied in its temporal and spatial aspects. He argues, for example, that the idea that time is a scarce and exploitable resource is one of the formative features of capitalism (Giddens, 1979). The measurement of time spent in labour and creation of the clearly defined working day have made possible the transformation of labour power into a commodity. Giddens has rejected the idea that society can be studied at one point in time, as if we could take a snapshot of it. This is an impossible idea, in Giddens' view, because nothing in society is fixed and all social events are the results of actions that unfold over time. For Giddens, therefore, there is no useful distinction to be made between the discipline of history and sociology. Similarly, Giddens wishes to remind us that all social events occur in space, and he thinks that there should be closer relationships between sociology and geography. For example, he thinks that we have not paid enough attention to urbanism, or in other words the ways in which the experience of living in cities has influenced social behaviour. Giddens has also pointed to Goffman's discussion of front regions and back regions as a useful instance of spatial analysis in sociology.

Giddens thinks that it is especially important to pay attention to what he calls 'time–space distanciation'. This is the tendency for interactions to occur between elements that are separated in time and space. For example, Giddens considers the development of writing as being a critical factor in the distancia-tion of interaction (Giddens, 1979). Writing enables messages to be carried unaltered across great distances, and it makes it possible for the written record of the past to be studied and interrogated in the present. Another example of time–space distanciation concerns the use of impersonal procedures in modern organizations (Giddens, 1987). Impersonal definitions of procedures permit the movement of individuals in and out of positions, without those positions necessarily changing over time. In this way modern organizations can endure over longer periods of time than was true of traditional organizations based on personal relationships. These examples illustrate a general point. The extension of social life in time and space is an overall characteristic of social development. According to Giddens, an important contemporary example of this is the world-wide spatial expansion of western industrial capitalism.

Critique of the Orthodox Consensus

Giddens developed some of his most important ideas out of a critique of what he calls the 'orthodox consensus' which existed in sociology in the 1950s and early 1960s. Influenced especially by structural functionalism and positivism, this orthodox consensus was never fully accepted, but it did dominate socio-logical theorizing. It has been some time since the orthodox consensus was broken, and Giddens wishes to tell us why that has happened, and to explain the lines along which he thinks sociology should develop in its aftermath.

Giddens thinks that there are four main criticisms to be made of the orthodox consensus. First, he criticizes the dualism of the concepts of structure and function in structural functionalism, and he proposes to put in their place the concept of the duality of structure. Giddens thinks that structure, as con-ventionally understood, is a static concept since it refers only to the enduring arrangement of the parts of a system. In other words, it refers only to those parts of a system which do not change. As a result, Giddens argues, the dynamic element in social life had to be added on in a separate concept, namely function. Giddens points out that the assumption underlying this conceptual dualism is that we can describe things (such as families) independently of what they do. He argues that this idea, which was borrowed by analogy from biology, cannot work in the social sciences. That is because in social life patterns 'only exist in so far as they are constantly produced and reproduced in human action' (Giddens, 1977: 114). For example, the very meaning of 'family' was redefined in the late 1960s and 1970s to include single-parent families, a category which did not exist before.

Giddens argues that what is needed is a concept of the duality of structure, which can explain how things sometimes change and sometimes stay the same. He finds this concept in the idea that structure consists of rules and resources which are used to generate lines of action, and which themselves are reconstituted in action. People use rules and resources which enable them to act in the same way, but the rules and resources themselves can be changed in ways that bring about a change in conduct.

Giddens' second criticism of the orthodox consensus is that he rejects the concept of function. Giddens argues that all forms of functional analysis are ultimately teleological. That is to say, they assume that a system of action operates with some end in view which is implicitly or explicitly conceived of as the needs of the system. In functionalism, the needs of the system are understood as being required for the survival or maintenance of the system. We have encountered this idea in the present book, in Talcott Parsons' work on the functional imperatives which all systems have to fulfil. Giddens objects to this point of view, because he says that it assumes that in some sense the system wants, or has an interest in, its survival. Giddens insists that it is only individuals who have wants, and he argues that individuals' wants are logically prior to any properties of systems. According to Giddens, 'Social systems, unlike organisms, do not have any need or interest in their own survival, and the notion of "need" is falsely applied if it is not acknowledged that system needs presuppose actors' wants' (Giddens, 1977: 110). In Giddens' view, sociology must pay serious attention to the ways in which individuals' wants are translated into social practices. This is the problem of agency in social theory.

Giddens' third criticism of the orthodox consensus is that it did not pay enough attention to the interpretation of meanings. He describes this as a hermeneutic task for sociology, and he argues that sociologists are inevitably caught up in a 'double hermeneutic'.

Giddens argues that the idea that sociology must take individuals' meanings seriously has important methodological implications. Sociology cannot follow the same logic of enquiry as that employed in the natural sciences. It is the job of the natural sciences to uncover the underlying laws of nature which are not visible to us through our ordinary experiences. Applying this idea to the social sciences, Giddens says, has given rise to the idea that social science is revelatory. In other words, it has given rise to the idea that social science is expected to reveal hidden patterns, such as latent functions, which are conceived of as the real truth. Giddens does believe that sociology can sometimes be revelatory. There are aspects of social action that may be unknown to the actors, such as the long-term consequences of their actions. Unintended consequences, and unacknowledged conditions, of action should be studied by sociologists, Giddens thinks. However, Giddens rejects the idea that this is all that sociologists do, for the same reason that Herbert Blumer and the symbolic interactionists have rejected it. Individuals act in terms of *their* beliefs and values, which they use in making decisions. Most human action is intentional. Furthermore, individuals have a great deal of knowledge about their own social world and their own behaviour. To confine sociology to revealing unconscious patterns would be to cut it off from the largest portion of its subject matter. Therefore, sociologists should take seriously the meanings that actors give to their lives, and they should actively seek to interpret their relations to action. Giddens therefore recommends a hermeneutic approach, in which the observer sets out to interpret the meanings employed by those whom he or she is studying, as a starting point for sociological analysis.

Giddens applies a hermeneutic approach not only to the actors who are studied by social scientists, but also to the work of social scientists themselves. Scientists' observations of phenomena are influenced by what they expect to see, and their expectations are grounded in the dominant point of view in the relevant scientific community. It follows from this that all observations are influenced by some theoretical framework. Therefore, any evaluation of research in the social sciences must include an evaluation of the theoretical ideas of the social scientists who have done the work. This is an interpretative task that goes beyond merely analysing the facts that support certain conclusions. The interesting point about this hermeneutic analysis of the social scientists' ideas is that those scientific ideas also draw upon the common sense ideas of the people whose lives are being studied. That is because in the social sciences most of our theories are elaborations of and commentaries upon the ideas of the people whose lives we are studying. The interpretation of ideas in the social sciences therefore has a dual aspect – the interpretation of the ideas of the actors who are being studied and the interpretation of the ideas of the observers who are doing the studying. This is the 'double hermeneutic' in sociology.

Finally, Giddens' fourth criticism of the orthodox consensus is that he thinks it is impossible to maintain a separation between facts and values. It will be recalled that Emile Durkheim urged sociologists to eradicate all preconceived ideas. Weber realized that values cannot be eradicated, but he believed that their effects could be limited. Values tell us what is important, and hence they define objects for study. But once the subject has been chosen, Weber argued that we should adopt a position of value neutrality and study the objective facts. It was this Weberian position that was incorporated into the orthodox consensus.

The position of the orthodox consensus on the fact/value distinction has come under increasing attack in recent years. It is argued that it is impossible to achieve, and that it is therefore necessary for sociologists to be conscious of the relations between their values and their research. Giddens accepts the general thrust of this argument, and he argues that it brings to light a general point about sociology as a discipline. Sociology is a critical discipline which calls into question the existence of practices that others have taken for granted. Giddens believes that sociology is an emancipatory discipline which frees individuals from accepting the inevitability of oppressive social structures. For example, Giddens himself has developed an account of recent changes in personal relationships as a process of the democratization of personal life (Giddens, 1992, 2000). He thinks that sociologists should generally be in favour of such democratization.

Giddens argues that there is an important conclusion to be drawn from this for our understanding of the double hermeneutic. Not only do social scientists draw on lay ideas in seeking to explain everyday behaviour, but actors may (and Giddens thinks they often do) draw on social scientific ideas to change their lives. The flow of ideas between everyday life and the social sciences is therefore a two-way street, in which social scientists are not at all separated from the objects of their study.

High Modernity

Many of Giddens' discussions are methodological, being intended to improve the ways in which sociologists theorize and conduct their research. That is not true, however, of his discussions of modernity (Giddens, 1990, 1991). Here Giddens wants to make a difference to substantive discussions about contemporary social life. In particular, he rejects the idea that contemporary social conditions are indicative of the emergence of a new era of postmodernity. Postmodernity is an era that comes after modernity, and it therefore begins with the end of modernity. Giddens insists that modernity has not come to an end, but it has entered a phase of super-development.

By 'modernity' Giddens understands the social world that was ushered into being by industrialization and capitalism. It is a world of constant change, in which traditions are eroded and replaced by open-ended possibilities for actions of many kinds. Giddens' views on modern society begin with the classical distinction between tradition and modernity. Traditional societies are static, governed by custom and slow to change. Modern societies are dynamic, influenced by responsive institutions such as the market economy and the democratic nation-state, and constantly changing. Giddens refers to the current phase of modernity as 'high modernity' or 'late modernity'. He thinks that the inherent features of modernity have been deepened, and they have been extended all around the world. Giddens thinks that the dynamism of modernity is due to three things: the separation of time and space; the disembedding of social institutions; and institutional reflexivity (Giddens, 1991).

Time and Space

The idea of the separation of time and space is Giddens' way of talking about the shift from a traditional society in which people lived in the 'here-and-now' to the more complex world that we live in today. Today, the present 'now' that we live in is no longer just a world of local experience, but it is influenced by a variety of factors some of which have origins that are very far away in space. Also, the local 'here' of our social world is not just located in the present, but we draw on ideas from the remote past as well as ideas about the future. In other words, modern social systems have been extended greatly in time and space.

Modern social institutions have undergone an enormous spatial extension. Thanks to the constant development of communications technologies, and the growth of national and international political institutions, as well as the growth of international markets and the expansion of capitalism, modern social institutions now reach people in widely dispersed locations. Giddens is especially interested in the effects of globalization, that is, the tendency for local issues to be affected by events on a world scale (Giddens, 2000). Giddens insists that globalization is not only economic, as it is about more than just international trade. It is also political, technological and cultural. In Giddens' view, modernity is multidimensional and the theory of modernity is not to be confused with economic determinism.

Modern social institutions have also been extended in time as well as in space. To begin with, they can trace their histories back in time and they use this knowledge to guide actions in the present. A good example of this is the use of legal precedents in court cases. Here, past decisions are referred to for the principles that can be drawn from them to help make decisions about current cases. As well, modern social institutions make projections into the future, which are also used to guide actions in the present. For example, business executives who have to make a decision about an investment will use projections about the future level of profit to be expected. Another example is the way in which governments who have to make decisions on health-care policies use projections about population ageing to estimate future demand for medical services. In all these ways, decisions made in the present are influenced by the past and the (projected) future.

Given the great extent of time–space distanciation in the contemporary world, the way in which activities are co-ordinated across time and space becomes a matter of some importance. Giddens points to the significance of timetables (Giddens, 1990). Timetables permit the co-ordination of the activities of large numbers of people across time and space; however, their efficiency is only made possible by a universal model of time. Giddens argues that in traditional societies there were a variety of models of time, each defining time within a particular region. For example, at one time there were rival calendars in Christendom: the Julian Calendar of the Orthodox Churches and the Gregorian calendar of the Roman Catholic Church. Eventually one of these, the Gregorian calendar, became the universal model. One model of time becomes the dominant one which is used by most modern institutions. Universal concepts of time, which extend through limitless space, permit what Giddens calls the 'disembedding' of social systems.

Disembedding

Giddens says that by disembedding he means the '"lifting out" of social relations from local contexts of interaction and their restructuring across indefinite spans of time-space' (Giddens, 1990: 21). As already noted, the rationalization of models of time is one very important condition for disembedding. In addition, there are two other principal developments which have historically facilitated the disembedding of social relations. One of these is the use of symbolic tokens, such as money. The advantage of money is that it can be exchanged between large numbers of people, without regard to their particular characteristics. Also, it permits borrowing on credit, in which goods are enjoyed in the present against the promise of future repayment.

The other factor which facilitates disembedding is reliance on expert systems. Expert systems are bodies of knowledge created by experts, upon which non-experts draw to construct their lines of action. It is characteristic of high modernity that people rely more and more upon expert systems. In the process, impersonal standards based on expert criteria standardize knowledge and practice across space. Giddens points out that in the late modern world most of the things that we use, and most of the knowledge that we learn, are based on standards which are defined in places which are spatially distant from the places where we live. The result of this is that local communities, and local systems of meaning, become less and less important in our everyday lives.

Institutional Reflexivity

Reflexivity is the capacity that all human beings possess to monitor their situation and to change their behaviour accordingly. What is different about modernity is that reflexivity becomes a property not only of individuals but also of the institutions that they organize. Modern life is therefore built up from the reflexive ordering and reordering of social relations in the light of continual inputs of knowledge. Sociology is one modern institution which has been very much affected by this process. It collects and analyses information that is distributed to people in various positions who use it to improve their own little piece of the world.

Institutional reflexivity transforms the impact of traditions, which must now justify themselves in the light of received knowledge. No longer simply taken for granted as the only way of doing things, tradition persists but in an altered context. Giddens claims that tradition is no longer lived in the traditional way, by which he means that tradition is no longer based exclusively on its own internal claims to truth (Giddens, 2000).

Traditions are not the only cultural elements whose standing is affected by institutional reflexivity. So also is scientific knowledge. Giddens points out that in societies which are thoroughly committed to the reflexivity of knowledge, expert systems are constantly being revised in the light of new information. As a result, all knowledge is subject to radical doubt since everyone knows that it will be changed sooner or later. According to Giddens, 'No knowledge under conditions of modernity is knowledge in the "old" sense, where "to know" is to be certain' (1990: 40). This applies equally to the natural sciences and the social sciences.

Risk and Trust

Giddens has argued that many features of social life in high modernity are shaped by the dynamic interplay of risk and trust. Risk is a pervasive feature of modern life, for two reasons. First, more and more decisions affecting people are made in places far away from them, and those decisions rely more and more on expert systems which they cannot know or understand. As a result, everyone in modern society faces increased risks that failures of other people will have serious negative consequences for them. For example, an economic collapse in a small country in a remote part of the world can trigger a major financial crisis with local effects. Second, risk becomes more and more a matter of calculation as individuals and groups seek to control the effects of possible future events on themselves. The obvious example here is the use of insurance to provide protection against possible financial losses in the future.

At the same time, the effectiveness of modern systems relies heavily upon the trust that people have in them. Or, to put the same point in a different way, these systems are very vulnerable to the withdrawal of trust. For example, financial crises are usually triggered by the withdrawal of trust, and subsequently the withdrawal of funds, by investors and money managers. This is true of relationships between individuals and institutions, and it is also true of personal relationships based on love, for example. In both cases, trust is related to absence and ignorance. We have no need to trust someone who is continually present, and whose actions can be watched over and supervised. Similarly, we have no need to trust systems that we know and understand in detail. Trust is necessary in the modern world because the scheduling of complex activities separates people more, and because more of our lives depends upon expert systems about which we know little.

Pure Relationships, Self-Identity and Anxiety

Trust is essential to personal relationships in modern society because more of them take the form of what Giddens calls 'pure relationships'. Giddens argues that an important dimension of change in high modernity is the emergence of the pure relationship as the foundation of personal life. A pure relationship is one which is not maintained by external forces, but its continuation depends upon the rewards that it delivers to the participants. The relationship is valued for itself, and it is constructed by the participants out of their own unaided efforts. As a result, interpersonal trust can no longer be based on factors outside the relationship, such as traditional obligations between the occupants of well-defined roles (Giddens, 1991). In a pure relationship trust can only be attained through a process of mutual disclosure of feelings and beliefs. There is therefore a great demand for intimacy in pure relationships. At the same time, the pure relationship becomes a context within which people try to define their self-identity.

According to Giddens, self-identity changes with the declining influence of tradition. The self is no longer something to be taken for granted, but it is something that must be constructed through organized activity. Social life today is more open, a greater diversity of lifestyle options are available, there is much greater social and cultural pluralism, and there is a greater diversity of authorities. Lifestyle choice is therefore increasingly important in the constitution of self-identity. Individuals have multiple choices, and they must choose their own lifestyles.

Having to choose, and making so many choices, can be a source of anxiety to many people. It is one of several causes of anxiety that Giddens identifies as characteristic of the late modern world (Giddens, 1991). First, there is the existential anxiety that is due to the openness of the self in contemporary conditions. In a post-traditional order, the self is not fixed but it can be many things. This can include making fundamental choices about sexual orientation and the sexual characteristics of the body. Under these conditions, people face multiple choices about what to do, and who to be. They may therefore turn to therapy in order to reconstruct an effective narrative of the self.

Second, there is the problem of authority, or its lack, under contemporary conditions. In searching for answers to their problems, people look to authorities for answers. In some cases, this leads to an extreme reliance on authoritative sources, as in religious fundamentalism. In most cases, however, it leads to new doubts because there are multiple, and contradictory, authorities. Furthermore, the advice of the authorities is constantly changing. Contemporary living is therefore characterized by a background of radical doubt.

Third, problems of defining the self and of finding suitable authorities are exacerbated by the fact that modernity produces a series of crises to which people must respond. Today we live in a 'runaway world' (Giddens, 2000). These crises may include an economic recession beginning in some remote part of the world, or a new disease which is introduced from a foreign country. These examples illustrate how contemporary problems are affected by globalization, a phenomenon with which Giddens is much concerned. Another example, which is of special interest to Giddens, is global warming. Here, the global environmental effects of industrialization require global solutions. Our final theorist, Zygmunt Bauman, also sees globalization as an important feature of the contemporary social world (Bauman, 1998).

Zygmunt Bauman

Zygmunt Bauman (1925–) has turned against the structural conception in sociology by emphasizing the fluidity and openness of contemporary social life. He has stressed that present-day life is fragmented, and he believes that this is more than just a temporary period of disorder. Bauman has embraced the idea that we have entered into a new era of history, which he prefers to call the postmodern. Postmodernity is a period in time which comes after modernity, and which therefore signifies the end of modernity. It is a new era in which important modern ideas like progress, and the institutions which have supported it, are called into question. In particular, Bauman believes that the state, which had claimed to guarantee progress for all through a variety of government programmes, has withdrawn from the leading role which it once played. Instead, there has been a trend towards deregulation and privatization, and more generally towards disengagement (Bauman, 1997). The result has been a kind of free-for-all, in which muggers and car thieves have flourished alongside tourists and sensation seekers.

The postmodern world, in Bauman's view, is one characterized by a new world disorder at the political level as the old power blocs have broken up. The results have included civil wars and new forms of political uncertainty. It also includes the weakening of neighbourhood and family ties, and the uncertain and temporary nature of relationships and identities.

Bauman's sociological work can be divided into four parts: the critique of modernity; the analysis of the changing role of intellectuals; the description of postmodernity; and the description of current forms of modernity. To summarize the main line of argument, Bauman's critique of modernity paves the way for his embrace of postmodernity: his analysis of the changing role of intellectuals includes a shift from the modern intellectual to the postmodern intellectual; Bauman analyses postmodernity as a new type of society; in recent writings Bauman has begun to refer to the new type of society as a variant of modernity.

Critique of Modernity

Bauman's critique of modernity is that rationality does not only lead to progress, but it can also lead to death and destruction. His example is the Holocaust in which Jews were killed in Nazi gas chambers. Bauman claims that the Holocaust was not an irrational creation of a few deranged individuals. Rather, he says that 'The Holocaust was born and executed in our modern rational society, at the high stage of our civilization and at the peak of human cultural achievement, and for this reason it is a problem of that society, civilization and culture' (Bauman, 1989: x). More pointedly, he claims that 'the exterminatory version of anti-Semitism ought to be seen as a thoroughly modern phenomenon; that is, something which could occur only in an advanced state of modernity' (Bauman, 1989: 73).

Bauman argues that the Holocaust was a unique outcome of a combination of factors, each of which by itself was quite ordinary and common. Together, these factors had the effect of weakening the pre-modern codes of morality. It is the absence or ineffectiveness of codes of morality which Bauman sees as permitting or facilitating the Holocaust. Contrary to theories of progress through increasing civilization, Bauman argues that modern society can have the effect of suppressing morality and making immoral conduct more plausible. There are four morality-eroding mechanisms in modern society that Bauman identifies. They are: rational criteria of choice; bureaucracy; technology and science; and the concentrated power of the state.

Rational Criteria of Choice

The most fundamental condition of modern society that tends to suppress the influence of morality is the dominance of a certain mode of reasoning, namely the logical choice of means towards ends, or in other words 'instrumental rationality'. Once the goals, or ends, of action have been decided, then there is a dispassionate process of selecting the most efficient means of achieving them. For example, Bauman claims that the decision to exterminate the Jews was made only after other alternatives, such as emigration, had been considered and discarded as ways of achieving a Germany free of Jews. In this process of rational decision-making, criteria of effectiveness and efficiency replaced moral criteria of good and evil.

Bauman argues that the impact of instrumental rationality is greatly expanded when it is combined with modern ideas of social engineering. In social engineering the goals which are set are ambitious plans for social improvement intended to produce the perfect society. Bauman suggests that rational criteria for bringing about the perfect society lead to the 'gardening' view of social engineering. According to this view, in order to allow the most productive plants to flourish it is necessary to nourish them, and also to pull out the 'weeds' that prevent the productive plants from flourishing. Hence, rational classifications are developed that distinguish productive from unproductive elements of society, and which define the different treatments that they should receive.

Bureaucracy

According to Bauman, the most important practical outcome of instrumental rationality is bureaucracy. It is the particular nature of bureaucracies everywhere, he argues, that they tend to subordinate thought and action to the pragmatics of economy and effectiveness. In so doing, they tend to suppress morality.

Bauman implies that many ordinary Germans had, or would have had, moral inhibitions against the extermination of the Jews and inflicting cruelty upon them. However, these inhibitions were overcome within the bureaucratized machinery for collecting, transporting, and killing the Jews. To begin with, violence against the Jews was authorized by legitimate authority figures in a hierarchy of authority. Also, evil actions were rendered normal by a process of routinization. That is to say, the process of following bureaucratic rules produced repetitive actions that came to take on the appearance of normality. Bauman suggests that the neutralization of morality was further enhanced by the discipline of working in a bureaucracy. In a bureaucracy, people are expected to, and do, place the organization's purposes before their own purposes. The neutralization of morality in a bureaucracy is also facilitated by the fact that few people in a bureaucracy see the end results of their actions. This is due to the functional division of labour, as well as the scale and complexity of large bureaucracies. As a result, there is a practical and mental distance between most individuals in a bureaucracy and the end results of the organization. Finally, objects in bureaucracies tend to be dehumanized by being identified in purely technical, ethically neutral terms. For example, Jews who were being transported to the concentration camps were simply referred to as 'cargo', and their progress was tracked on morally neutral graphs identifying the numbers of units transported.

Technology and Science

Bauman argues that technology and science have a similar morally neutralizing effect to bureaucracy. Science tends to replace religion and ethics with morally neutral criteria for judgement and decision-making. As such, it has tended to weaken the authority of all normative thinking. Scientists also helped the perpetrators of the Holocaust directly, for example through devising efficient means of mass extermination and through establishing a body of supporting knowledge on racial issues. Scientists, Bauman suggests, were eager to expand their research and to accept the major sources of funding open to them for research.

The significance of this is that science has generally been seen as a source of enlightenment leading to progress. It produces the objective knowledge needed to improve the human condition. However, Bauman claims that with the Holocaust: 'The deadly potential of the most revered principles and accomplishments of modern science has been exposed' (1989: 108). Among other things, science has been connected to the activist attitude towards nature and human society which culminated in social engineering. Thus the language of Hitler and the Nazis drew on medical and scientific terminology. Christianity and communism were likened to syphilis and the plague, and the Jews were said to be bacilli or decomposing germs that undermined the health of the German people.

Concentrated Power of the State

Along with science, the state is another of the social institutions associated with modernity and projects of modernization. It is the principal collective instrument through which power is organized to achieve collective goals for the society as a whole. Bauman claims that the Holocaust shows us the state can be an instrument of evil, as well as an instrument of progress. The extermination of the Jews was planned, organized and administered through the state.

The main problem with the state in Nazi Germany, according to Bauman, is that there were no independent sources of power which could have deflected the state from its goal of removing the Jews from Germany. That is because the state, as the ultimate source of power and authority within a territory, is largely free of external controls. Bauman argues that the vacuum which is created by the collapse of communities in modern society is filled by the state. The result is the supremacy of the state over society.

Furthermore, Bauman argues that the rise of the identity between the state and the nation in nation-states has created special problems for groups, such as the Jews, who have significant ties outside the nation. Such groups are likely to be seen as disloyal to the state. Bauman argues that this was a contributory factor in the rise of anti-Semitism.

Changing Role of Intellectuals

Bauman is clearly critical of the part played by scientists in the 'gardening' model of society. In his opinion, scientists have lent their expertise, and their authority, to creating distinctions and classifications that have proven to be harmful, and eventually destructive. Bauman's critique of the contributions made by scientists to Nazism does not lead him to a pessimistic view of the intellectuals, however. He thinks that the role of intellectuals in society has been changing, from that of the modern legislator to the postmodern interpreter (Bauman, 1987, 1991, 1992).

Bauman argues that intellectuals in modernity have occupied a particular type of role that he refers to as 'legislative reason', or simply the legislator. Ultimately, he thinks that this role has failed, and it has been replaced by a new role for the intellectual which he refers to as the interpreter. He describes this new role for the intellectuals as being associated with postmodernity.

The modern strategy of intellectual work is a strategy in which the intellectual pronounces, or legislates, on questions of truth pertaining to major issues of the day. The 'legislator' intervenes in controversies of opinion, and makes authoritative statements which are accepted as correct and binding because of the superior knowledge to which the intellectual lays claim. This strategy rests on the assumption that objective, universal truth exists to be discovered, and that it is possible for the intellectuals to discover it.

In contrast, the postmodern role of the interpreter is based on a position of cultural relativism. Knowledge is construed as being created within communally based traditions which give statements their meanings. The task of the postmodern intellectual faced with the differences between intellectual traditions is not to adjudicate which one is true or which one is false. Rather, the postmodern task is to interpret one set of meanings from one community so that they can be understood by a different set of people in a different community.

The Rise of the Legislator

Bauman maintains that different intellectual strategies were formulated under different historical conditions. The modern strategy of intellectual work began in the eighteenth century, especially in France. Its emergence was due to a unique combination of circumstances. First, absolutist monarchy was reaching its peak, with claims to pronounce laws and regulations on a wide range of matters across large territories. Second, the old ruling class of the nobility was in decline, creating a power vacuum and a demand for new legitimations. Third, no new class had yet emerged to gain control. Fourth, the intellectuals had no fixed place in society, as they came from different groups. They could therefore conceive of themselves as a group serving the entire society. Fifth, the intellectuals were linked through ties of communication in social networks. And sixth, all of this occurred in a period of rapid social change when new solutions were demanded to many problems. The result was a situation in which the intellectuals became politically influential, and power and knowledge were united in new ways. Knowledge became an instrument for gaining power over others, and those in power became dependent on knowledge and the legitimations that it had to offer.

As a result of the changes outlined above, the role of the state expanded and a new structure of domination emerged which Bauman refers to as 'the rule of the knowledgeable and knowledge as the ruling force' (1987: 67). In this system, education and the educators took on a much more important role.

The Fall of the Legislator

Bauman argues that today intellectuals no longer act as legislators, for the most part, because they no longer have the confidence to do so. In particular, they have lost the sense of absolute certainty about the superiority of the modern western way of life. As a result, they no longer feel entitled to legislate universal knowledge and standards of behaviour.

Bauman sees the decline of legislative reason as being due to a number of factors. First, there is the resistance of oppressed and marginal groups who have claimed the right to speak with their own voices. The representatives of subordinate races, underdeveloped countries, the poor, the mentally ill, the disabled and women have all challenged the dominant points of view, and in so doing they have shattered the old certainties. Second, demand from the state for legitimations as a way of bolstering support for its programmes has declined. That is because the state has devised new and more detailed means of social control, such as administrative regulation and surveillance. Third, there is increasing disenchantment with the rational, science-based world and the problems it creates, such as pollution and the lack of meaning. Fourth, markets, such as the art market, have tended to replace authority figures as the ultimate arbiters of tastes and values. And fifth, the dominance of markets is reflected in the importance of consumerism. The state no longer needs the legitimations of intellectuals, because citizens are 'seduced' by all the pleasures of consumption in a consumer society. The result of all these factors has been a crisis of the traditional role of the legislator.

The Rise of the Interpreter

Under contemporary conditions, intellectuals have tended to adopt an interpretative role, mainly because of the increased awareness of pluralism in postmodern society. Pluralism as such has always existed. What is new is an intensified awareness that cultural pluralism is not going to disappear with more modernization. Today, we face the unavoidable situation that different groups live in different worlds, based on different systems of meaning. This realization has undermined the modern project of establishing an objective, universal truth that is equally true for all humanity. Instead, we witness the emergence of new forms of relativism.

Faced with the inevitability of pluralism and relativism, the most urgent problem becomes one of communicating across traditions. Specialists in translating across traditions are called for, who can open up for communication worlds of meaning that would otherwise be closed. Bauman thinks this is specifically the task of postmodern sociology. The postmodern sociologist is one who mediates between intellectual traditions in a way that is intended to enrich all sides.

Postmodernity

Postmodernity is a subject of great interest to Bauman (1988, 1991, 1992). It is therefore interesting that he defines postmodernity in two rather different ways. On one hand, he regards postmodernity as a definite period of history in a definite place (Bauman, 1988, 1992). It is the kind of social world that emerged in the second half of the twentieth century, in the affluent countries of Europe and of European descent. This kind of social world is thought to have replaced the modern type of society that emerged between the seventeenth and nineteenth centuries. On the other hand, Bauman sees postmodernity as a kind of consciousness of modernity (Bauman, 1991). It is a way of looking back at modernity from a new, more self-conscious and more critical perspective. Seen from this vantage point, modernity has not disappeared but it is still present and may continue into the future. Defined in this way, 'Postmodernity is no more (but no less either) than the modern mind taking a long, attentive and sober look at itself, at its condition and its past works, not fully liking what it sees and sensing the urge to change' (Bauman, 1991: 272). For example, Bauman's own critique of the rationality of modernity in the Holocaust would count as a piece of postmodern work.

In this section, we will be concerned with postmodernity in the first sense, as a type of social world with a definite position in time and space. Regarded in this way, Bauman has identified ten characteristics of postmodernity. First, the most fundamental characteristic of postmodernity in Bauman's account is the dominant role played by consumerism. Because of this, Bauman claims that while the postmodern social world is still capitalist, it is a different type of capitalism. Modern capitalism was characterized by the central position occupied by work. In postmodern capitalism, consumerism has replaced work as the crucial link which fastens together the lifeworlds of individuals and the properties of social systems. At the individual level, the joys of consumption become the centre of the lifeworld. At the social level, consumer choices become the basis for lifestyles and the formation of symbolic communities. At the systemic level, merchandising companies dominate the definition of the good life, and the reproduction of capital now depends much more on the manipulation of the market than it does on the exploitation of labour. Profit making by corporations now depends upon a social world in which the motives of spending and consuming dominate those of earning and saving. The 'work ethic' therefore has an ever-diminishing relevance to contemporary social life.

The second feature of postmodernity is permanent cultural pluralism. A variety of lifestyles flourish, each with its own system of meaning. This is partly due to the growth of consumerism, since Bauman says that: 'The market thrives on variety' (1992: 52). In postmodernity, individuals have greater freedom of choice, and corporations compete with one another to appeal to different segments of the market.

In the pluralism of postmodernity, different tastes do not stand in a hierarchical relationship and there is no evolutionary sequence of cultures. There are no 'right' or 'wrong' styles of life, only different lifestyles. Each system of meaning is autonomous, and in the absence of an overarching framework of meaning there are problems of communication between cultural traditions. It is the task of sociology to try to overcome these communication problems.

The third feature of postmodernity is that it is characterized by a division between those who are well integrated into the system of consumption and the poor and marginalized individuals who Bauman refers to as 'flawed consumers'. He calls the former group the 'seduced' and the latter group the 'repressed'. Because the latter cannot be integrated into the system through consumption, they must be integrated through repression. The repressed in postmodernity are the 'new poor'. They are not a uniform class like the class of workers in early capitalism, but they are all those who are unable to find a place within the system. For example, they are those who rely on benefits and welfare payments, the unemployed, casual workers, the handicapped, and those who are illiterate and unskilled. They are subject to surveillance and normative regulation.

Fourth, Bauman thinks that the nature of postmodernity cannot be captured by the sociological concept of structure as 'a cohesive totality with a degree of stiffness and resilience against change' (Bauman, 1992: 54). Connections between individuals are weak, since each one possesses considerable autonomy, and social life is fluid and changeable. Bauman therefore places a greater emphasis on agency.

Fifth, the postmodern world is a world in which the triumph of capitalism is exemplified by the fall of communism. Bauman attributes the fall of communism to the rise of consumerism, and the inability of communism to respond to new consumer demands. The decline of communism also illustrates the retreat from social engineering that Bauman thinks has gone on everywhere. There are no grand visions and no grand designs for a new social order. According to Bauman, 'the fall of communism signalled the final retreat from the dreams and ambitions of modernity' (1992: 178).

The sixth characteristic of postmodernity is that discontents have become privatized, and instead of threatening the system they aid in its reproduction. For example, the problems and risks of computer technology that many people find so frustrating merely lead to demands for more technology to solve the problems. Bauman therefore does not see the postmodern world as a world in crisis, but as one that will continue to go on in the same way.

Seventh, individuals in the postmodern world are actively engaged in constructing their own identities. As a result, identities are not fixed but they are often undecided and without any clear foundation in the world around them.

Eighth, as there is no pre-determined basis for constituting self-identity, individuals need guidance and reassurance at each stage in their lives from other people or groups who serve as orientation points. These groups do not lay down rules for their members, because they do not seek to control the behaviour of individuals. Rather, they are adopted by individuals as what Bauman refers to as 'symbolic tokens'. The use of symbolic tokens depends on their availability and accessibility. The availability of symbolic tokens in turn depends upon their visibility and authority. For example, credited expertise contributes to authority, and having a mass following contributes to visibility. Accessibility, on the other hand, depends upon having resources, especially knowledge. The possession of knowledge therefore becomes the major index of social standing in postmodernity.

The ninth feature of postmodernity is that postmodern politics is different from modern politics. Throughout the modern era, politics was mainly concerned with inequality and hence with conflicts over the distribution of resources. In the postmodern era, politics is mainly concerned with increasing the individual's autonomy and hence with human rights. This shift has occurred partly because the ambitions of the state have been shrinking, and partly because of the importance of self-constitution in postmodernity.

And tenth, Bauman thinks that there is a heightened interest in ethical debates in postmodernity. This development has occurred for two reasons. On one hand, there are effects of the pluralism of authority. Since there is no single authority who can be called on to provide unequivocal answers to questions, individuals must negotiate with one another and they must reach an understanding on the rules that they agree to recognize. On the other hand, there is the centrality of choice in the self-constitution of postmodern individuals. Because individuals must construct their own lives, they are constantly faced with moral choices, such as whether or not to use contraceptives and whether or not to have an abortion. Choice always means the assumption of responsibility, and making choices therefore involves making claims about the individual's construction of the self as a moral actor.

Modernity

Bauman has presented a detailed account of postmodernity, but he has not been consistent in his terminology of periodization. In his most recent writings, he sometimes drops the use of the term 'postmodern' and instead he talks about different stages of modernity. While he seems to continue to prefer to refer to the contemporary world as postmodern, he is prepared to use other terminology if that will evoke general agreement (Bauman, 2001). Bauman claims that in one sense modernity has continued to the present day. The modern world is a world of ceaseless change, brought on by the constant desire to bring about improvements such as economic growth. If modernization is a constant force for change, Bauman nevertheless thinks that contemporary modernity is different from early modernity. Any hope of constructing the perfect society has been dropped, and the role of the state has changed thanks to deregulation and privatization. We have entered a new stage of modernity, Bauman now claims, which he calls the fluid stage of modernity in contrast with the earlier solid stage (Bauman, 2000). This 'liquid modernity' has the following characteristics.

First, there is greater mobility of all kinds, which is a phenomenon that is bringing about greater globalization (Bauman, 1998). Travel has become much easier and faster, and barriers to movement have been increasingly removed. Also, electronic communications such as e-mail and cell phones now make it possible to be connected almost instantaneously to any point on earth from any other point on earth. Among the results of this new mobility is the emergence of an 'exterritorial elite' of people who direct events in various territories in which they do not live, but between which they constantly move in search of better opportunities. Here, power no longer consists of the ability to control local populations, but it consists of the ability to withdraw from them without cost, for example by shutting down factories and moving them elsewhere.

Second, as a result of this new mobility there is a loosening of ties linking capital and labour. Relations between the owners of capital and local labour forces are temporary, and they may be broken at any time for any reason. The profitability of corporations is no longer dependent on developing a relationship with the local labour force, but it depends on the ability to play one labour force off against another to see where the largest concessions can be extracted.

Third, the new mobility of capital exerts pressure on local governments to become more hospitable to capital and to place fewer constraints on it. Faced with the implicit or explicit threat of capital flight and therefore loss of jobs, governments are forced to make tax cuts, remove onerous regulations and reduce the power of organized labour.

Fourth, the forms of organization become looser. Forms of organization are developed that can be put together, dismantled and reassembled in short periods of time. As a result, more people are hired on short-term positions, and more people find themselves laid off due to corporate downsizing and streamlining. This leads to a general increase in insecurity.

Fifth, precarious economic and social conditions train men and women to perceive the world as full of disposable objects. This applies to consumer goods, which are now thrown away and replaced instead of being repaired, and it also applies to people and their relationships. Marriage, for example, ceases to be a relationship that is intended to last until death separates the partners. Instead, it becomes a contractual relationship that is entered into only for as long as both partners continue to derive gratifications from it. Relationships therefore become temporary and are subject to sudden termination.

Sixth, Bauman maintains that the chronic tendency of modernity to erode established social forms has shifted in recent years. It has changed from eroding social forms at the macro-level to the micro-level. In the past, what were broken down were the traditional customs and obligations that made up traditional society. Today, in a more mobile social world, what are being broken down are the connections between individuals and normative groups.

Seventh, contemporary modernity is an individualized and privatized modernity. Individuals have greater freedom of choice, but at the same time they face the pressures of taking greater responsibility for how they construct their lives. Failure becomes a personal responsibility, and individuals are left alone to cope with its consequences.

Conclusion

In this chapter we have examined the contributions of three authors who have attempted to rethink the discipline of sociology, including the relationship between structure and agency. Those authors are Pierre Bourdieu, Anthony Giddens and Zygmunt Bauman.

Pierre Bourdieu integrated structure and agency through a combination of key concepts. The structure of social life is defined by the concepts of field and capital, and agency is defined by the concept of habitus. The concept of field refers to a structure of relationships between positions. These positions have unequal amounts of capital associated with them, and the result is that fields are structured by systematic patterns of inequality. Inequality also exists at a more fundamental level, in processes of inclusion and exclusion, through which some people are allowed into the field and others are kept out.

The concept of capital refers to a possession that gives individuals the ability to do certain things, such as exercising domination over others. There are four types of capital: economic capital, social capital, cultural capital and symbolic capital. Economic capital consists of material wealth in the form of money or things that can be converted into money, such as stocks and shares, or property. Social capital is all the resources that are gained through social ties with other people. Cultural capital is the knowledge and tastes that are transmitted within families and in schools, and that mark those who possess them as socially superior to those who do not. And, symbolic capital is the capacity to construct beliefs about the world and to make them seem real. Bourdieu thinks that economic capital is the most important of these four types of capital. However, it does not determine the other types of capital. All species of capital need to be studied separately in order to arrive at a complete picture of society.

Finally, habitus is the set of dispositions which incline individuals to act and react in certain ways. It is internalized as a result of occupying a particular position in a field, but it is filtered through the habitus that remains from earlier experiences. As a result, early habitus have a stronger effect on behaviour than later habitus.

Anthony Giddens criticizes structural sociologists who do not pay enough attention to people's own knowledge of the world and the use that they make of it. In reaction, he redefines the concept of structure. By structure Giddens means the rules and resources that individuals draw on in constructing their lines of action. Giddens' redefined concept of structure is the central point for a body of theory that he refers to as structuration theory.

One of the principal features of structuration theory is the importance that Giddens attaches to the study of time and space. In particular, he pays special attention to time–space distanciation. Time–space distanciation is the tendency for interactions to occur between elements that are separated in time and space. Giddens believes that time–space distanciation has been increasing in that complex of social changes which he refers to as modernity.

Another key idea in structuration theory is that of reflexivity. By reflexivity Giddens means the process in which people monitor their own conduct and use the knowledge that they gain from monitoring to revise their behaviour. Giddens sees reflexivity as a fundamental feature of action. It is through reflexivity that people control their own behaviour and are not simply determined by social forces. In addition, institutions have also become reflexive in the modern world, and institutional reflexivity is a principal characteristic of modernity.

Giddens refers to the current stage of modernity as high modernity or late modernity. It is the stage of modernity when institutional reflexivity and time–space distanciation have both been developed to a high degree. Giddens' generally optimistic analysis of high modernity is that it brings about tremendous potential for improvements in the human condition, but at the cost of problems such as increased risk and heightened anxieties.

Zygmunt Bauman rejects the structural approach in sociology as no longer being very useful. Connections between individuals are weak, and social life is fluid and changeable. He thinks that a new approach is needed to a new type of social world which he prefers to call postmodernity, but that he has also called liquid modernity.

Bauman's sociological work falls into four categories: the critique of modernity; the analysis of the changing role of intellectuals; the description of postmodernity; and the description of current forms of modernity. His critique of modernity is that reason and rationalization can have destructive consequences. Bauman's example is the Holocaust. He argues that the Holocaust was not an isolated creation of deranged individuals, but it was the product of normal features of modern society. Such features as bureaucracy and science contributed to the destruction of the Jews and must therefore be held responsible for their fate.

Bauman's analysis of the changing role of intellectuals is that intellectuals have changed from being legislators to being interpreters. In modernity, the intellectuals were expected to pronounce on important issues of the day and to provide authoritative guidance for the solution of social problems. In postmodernity, intellectuals no longer play that role, mainly because they have lost the confidence to do so. Instead, intellectuals act as mediators between cultural traditions. They interpret the meaning of one cultural tradition for the followers of another cultural tradition. This task has become a matter of some urgency due to the irreducible cultural pluralism of postmodernity.

Bauman's description of postmodernity is that it is a type of social world characterized by increasing fragmentation. Insofar as there is any linking theme in this fragmentary universe it is consumerism. Consumption has replaced work as the central life activity, and the reproduction of capital now depends on access to markets rather than access to labour. The growth of consumerism has also contributed to increased cultural pluralism as markets thrive on variety. Frustrated consumerism also played a major part in the fall of communism, which Bauman sees as a significant event. Communism was the last instance of the modern dream of designing and managing a perfect society. With the fall of communism, and privatization and deregulation in non-communist societies, the state now plays a much diminished part in social life.

Finally, Bauman's description of current forms of modernity is that it is a flexible social world. The linking theme here is mobility. In the fluid stage of modernity, people, goods, communications and capital are all moving further and faster. This contributes to increased globalization. It also contributes to a number of specific features of liquid modernity, such as individualization and the weakening of social supports.

Further Reading

Bauman, Zygmunt, 1987, *Legislators and Interpreters: On Modernity, Post-modernity and Intellectuals*, Ithaca: Cornell University Press.

Bauman, Zygmunt, 1989, *Modernity and the Holocaust*, Ithaca: Cornell University Press.

Bauman, Zygmunt, 1992, *Intimations of Postmodernity*, London: Routledge.

Bauman, Zygmunt, 2000, *Liquid Modernity*, Cambridge: Polity Press.

Bourdieu, Pierre, 1984, *Distinction: A Social Critique of the Judgement of Taste*, trans. Richard Nice, Cambridge, MA: Harvard University Press.

Bourdieu, Pierre, 1986, 'The Forms of Capital', in John G. Richardson, ed., *Handbook of Theory and Research for the Sociology of Education*, New York: Greenwood, pp. 241–258.

Bourdieu, Pierre and Loïc J. D. Wacquant, 1992, *An Invitation to Reflexive Sociology*, Chicago: University of Chicago Press.

Bryant, Christopher G. A. and David Jary, 'Anthony Giddens', in George Ritzer, ed., *The Blackwell Companion to Major Social Theorists*, Oxford: Blackwell, pp. 670–695.

Calhoun, Craig, 2000, 'Pierre Bourdieu', in George Ritzer, ed., *The Blackwell Companion to Major Social Theorists*, Oxford: Blackwell, pp. 696–730.

Clark, Jon, Celia Modgil and Sohan Modgil, 1990, *Anthony Giddens: Consensus and Controversy*, London: Falmer Press.

Craib, Ian, 1992, *Anthony Giddens*, London: Routledge.

Giddens, Anthony, 1984, *The Constitution of Society: Outline of the Theory of Structuration*, Berkeley: University of California Press.

Giddens, Anthony, 1990, *The Consequences of Modernity*, Stanford: Stanford University Press.

Giddens, Anthony, 1992, *The Transformation of Intimacy: Sexuality, Love and Eroticism in Modern Societies*, Stanford: Stanford University Press.

Grenfell, Michael and Michael Kelly, eds, 2001, *Pierre Bourdieu: Language, Culture and Education: Theory into Practice*, Oxford: Peter Lang.

Jenkins, Richard, 1992, *Pierre Bourdieu*, London: Routledge.

Kaspersen, Lars Bo, 2000, *Anthony Giddens: An Introduction to a Social Theorist*, trans. Steven Sampson, Oxford: Blackwell.

Lane, Jeremy F., 2000, *Pierre Bourdieu: A Critical Introduction*, London: Pluto Press.

Smith, Dennis, 1999, *Zygmunt Bauman: Prophet of Postmodernity*, Cambridge: Polity Press.

Tucker, Kenneth H., Jr, 1998, *Anthony Giddens and Modern Social Theory*, London: Sage.

Webb, Jen, Tony Schirato and Geoff Danaher, 2002, *Understanding Bourdieu*, London: Sage.

Conclusion

Sociological theory has developed along a number of different dimensions. We have seen in this book how sociology has unfolded along five dimensions, each with its own distinctive trajectory. In the conclusion to this book we will identify broad trends in these developments as a way of summarizing what we have learned.

The first dimension of sociological theory was that of the unit of analysis to be adopted at the outset of inquiry. Here we saw that there have been three positions that have been taken with respect to the unit of analysis. First, the individual may be taken as the basic unit. This was the position initially taken by John Stuart Mill, and later by the phenomenological sociologist Alfred Schutz as well as the exchange and rational choice theorists George Homans, Peter Blau and James Coleman. Second, the unit of analysis may be a complex whole. This was the approach taken by Emile Durkheim in his discussion of social facts. And third, the unit of analysis may be given as the set of interactions that take place between individuals. This was the definition of sociology employed by Georg Simmel.

All of the approaches to defining the unit of analysis can still be found in sociological theory today. However, there has been a trend over time in the relative importance of these three approaches. By the beginning of the second half of the twentieth century, the holistic approach derived from the work of Emile Durkheim had become the dominant approach in sociological theory. This was the direction taken by Talcott Parsons. For Parsons, the social system was the basic unit of analysis, and the individual as such received very little attention.

In opposition to Parsonian systems theory, and continuing into the present day, there has been the tradition of symbolic interactionism. Symbolic interactionism inherited the approach of Georg Simmel that focused on the phenomenon of interaction. In the work of Herbert Blumer, for example, the joint act is taken as the unit of analysis, which is the interaction produced by the fitting together of the lines of action of the separate participants. Symbolic interactionism has remained a minority approach, however.

When Parsonian systems theory declined in influence, its dominant position was taken over by new forms of individualism. This trend has continued to the present day. We have seen in the work of Anthony Giddens, for example, how he rejects the concept of function because it assumes that systems rather than individuals have wants. For Giddens, it is individual wants that are basic, and we must therefore pay attention to individuals as knowledgeable actors who reflexively construct their own lives. Similarly, we have seen in the work of Zygmunt Bauman how postmodern processes of fragmentation have produced a new individualization in which individuals have a previously unimagined degree of autonomy of action. The individual is the most common unit of analysis in sociology today, and that trend seems likely to continue for some time.

The second dimension of sociological theory considered in this book was that of modes of explanation. Here, again, three approaches were identified. First was the analysis of causal relationships to be found in Durkheim's positivism. Second was the analysis of functions to be found in Durkheim's functionalism, and in the structural functionalism of Robert Merton and Talcott Parsons. And third was the interpretation of meanings to be found in Max Weber's sociology.

The main trend here has clearly been the decline of functionalism. From its high point in the structural functionalism of Parsons and Merton, interest in functionalism has declined to reach a low point today. Causal analysis, and its successor variable analysis, remains important, especially in quantitative sociology. Of equal interest today, however, is the emergence of interpretive sociologies, exemplified by the growing importance of qualitative research methods. Here symbolic interactionism has had an impact, illustrated in this book by Blumer's critique of variable analysis. According to Blumer, what is wrong with variable analysis is that it ignores the interpretive process through which individuals analyse their attitudes and behaviour as well as considering alternative lines of action. Also of interest in this regard is Anthony Giddens' hermeneutic approach to sociological studies. According to Giddens, sociology engages in the interpretation of the meanings employed by those whose lives we are studying, as a starting point for sociological analysis.

The third dimension of sociological theory is that of the key factors that are used in sociological explanation. The first approach considered here was the historical materialism of Karl Marx. Second, we studied Talcott Parsons' cultural determinism, according to which it is the cultural codes that occupy the pre-eminent position in the cybernetic hierarchy that organizes life. Third, we discussed the approach of Jürgen Habermas, who places the stress upon communicative action.

The underlying theme in this section of the book was to examine theories of social evolution, and to consider the nature of the explanations that are offered. The principal trend here has been one of a shift away from monocausal theorizing focused on the economy to multicausal theorizing. The prime example of this is Jürgen Habermas's complex model of evolutionary change. Habermas sees the significance of the economy in social change as itself changing over time. Only in modern society has the economy become the dominant factor, yet even here it is not the only factor. Science and politics influence economic developments, and they therefore have an independent role in contemporary social change. We have also seen how Pierre Bourdieu and Anthony Giddens recognize the influence of the economy, but as only one factor among many others. In Bourdieu's case, economic capital is seen as being the most important type of capital, but it does not determine social behaviour on its own. There are also social capital, cultural capital and symbolic capital, which all need to be taken into account. Similarly, Anthony Giddens sees globalization as being a question not only of the growth of international markets, but it also reflects cultural, political and technological developments.

The fourth dimension of sociological theorizing is the relationship between sociology and ideology. To what extent is sociology an ideology, and what are the implications of the different answers to this question? Here we considered Karl Mannheim's sociology of knowledge, Michel Foucault's rejection of the concept of ideology and Dorothy Smith's analysis of the relations of ruling. The underlying theme in this section was the opposition between philosophical realism and philosophical relativism. Philosophical realism is the belief that it is possible to comprehend the nature of reality through scientific methods which replace myths and errors with truths, and which probe beneath surface appearances to reveal the underlying structures of the real world. Philosophical relativism is the belief that all understandings, including scientific knowledge, are relative to some point of view, and that there is no position from which absolute truth can be discovered.

The general trend here has been towards cultural relativism, culminating in Zygmunt Bauman's claim that sociologists have ceased to be legislators and are now interpreters. That is to say, sociologists no longer have the confidence to pronounce universal truths, but instead they translate meanings between cultural traditions which are now formally equal. No tradition can support a special claim to truth in a context of cultural pluralism, and there is no hierarchy of knowledge in postmodernity. However, there is an important exception to this trend, illustrated here by the work of Dorothy Smith. If the members of previously dominant groups have lost the confidence to pronounce universal truths, that is not necessarily so for those who have challenged them. Dorothy Smith argues that those people who speak from the subordinate position of the 'servant' have the capacity to see their social world in the way that it really is, in a manner that is impossible for their social superiors. Here, philosophical realism returns in a strong form, and the debate continues.

Finally, the fifth dimension of sociological theory discussed in this book is that of structure and agency. The underlying question here is the extent to which individuals are constrained in their actions by social structures, as compared to being free to construct their actions along lines of their own choosing. In this section we contrasted the conservative and radical structural approaches of Robin Williams and Mary O'Brien with a variety of critical alternative approaches. The first critical approach considered was the symbolic inter-actionism of Herbert Blumer. Blumer rejected the structural approach to society because it paid insufficient attention to the ways in which individuals give meanings to the objects in their environment. The next critical approach considered was that of Anthony Giddens, who rejects the structural approach because it is unable to integrate the study of stasis and change. Instead, he redefines structure as the rules and resources that actors draw on in constructing their lines of action. The final critical approach is that of Zygmunt Bauman. He concludes that the structural approach is no longer useful because it cannot comprehend the fluidity and changeability of contemporary social life. Also, two alternative approaches were considered, in the work of Pierre Bourdieu and Erving Goffman. Bourdieu integrated structure and agency in the concepts of field, capital and habitus, and Goffman provided a micro-structural account of behaviour in the rules that govern face-to-face interaction.

Trends are somewhat harder to detect here, but if there has been a trend it has been towards a greater emphasis on agency. This is exemplified by Anthony Giddens account of actors engaging in the reflexive construction of their lives. Yet even here, the trend towards agency is not complete, since Giddens believes that individuals do not always construct their lives under conditions of their own choosing. Furthermore, the existence of unintended consequences and unacknowledged conditions of action means that individuals do not always exercise conscious control over the things that they do. On the dimension of structure and agency, debates between different sociological positions are still very much alive.

References

Bauman, Zygmunt, 1987, *Legislators and Interpreters: On Modernity, Post-modernity and Intellectuals*, Ithaca: Cornell University Press.

Bauman, Zygmunt, 1988, 'Sociology and Postmodernity', *The Sociological Review*, 36: 4, 790–813.

Bauman, Zygmunt, 1989, *Modernity and the Holocaust*, Ithaca: Cornell University Press.

Bauman, Zygmunt, 1991, *Modernity and Ambivalence*, Ithaca: Cornell University Press.

Bauman, Zygmunt, 1992, *Intimations of Postmodernity*, London: Routledge.

Bauman, Zygmunt, 1997, *Postmodernity and its Discontents*, New York: New York University Press.

Bauman, Zygmunt, 1998, *Globalization: The Human Consequences*, New York: Columbia University Press.

Bauman, Zygmunt, 2000, *Liquid Modernity*, Cambridge: Polity Press.

Bauman, Zygmunt, 2001, *The Individualized Society*, Cambridge: Polity Press.

Blau, Peter, 1964, *Exchange and Power in Social Life*, New York: John Wiley.

Blumer, Herbert, 1960, 'Early Industrialization and the Laboring Class', *The Sociological Quarterly*, 1, 5–14.

Blumer, Herbert, 1962, 'Society as Symbolic Interaction', in Arnold M. Rose, ed., *Human Behavior and Social Processes*, London: Routledge & Kegan Paul, pp. 179–192.

Blumer, Herbert, 1964, 'Industrialization and the Traditional Order', *Sociology and Social Research*, 48: 2, 129–138.

Blumer, Herbert, 1969, *Symbolic Interactionism: Perspective and Method*, Englewood Cliffs: Prentice-Hall.

Blumer, Herbert, 1990, *Industrialization as an Agent of Social Change: A Critical Analysis*, New York: Aldine de Gruyter.

Bottomore, T. B. and Maximilien Rubel, eds, 1963, *Karl Marx: Selected Writings in Sociology and Social Philosophy*, trans. T. B. Bottomore, Harmondsworth: Penguin.

Bourdieu, Pierre, 1984, *Distinction: A Social Critique of the Judgement of Taste*, trans. Richard Nice, Cambridge, MA: Harvard University Press.

Bourdieu, Pierre, 1986, 'The Forms of Capital', in John G. Richardson, ed., *Handbook of Theory and Research for the Sociology of Education*, New York: Greenwood, pp. 241–258.

Bourdieu, Pierre, 1990, *The Logic of Practice*, trans. Richard Nice, Stanford: Stanford University Press.

Bourdieu, Pierre, 1991, *Language and Symbolic Power*, trans. Gino Raymond and Matthew Adamson, Cambridge, MA: Harvard University Press.

Bourdieu, Pierre, 1993, *Sociology in Question*, trans. Richard Nice, London: Sage.

Bourdieu, Pierre and Jean-Claude Passeron, 1977, *Reproduction in Education, Society and Culture*, trans. Richard Nice, London: Sage.

Bourdieu, Pierre and Loïc J. D. Wacquant, 1992, *An Invitation to Reflexive Sociology*, Chicago: University of Chicago Press.

Coleman, James S., 1990, *Foundations of Social Theory*, Cambridge, MA: Belknap Press.

Durkheim, Emile, 1964a, *The Rules of Sociological Method*, trans. Sarah Solovay and John Mueller, ed., George E. G. Catlin, New York: Free Press.

Durkheim, Emile, 1964b, *The Division of Labor in Society*, trans. George Simpson, New York: Free Press.

Durkheim, Emile, 1965, *The Elementary Forms of Religious Life*, trans. Joseph Ward Swain, New York: Free Press.

Durkheim, Emile, 1966, *Suicide*, trans. John A. Spaulding and George Simpson, ed., George Simpson, New York: Free Press.

Durkheim, Emile, 1995, *The Elementary Forms of Religious Life*, trans. Karen Fields, New York: Free Press.

Durkheim, Emile, 1997, *The Division of Labor in Society*, trans. W. D. Halls, New York: Free Press.

Feuerbach, Ludwig, 1969, 'The Truth of Religion', in Norman Birnbaum and Gertrud Lenzer, eds, *Sociology and Religion*, Englewood Cliffs, NJ: Prentice-Hall, pp. 87–91.

Foucault, Michel, 1979, *Discipline and Punish: The Birth of the Prison*, trans. Alan Sheridan, New York: Vintage Books.

Foucault, Michel, 1980, *Power/Knowledge: Selected Interviews and Other Writings 1972–1977*, trans. Colin Gordon, Leo Marshall, John Mepham and Kate Soper, New York: Pantheon Books.

Gerth, H. H. and C. Wright Mills, eds, 1948, *From Max Weber: Essays in Sociology*, trans. H. H. Gerth and C. Wright Mills, London: Routledge & Kegan Paul.

Giddens, Anthony, 1977, *Studies in Social and Political Theory*, London: Hutchinson.

Giddens, Anthony, 1979, *Central Problems in Social Theory: Action, Structure and Contradiction in Social Analysis*, London: Macmillan.

Giddens, Anthony, 1984, *The Constitution of Society: Outline of the Theory of Structuration*, Berkeley: University of California Press.

Giddens, Anthony, 1987, *Social Theory and Modern Sociology*, Stanford: Stanford University Press.

Giddens, Anthony, 1990, *The Consequences of Modernity*, Stanford: Stanford University Press.

Giddens, Anthony, 1991, *Modernity and Self-Identity: Self and Society in the Late Modern Age*, Stanford: Stanford University Press.

Giddens, Anthony, 1992, *The Transformation of Intimacy: Sexuality, Love and Eroticism in Modern Societies*, Stanford: Stanford University Press.

Giddens, Anthony, 2000, *Runaway World*, New York: Routledge.

Goffman, Erving, 1959, *The Presentation of Self in Everyday Life*, Garden City: Doubleday.

Goffman, Erving, 1961, *Asylums: Essays on the Social Situation of Mental Patients and Other Inmates*, Chicago: Aldine.

Goffman, Erving, 1963, *Behavior in Public Places: Notes on the Social Organization of Gatherings*, New York: Free Press.

Goffman, Erving, 1967, *Interaction Ritual: Essays on Face-to-Face Behavior*, Garden City: Doubleday.

Goffman, Erving, 1971, *Relations in Public: Microstudies of the Public Order*, New York: Basic Books.

Habermas, Jürgen, 1970, *Toward a Rational Society*, trans. Jeremy Shapiro, Boston: Beacon Press.

Habermas, Jürgen, 1975, *Legitimation Crisis*, trans. Thomas McCarthy, Boston: Beacon Press.

Habermas, Jürgen, 1979, *Communication and the Evolution of Society*, trans. Thomas McCarthy, Boston: Beacon Press.

Habermas, Jürgen, 1987, *The Theory of Communicative Action, Volume 2: Lifeworld and System: A Critique of Functionalist Reason*, trans. Thomas McCarthy, Boston: Beacon Press.

Homans, George C., 1958, 'Human Behavior as Exchange', *American Journal of Sociology*, 63: 6, 597–606.

Homans, George C., 1961, *Social Behaviour: Its Elementary Forms*, London: Routledge & Kegan Paul.

Homans, George C., 1974, *Social Behavior: Its Elementary Forms*, Revised Edition, New York: Harcourt Brace Jovanovich.

Mannheim, Karl, 1960, *Ideology and Utopia*, London: Routledge & Kegan Paul.

Marx, Karl, 1963, *Early Writings*, trans. T. B. Bottomore, London: C. A. Watts.

Marx, Karl, 1970, *A Contribution to the Critique of Political Economy*, ed., Maurice Dobb, trans. S. W. Ryazanskaya, New York: International Publishers.

Marx, Karl, 1971, *Karl Marx: Early Texts*, trans. David McLellan, Oxford: Blackwell.

Marx, Karl, 1976a, 'Theses on Feuerbach', in Karl Marx and Frederick Engels, eds, *Collected Works, Volume 5: Marx and Engels: 1845–47*, New York: International Publishers, pp. 3–5.

Marx, Karl, 1976b, 'Speech on the Question of Free Trade', in Karl Marx and Frederick Engels, eds, *Collected Works, Volume 6: Marx and Engels: 1845–48*, New York: International Publishers, pp. 450–465.

Marx, Karl, 1977, *Capital: A Critique of Political Economy*, Volume 1, trans. Ben Fowkes, New York: Vintage Books.

Marx, Karl and Frederick Engels, 1964a, *The German Ideology*, ed., S. Ryazanskaya, Moscow: Progress Publishers.

Marx, Karl and Frederick Engels, 1964b, *On Religion*, New York: Schocken.

Marx, Karl and Frederick Engels, 1973, *Manifesto of the Communist Party*, Peking: Foreign Languages Press.

Merton, Robert K., 1957, *Social Theory and Social Structure*, New York: Free Press.

Mill, John Stuart, 1969, *Collected Works of John Stuart Mill, Volume X: Essays on Ethics, Religion and Society*, ed., J. M. Robson, Toronto: University of Toronto Press.

Mill, John Stuart, 1974, *Collected Works of John Stuart Mill, Volume VIII: A System of Logic*, ed., J. M. Robson, Toronto: University of Toronto Press.

O'Brien, Mary, 1981, *The Politics of Reproduction*, London: Routledge & Kegan Paul.

O'Brien, Mary, 1989, *Reproducing the World: Essays in Feminist Theory*, Boulder: Westview Press.

Parsons, Talcott, 1949, *The Structure of Social Action*, Glencoe: Free Press.

Parsons, Talcott, 1951, *The Social System*, Glencoe: Free Press.

Parsons, Talcott, 1954, *Essays in Sociological Theory*, New York: Free Press.

Parsons, Talcott, 1961, 'An Outline of the Social System', in Talcott Parsons, Edward Shils, Kaspar D. Naegele and Jesse R. Pitts, eds, *Theories of Society: Foundations of Modern Sociological Theory*, Volume 1, New York: Free Press, pp. 30–79.

Parsons, Talcott, 1966, *Societies: Evolutionary and Comparative Perspectives*, Englewood Cliffs: Prentice-Hall.

Parsons, Talcott, 1967, *Sociological Theory and Modern Society*, New York: Free Press.

Parsons, Talcott, 1971, *The System of Modern Societies*, Englewood Cliffs: Prentice-Hall.

Poggi, Gianfranco, 2000, *Durkheim*, Oxford: Oxford University Press.

Schutz, Alfred, 1964, *Collected Papers, Volume II: Studies in Social Theory*, ed., Arvid Brodersen, The Hague: Martinus Nijhoff.

Schutz, Alfred, 1966, *Collected Papers, Volume III: Studies in Phenomenological Philosophy*, ed. I. Schutz, The Hague: Martinus Nijhoff.

Schutz, Alfred, 1967, *Collected Papers, Volume I: The Problem of Social Reality*, ed., Maurice Natanson, The Hague: Martinus Nijhoff.

Schutz, Alfred, 1970, *On Phenomenology and Social Relations*, ed., Helmut R. Wagner, Chicago: University of Chicago Press.

Schutz, Alfred and Thomas Luckmann, 1974, *The Structures of the Life-World*, trans. Richard M. Zaner and H. Tristram Engelhardt, Jr, London: Heinemann.

Simmel, Georg, 1955, *Conflict and the Web of Group-Affiliations*, trans. Kurt H. Wolff and Reinhard Bendix, Glencoe: Free Press.

Simmel, Georg, 1971, *On Individuality and Social Forms*, ed., Donald N. Levine, Chicago: University of Chicago Press.

Simmel, Georg, 1978, *The Philosophy of Money*, trans. Tom Bottomore and David Frisby, London: Routledge & Kegan Paul.

Smelser, Neil J., 1988, 'Social Structure', in Neil J. Smelser, ed., *Handbook of Sociology*, Newbury Park: Sage, pp. 103–129.

Smith, Dorothy E., 1979, 'A Sociology for Women', in Julia A. Sherman and Evelyn Torton Beck, eds, *The Prism of Sex*, Madison: University of Wisconsin Press, pp. 135–187.

Smith, Dorothy E., 1987, *The Everyday World as Problematic: A Feminist Sociology*, Boston: Northeastern University Press.

Smith, Dorothy E., 1999a, 'From Women's Standpoint to a Sociology for People', in Janet L. Abu-Lughod, ed., *Sociology for the Twenty-first Century: Continuities and Cutting Edges*, Chicago: University of Chicago Press, pp. 65–82.

Smith, Dorothy E., 1999b, *Writing the Social: Critique, Theory, and Investigations*, Toronto: University of Toronto Press.

Spykman, Nicholas J., 1965, *The Social Theory of Georg Simmel*, New York: Atherton Press.

Weber, Max, 1947, *Max Weber: The Theory of Social and Economic Organization*, trans. A. M. Henderson and Talcott Parsons, Glencoe: Free Press.

Weber, Max, 1949, *The Methodology of the Social Sciences*, trans. Edward A. Shils and Henry A. Finch, Glencoe: Free Press.

Weber, Max, 1958, *The Protestant Ethic and the Spirit of Capitalism*, trans. Talcott Parsons, New York: Charles Scribner's Sons.

Weber, Max, 1961, *General Economic History*, trans. Frank H. Knight, New York: Collier.

Williams, Robin M., Jr, 1951, *American Society: A Sociological Interpretation*, New York: Knopf.

Wolff, Kurt H., 1964, *The Sociology of Georg Simmel*, New York: Free Press.

Index